This book is very timely and provides a comparative take on judicial review in relation to elections in nine Asian jurisdictions whose constitutional systems are based on common law or civil law principles.

Po Jen Yap is highly qualified to undertake the task of bringing relevant scholars together to discuss the relevant issues in a comparative frame of reference. He has done so superbly and this book is to be highly recommended.

Andrew Harding, *Professor of Law & Director of Centre for Asian Legal Studies, National University of Singapore*

Professor Po Jen Yap has assembled a formidable group of legal thinkers from Asia, joined them with their counterparts from Canada, Australia, and South Africa, and produced a unique and provocative collection of essays on an understudied area of public law, the law governing the elections process. This collection of essays invites us to think afresh about the role of courts and, in some instances, election commissions—and the legal and political constraints they face—in supervising the integrity of the elections process. The collection manages both to focus in on the nuances of particular jurisdictions and to pan out for a wide-angle view across the political spectrum from the politically fragile to the dominant-party to the vibrant, multi-party democracies of Asia.

Victor V. Ramraj, *Professor of Law & Chair in Asia-Pacific Legal Relations, University of Victoria, Canada*

The paradox of democracy is that its flourishing depends on judicial institutions that are insulated from politics. Yet until recently, there has been scant attention to the role of courts in making Asian democracies work. This book fills that void, offering fascinating perspectives from top-notch scholars on how courts have intervened in Asian elections, sometimes constructively and sometimes disastrously. It is essential reading for anyone who cares about democracy and wants to see it thrive, in Asia and across the globe.

Daniel Tokaji, *Charles W. Ebersold and Florence Whitcomb Ebersold Professor of Constitutional Law, The Ohio State University*

Judicial Review of Elections in Asia

In the past century, Asian nations have experienced a wave of democratisation as countries in the region have gained independence or transitioned from authoritarian military rule towards more participatory politics. At the same time, there has been an expansion of judicial power in Asia, whereby new courts or empowered old ones emerge as independent constraints on governmental authority.

This is the first book to assess the judicial review of elections in Asia. It provides important insights into how Asian courts can strategically engage with the political actors in their jurisdictions and contribute to a country's democratic discourse. Each chapter in the book sheds light on the judicial review of elections and the electoral process in a specific Asian jurisdiction, including Common Law Asia, namely Hong Kong, India, Malaysia, and Singapore, as well as jurisdictions in Civil Law Asia, namely Indonesia, Japan, the Republic of Korea, Taiwan, and Thailand. It fills a gap in the literature by addressing a central challenge to democratic governance, namely the problem of partisan self-dealing in the electoral processes.

By exploring the constantly evolving role of the courts in addressing pivotal constitutional questions, this book will be of interest to students and scholars of Asian Law, Governance, and Politics.

Po Jen Yap is an Associate Professor at the Faculty of Law, University of Hong Kong.

Routledge studies in Asian law

Asian Law in Disasters
Toward a human-centered recovery
Edited by Yuka KANEKO, Katsumi MATSUOKA and Toshihisa TOYODA

Judicial Review of Elections in Asia
Edited by Po Jen Yap

Judicial Review of Elections in Asia

Edited by Po Jen Yap

Routledge
Taylor & Francis Group
LONDON AND NEW YORK

First published 2016
by Routledge

2 Park Square, Milton Park, Abingdon, Oxfordshire OX14 4RN
711 Third Avenue, New York, NY 10017

Routledge is an imprint of the Taylor & Francis Group, an informa business

First issued in paperback 2017

British Library Cataloguing in Publication Data
A catalogue record for this book is available from the British Library

Library of Congress Cataloging in Publication Data
Names: Yap, Po Jen, editor.
Title: Judicial review of elections in Asia / Edited by Po Jen Yap.
Description: New York, NY : Routledge, 2016. | Includes bibliographical references and index.
Identifiers: LCCN 2015044179| ISBN 9781138950283 (hardback) | ISBN 9781315668567 (ebook)
Subjects: LCSH: Elections–Asia. | Election law–Asia. | Judicial review–Asia.
Classification: LCC KNC585 .J83 2016 | DDC 342.5/07–dc23
LC record available at http://lccn.loc.gov/2015044179

ISBN: 978-1-138-95028-3 (hbk)
ISBN: 978-0-8153-6882-3 (pbk)

Typeset in Times New Roman
by Wearset Ltd, Boldon, Tyne and Wear

Contents

Tables

Contributors

Wen-Chen Chang is a Professor at the National Taiwan University, College of Law. She received her LLB and LLM degrees from National Taiwan University and holds an LLM and JSD from Yale Law School. She is a leading authority on constitutional law in Taiwan and has published and edited major scholarly works on comparative constitutional law, including *Asian Courts in Context*, with Jiunn-rong Yeh (Cambridge University Press, 2015) and *Constitutionalism in Asia: Cases and Materials*, with Kevin Y.L. Tan, Li-ann Thio, and Jiunn-rong Yeh (Hart Publishing, 2014).

Moeen H. Cheema is a Lecturer at the ANU College of Law, Australian National University. He is especially interested in constitutional law, politics, judicial review, and criminal justice systems in South Asia. He completed an LLM from Harvard Law School and an LLB (Hons) from the University of London. He is also a PhD candidate at the ANU. Prior to joining the ANU College of Law he taught law in Pakistan from 2004 to 2008.

Kareem Crayton is an expert and scholar on election law and constitutional design. He has served on faculties including Harvard, the University of Southern California, and the University of North Carolina and is widely published in both law and political science journals. He is currently Visiting Professor at Vanderbilt University Law School and manages Crimcard Consulting Services which provides guidance to entities worldwide about election-related issues. He graduated in Government with high honours from Harvard College, and he later earned a JD as well as a PhD in Political Science from Stanford University.

Yasmin Dawood is an Associate Professor at the Faculty of Law, University of Toronto, and is cross-appointed in the Department of Political Science. She has published widely on election law, comparative constitutional law, and democratic theory. She has testified before a Parliamentary committee as an election law expert, and is a frequent media commentator. She received a PhD in Political Science from the University of Chicago, a JD from Columbia Law School, and a BA from the University of Toronto.

Surya Deva is an Associate Professor at the School of Law of City University of Hong Kong. His primary research interests lie in Business and Human

Rights, Corporate Social Responsibility, and India–China Constitutional Law. His books include *Regulating Corporate Human Rights Violations: Humanizing Business* (Routledge, 2012). He is one of the founding Editors-in-Chief of the *Business and Human Rights Journal* (Cambridge University Press), and he sits on the Editorial Board of the *Netherlands Quarterly of Human Rights* and the *Vienna Journal on International Constitutional Law*. In 2014, he was elected a Member of the Executive Committee of the International Association of Constitutional Law.

Stefanus Hendrianto, SJ, is a visiting scholar at the Kellogg Institute of International Studies, University of Notre Dame. Previously he was an Adjunct Professor at Santa Clara University Law School and the Political Science Department. Born and raised in Indonesia, he holds a PhD degree from the School of Law, University of Washington, Seattle and LLM degree from Utrecht University, Netherlands, in addition to his LLB degree from Gadjah Mada University, Indonesia.

Yi-Li Lee is a post-doctoral fellow at the National Taiwan University, College of Law. She obtained her PhD degree from National Taiwan University College of Law and was a Visiting Fellow at the European Research Center on Contemporary Taiwan (ERCCT) at Tübingen University in 2015. Her research interests include transitional justice, comparative constitutions, international human rights, international humanitarian law, and international criminal law.

Shigenori Matsui is a Professor of Law at the University of British Columbia, Peter A. Allard School of Law, and is the Director of the Japanese Studies programme at the Centre for Asian Legal Studies and a Co-director of the Centre for Japanese Research of the Institute of Asian Research. Before joining the University of British Columbia, he was teaching at the Osaka University for over twenty-five years.

Sarah Murray is a constitutional law academic at the University of Western Australia and is a co-convenor of the Electoral Regulation and Research Network for Western Australia. She is the author of *The Remaking of the Courts: Less-Adversarial Practice and the Constitutional Role of the Judiciary in Australia* (Federation Press, 2014), the editor of *Constitutional Perspectives on an Australian Republic: Essays in Honour of Professor George Winterton* (Federation Press, 2010), and a co-author of *The Constitution of the Commonwealth of Australia: History, Principle and Interpretation* (Cambridge University Press, 2015).

Woo-Young Rhee is a Professor of Public Law at Seoul National University (SNU) School of Law in Korea. After graduation (LLB, Seoul National University; LLM, Harvard Law School; JSD, Stanford Law School), she practised law in California, until she joined the faculty of SNU Law School in 2004. While teaching and conducting research in the area of constitutional law, she has served in advisory committees for the Constitutional Court, the Supreme Court, the Ministries of Justice and Legislation of Korea, and the Korean Bar Association.

Kevin Y.L. Tan, is a Singaporean scholar who specialises in the constitutional law and legal history of Malaysia and Singapore. He graduated from the National University of Singapore with an LLB (Hons) degree and obtained his LLM and JSD degrees from Yale Law School. He is the author/editor of over thirty books on the law, history, and politics of Singapore and is currently Adjunct Professor at both the Faculty of Law, National University of Singapore and the S Rajaratnam School of International Studies, Nanyang Technological University.

Khemthong Tonsakulrungruang is a Lecturer at the Faculty of Law, Chulalongkorn University, where he teaches Constitutional and Administrative Law. He graduated from Chulalongkorn before earning his LLM degree at Yale Law School. His area of interest includes freedom of expression, law and religion, and environmental law. In addition to teaching, he also blogs on Thailand's democratic process and works with local environmental advocate groups.

Po Jen Yap is an Associate Professor at the University of Hong Kong, Faculty of Law, where he specialises in constitutional and administrative law. He graduated from the National University of Singapore with an LLB degree and he obtained LLM qualifications from both Harvard Law School and University College London. He also has a PhD degree from the University of Cambridge. He is the sole author of the monograph *Constitutional Dialogue in Common Law Asia* (Oxford University Press, 2015).

Simon N.M. Young is Professor and Associate Dean (Research) in the Faculty of Law, University of Hong Kong, a practising barrister at Parkside Chambers, and Co-Editor-in-Chief of the *Asia Pacific Journal on Human Rights and the Law* (Brill). He was junior counsel in Hong Kong's first prisoners' right to vote case. In 2014–2015, he testified before parliamentary committees in the United Kingdom and Canada on the political situation in Hong Kong.

1 Courts and elections in Asia

Po Jen Yap[1]

Introduction

In the past century, as the winds of political change swept across the globe, Asian nations too experienced a wave of democratisation as countries in the region gained independence or transitioned from authoritarian military rule towards more participatory politics. In tandem with this democratisation trend, we may also witness a concomitant expansion of judicial power in Asia, whereby new courts or empowered old ones emerge as independent constraints on governmental authority.[2] The rise of the courts, and the accompanying 'judicialisation of politics',[3] is as much an Asian phenomenon, as it is a prevalent trend in the West.

There is now a rich corpus of literature on how Asian courts have participated in and even reshaped the human rights discourse in their respective jurisdictions.[4] However, little academic literature has examined how Asian courts have responded to deficiencies in the electoral processes and the concomitant problem of partisan self-dealing. Specifically, partisan self-dealing occurs when the political actors devise electoral rules that govern voting, political parties, electoral boundaries, apportionment, the administration of elections, and campaign finance that are designed to entrench themselves in power.[5] The purpose of this book is to redress this gap in the scholarship by exploring how courts in Asia have addressed this central challenge to democratic governance.

The chapters in this volume stemmed from a symposium held at the University of Hong Kong in July 2015. Each of the ten chapters profiled in Part I and Part II of this book sheds light on the judicial review of elections and the electoral process in a specific Asian jurisdiction. Part I examines the common law jurisdictions of Hong Kong, India, Malaysia, Pakistan, and Singapore. Part II explores the civil law jurisdictions of Indonesia, Japan, South Korea, Taiwan, and Thailand. To allow readers to draw insights from judicial practices in non-Asian jurisdictions, Part III includes, as a comparative foil, a brief account of the state of play in Australia, Canada, and South Africa.

A survey of the ten Asian jurisdictions under study herein illuminates an interesting phenomenon. In states like Malaysia and Singapore where a dominant party or coalition is in control, their courts perform their supervisory functions of the democratic process, but they only operate at the fringes of the country's political life. On the other hand, in dynamic democracies where there have been extended periods of competing political parties taking turns in office, their courts play a more central role in democratic consolidation. Such courts as those found in Indonesia, South Korea, and Taiwan would ameliorate systemic inequalities in electoral systems and provide constitutional redress for vulnerable or unpopular groups that have been excluded from the voting process. But even then, successful courts in these dynamic democracies would attempt to be neutral arbiters between rival political parties and steer clear of overturning key electoral results or removing key politicians. Finally, for Asian courts that get too close to the 'live wire of electoral politics'[6] and become partisan tools that assist one political camp to dislodge its rivals, as the Constitutional Court in Thailand did, their actions would only accelerate a political crisis that may send the country over the constitutional cliff. In fragile or unstable democracies, where the country oscillates regularly between military rule and civilian governments, prudent judges may prefer to insulate the courts against political attacks rather than engage in strong-form judicial review.

My fundamental point is that all courts operate within political parameters and the task of scholars is to explain how these parameters can both empower or constrain courts.[7] As Professor Tom Ginsburg has observed, the extent of political diffusion within the legislative and executive structures determines how successfully courts can assert their judicial power.[8] Where divided government exists, the 'policy space'[9] of the courts is greater as the opposing parties in the legislature have to cooperate to effectuate any disagreement with the judiciary. On the other hand, in dominant-party or fragile democracies, courts can only take a limited range of actions before they outrun the government's 'zone of tolerance'[10] as the government can respond to confrontational judicial decisions by deploying constitutional or unconstitutional means to overrule or 'punish' the courts. Bipartisan legislative agreement to overrule or punish judges would be less likely and frequent in dynamic democracies. In such systems, courts can play a more major role in the country's political life by consolidating the democratic processes and actively facilitating electoral *systemic* change. Naturally, the role of any court is not static, it can change and will change, as the jurisdiction in question evolves and democratises further.

Dominant-party democracies

In dominant-party democracies, the main obstacle to electoral competition is not fraud or violence associated with fragile or unstable democracies, but the overwhelming control asserted by one party/coalition that has successfully consolidated its political apparatus in office.[11] Malaysia has been ruled by the same political coalition since its independence, i.e. the Alliance Party, which was renamed *Barisan Nasional* (National Front) in 1974. The People's Action Party has been the ruling party in Singapore since its independence and the party has controlled over 90 per cent of the elected seats in Parliament since 1968. In turn, their courts have acquiesced to the state of affairs by playing a more limited role in their countries' political life as their judges will be unable to rely on the support of other strong institutional actors to counter any backlash from the dominant party if they engage in robust judicial review over electoral disputes. Therefore, it is perhaps unsurprising that the Malaysian courts, as explored in Kevin Y.L. Tan's chapter on Malaysia, have accepted that its Election Commission does not have a duty to arrange for persons in detention to vote at the requisite polling centres,[12] nor is it obliged to allow Malaysian citizens living abroad to be registered as absentee voters.[13] In the same vein, as explored in my chapter on Singapore, judicial intervention in election cases in Singapore would arise only in the most exceptional cases;[14] and so long as its Prime Minister does not openly reject the possibility of a by-election when a casual vacancy arises, it would appear that there are no other constitutional limits laid down by the Court of Appeal on the Prime Minister's exercise of his discretion to call for a by-election to fill a vacancy.

Turning to Japan, we may notice a similar phenomenon. The dominant Liberal Democrat Party (LDP) has ruled Japan since 1955, except for a brief 11-month period between 1993 and 1994 and also between 2009 and 2012. As detailed in Shigenori Matsui's chapter on Japan, the country implements the most restrictive regulatory regime on election campaigns in the world, which includes limits on the number of permissible electoral posters that may be distributed and a blanket ban on door-to-door canvassing, but its Supreme Court has upheld all these restrictions as reasonable limitations on free speech.

Hong Kong provides yet another fascinating case study. As examined in Simon N.M. Young's chapter on Hong Kong, China has deliberately retained the Functional Constituencies (FC) electoral method in Hong Kong, a system in which the right to vote depends upon a person's membership or registration in a recognised social, economic, industrial, commercial, political advisory, or professional body represented in the legislature. In many of these FCs, e.g. Insurance, Transport, Tourism, Finance, Labour etc., it is not individuals working in these professions that are eligible to vote; instead, it is only the recognised corporate bodies operating in these professions that are eligible to vote. It is significant that since the establishment of the Hong Kong Special Administrative Region, the pro-Beijing/pro-establishment camp has relied on these 'corporate' votes to dominate the FC elections, such that the pro-establishment camp is able to command an overall majority of the seats in the Legislative Council, even though it lags behind in the Geographical Constituencies (GC) elections that are constituted via universal suffrage.[15] (One may note that since the Hong Kong executive government is heavily reliant on the support of the pro-establishment camp in the legislature for the passage of its bills, unrestricted elections by universal suffrage for all of the seats in the Legislative Council would unlikely be allowed till the pro-establishment camp is able to form a clear majority in the Legislative Council, without the use of the FC system as a political crutch.) Furthermore, the Standing Committee of the National People's Congress (SCNPC) is empowered under Hong Kong's Basic

Law to overrule the Court of Final Appeal's decision via a Legislative Interpretation. In light of these political realities, it is thus unsurprising that the Hong Kong judiciary has adopted, as Young puts it, a 'contradictory approach to judicial review': its traditionally active judiciary has been willing to extend voting rights writ small to disenfranchised prisoners[16] or those who had been convicted of minor offences;[17] but the courts have been unwilling to make *systemic* changes that invalidate 'corporate voting',[18] a cardinal feature of the FC electoral system.

Dynamic democracies

On the other hand, courts operating within dynamic democracies function differently. Where there have been extended periods of competing political parties taking turns in office, courts have less to fear as bipartisan legislative agreement to overrule or punish judges are less likely and frequent in such contested environments. In turn, their courts would have more opportunity to innovate and can play a more central role in democratic consolidation by making larger systemic changes to the electoral systems.

In India, as examined by Surya Deva in his chapter on India, its Supreme Court has been zealous in rooting out systemic and prevalent corrupt practices amongst politicians and their allies by adopting a very robust reading of the Representation of the People Act (RPA). Politicians are required to prove that any expenditure by a political party was in fact incurred by the political party and not by them; otherwise such expenditures relating to their candidacies would be presumed to be authorised by them.[19] In its bid to drive out criminals from politics, the Court also invalidated a law that protected incumbents by exempting convicted criminals from disqualification as members of Parliament if they were *continuing* in that office,[20] and has held that the failure to declare one's criminal antecedents when running for office was a corrupt practice under the RPA.[21]

More significantly, as detailed in Woo-Young Rhee's chapter on South Korea, its Constitutional Court of Korea has directly intervened in the electoral process by mandating that each voter be allowed to cast two votes in the National Assembly election: one for his/her preferred individual candidate in the electoral district and the other for his/her preferred political party that elects the proportional representative.[22] Furthermore, the Constitutional Court of South Korea has also held that the population ratio of the most populous electoral district to the least populous district must not deviate from a ratio of two-to-one,[23] and this population ratio would take effect in the upcoming 2016 National Assembly Election.

In the same vein, as discussed by Stephanus Hendrianto in his chapter on Indonesia, its Constitutional Court scrapped an electoral scheme that awarded electoral seats in the national legislature to candidates who were ranked highest on their political party's list when none of the candidates could obtain a requisite percentage of the popular vote.[24] Now, these electoral seats are simply awarded to persons with the highest number of votes. Furthermore, the Court indirectly facilitated smaller political parties to obtain more electoral seats in the national legislature when it held that votes that were already counted in the first-round allocation of electoral seats could not be 'reused' to determine the allocation of the remaining unfilled seats in the second phase.[25] More recently, the Court held that the legislative and presidential elections had to be simultaneously held[26] so that the political parties would not have excessive leverage and control over their presidential nominees, which existed under the prior system where the presidential election was held a few months after the legislative election.

While courts in these dynamic democracies have creatively consolidated the democratic process by amplifying the competitiveness and fairness of elections and electoral institutions, they have also displayed remarkable restraint insofar as their judges seek to be non-partisan arbiters. As argued by Wen-Chen Chang and Yi-Li Lee in their chapter on Taiwan, its courts have empowered the independent Central Election Commission to uphold the integrity of elections impartially and have also prevented political rivals from seeking retaliation against one another by limiting the use of criminal libel suits.[27] More importantly, the Taiwanese judiciary has also adopted a strategy of upholding key election results. The *Pan-Blue* camp, affiliated with the Kuomintang, had refused to accept the re-election of President Chen Shui-bian in 2004, but their courts, with great care, upheld the validity of that presidential election. Likewise, the Indonesian Constitutional Court in 2014 has also upheld the election of President Joko Widodo. Even in impeachment proceedings, the Constitutional Court of South Korea has strategically avoided removing President Roh Moon-Hyun from power after Roh's party won resoundingly at the 2004 National Assembly election during the deliberations of the impeachment case.[28]

Fragile democracies

In contrast, courts that have come too close to the 'live wire of electoral politics'[29] may end up doing a disservice to their country's transition to a stable democracy, and the state may, as a consequence, backslide to some variant of autocratic military rule. As discussed by Khemthong Tonsakulrungruang in his chapter on Thailand, since 2006, the Constitutional Court had invalidated two Parliamentary elections and six political parties affiliated with Thaksin Shinawatra, and the ensuing political impasse had only precipitated two military coups. The most recent military coup in 2014 saw the rise of General Prayut Chan-o-cha as the country's premier and the abolition of the Thai Constitution. If courts become mere partisan tools that assist one political camp to remove its enemies from the country's political life, as the Constitutional Court in Thailand did, the country's transition to a stable democracy can be easily derailed.

Therefore, for countries that regularly oscillate between military rule and civilian government, the judiciary's primary and basic goal should arguably *not* be strong-form judicial review but the maintenance of its institutional independence instead.[30] As detailed in Moeen Cheema's chapter on Pakistan, its Supreme Court's exercise of active judicial review under the leadership of Chief Justice

Iftikhar Chaudhry unnerved General Pervez Musharraf's regime and the government dismissed more than 60 judges on the superior courts in 2007 and the Chief Justice himself was removed twice from office that year! The precarious state of judges in fragile democracies may thus, in part, explain the post-Chaudhry Supreme Court's recent reluctance to review the 2013 Parliamentary election, even though there had been allegations of widespread electoral fraud.

Conclusion

This volume seeks to provide important insights on how Asian courts can strategically engage with the political actors in their jurisdictions and contribute to the country's democratic discourse. In dominant-party democracies, genuine political competition is absent. Nevertheless, even if their courts are unable to challenge the hegemonic dominant player by ushering in *systemic* electoral reforms, they can seek to extend voting rights writ small to marginalised groups, such as prisoners or convicts, as the Hong Kong judiciary has done. Courts in dynamic democracies have more political space to operate. They can facilitate their countries' democratic transformation by making *systemic* changes that enhance the competitiveness and fairness of voting procedures and electoral institutions. But, even then, judges should remain non-partisan and not be viewed as proxies that merely aid one political camp to remove its enemies from the country's political life. This concern is especially pronounced in unstable democracies where the country has been oscillating between military rule and civilian governments. Where the democracy's institutional processes are functioning poorly, and judicial independence is fragile, courts should reduce the potential pressures they face and not maximise them.[31]

There is a symbiotic relationship between a country's state of democratisation and the long-term sustainability of the political power that its judges can wield. A stable and dynamic democracy can empower its judges to shape their political environment and further contribute to democratic politics. On the other hand, judges in dominant-party, or even fragile, democracies, may not act with impunity. Therefore, prudent and wise judges must always design constitutional rules and doctrines that keep 'democratic transitions on course rather than contributing to pushing them off the rails'.[32]

Notes

1 The author is very grateful for the research assistance rendered by Sophie Mayatt-Simmons and Florence Sit in the preparation of this edited volume.
2 Ginsburg (2012); Ginsburg (2008); Harding and Nicholson (2011).
3 Hirschl (2004); Dressel (2012).
4 Yap (2015); Yap and Lau (2001); Chen (2014).
5 Dawood (2012) 500.
6 Issacharoff (2014) 610.
7 Ginsburg (2012) 738.
8 Ginsburg (2003) 19.

9 Ibid. 81.
10 Epstein (2001) 127–9; Landau (2014) 1541.
11 Issacharoff (2014) 588.
12 *Yazid bin Sufaat & Ors* v. *Suruhanjaya Pilihanraya* [2009] 6 MLJ 152.
13 *Teo Hoon Seong & Ors* v. *Suruhanjaya Pilihanraya* [2012] 4 MLJ 245.
14 *Vellama d/o Marie Muthu* v. *Attorney-General* [2013] SGCA 39, [2013] 4 SLR 1.
15 Currently, 35 seats in the Legislative Council are constituted via universal suffrage in GC elections while another 35 seats are constituted via FC elections. Ma (2007). See also Lo (2010) 130–1.
16 *Chan Kin Sum* v. *Secretary of Justice* [2009] 2 HKLRD 166 (Hong Kong Court of First Instance).
17 *Wong Hin Wai* v. *Secretary of Justice* [2012] 4 HKLRD 70 (Hong Kong Court of First Instance).
18 *Chan Yu Nam* v. *Secretary of Justice* [2012] HKCFA 17 (Hong Kong Court of Final Appeal).
19 *Common Cause* v. *Union of India* (1996) 2 SCC 752.
20 *Lily Thomas* v. *Union of India* (2013) 7 SCC 653.
21 *Krishnamoorthy* v. *Sivakumar* (2015) 3 SCC 467.
22 Constitutional Court Decision issued 19 July 2001, 2000 Hun-Ma 91, Constitutional Complaint on the Constitutionality of Article 56, 146(2) and 189 of the Public Election Act.
23 Constitutional Court Decision issued 30 October 2014, 2012 Hun-Ma 190, Constitutional Complaint on the Constitutionality of [Table 1] incorporated in and attached to Article 25(2) of the Public Election Act.
24 Constitutional Court Decision No. 22–24/PUU-VI/2008 (the *Muhammad Sholeh* case).
25 Constitutional Court Decision No. 110–111–112–113/PUU-VII/2009 (the *Left over Votes* case).
26 Constitutional Court Decision No. 14/PUU-XI/2013 (the *General Election Schedule* case).
27 See Judicial Yuan Interpretation No. 509 [2000] Constitutional Court of Taiwan.
28 See Chang (2010).
29 Issacharoff (2014) 610.
30 Gardbaum (2015).
31 Ibid. 306.
32 Ibid. 320.

References

Chang W.C., ‘Strategic Judicial Responses in Politically Charged Cases: East Asian Experiences’ (2010) 8 *International Journal of Constitutional Law* 885.

Chen A.H.Y. (ed.), *Constitutionalism in Asia in the Early Twenty-First Century* (Cambridge, Cambridge University Press 2014).

Dawood Y., ‘Electoral Fairness and the Law of Democracy: A Structural Rights Approach to Judicial Review’ (2012) 62 *University of Toronto Law Journal* 499.

Dressel B. (ed.), *Judicialization of Politics in Asia* (London, Routledge 2012).

Epstein L., ‘The Role of Constitutional Courts in the Establishment and Maintenance of Democratic Systems of Government’ (2001) 35 *Law and Society Review* 117.

Gardbaum S., ‘Are Strong Constitutional Courts Always a Good Thing for New Democracies?’ (2015) 53 *Columbia Journal of Transnational Law* 285.

Ginsburg T., *Judicial Review in New Democracies: Constitutional Courts in Asian Cases* (Cambridge, Cambridge University Press 2003).

Ginsburg T., 'Constitutional Courts in East Asia: Understanding Variation' (2008) 3 *Journal of Comparative Law* 80.

Ginsburg T., 'Courts and New Democracies: Recent Works' (2012) 37 *Law and Society* 720.

Harding A. and Nicholson P. (eds), *New Courts in Asia* (London, Routledge 2011).

Hirschl R., *Towards Juristocracy* (Cambridge, Harvard University Press 2004).

Issacharoff S., 'Constitutional Courts and Consolidated Power' (2014) 62 *American Journal of Comparative Law* 585.

Landau D., 'A Dynamic Theory of Judicial Role' (2014) 55 *Boston College Law Review* 1501.

Lo S., *Competing Chinese Political Visions* (Westport CT, Praeger 2010).

Ma N., 'Political Parties and Elections' in W.-M. Lam, W. Wong, and I. Holliday (eds), *Contemporary Hong Kong Politics: Governance in the Post-1997 Era* (Hong Kong, Hong Kong University Press 2007).

Yap P.J., *Constitutional Dialogue in Common Law Asia* (Oxford, Oxford University Press 2015).

Yap P.J. and Lau H. (eds), *Public Interest Litigation in Asia* (London, Routledge 2001).

Part I

Common Law Asia

2 Judicial review of elections in Hong Kong

Resolving a contradiction

Simon N.M. Young[1]

Introduction

The judicial review of elections in Hong Kong is a relatively recent phenomenon.[2] It occurs in a unique milieu of entrenched political rights[3] and political institutions that are on an evolving course to becoming fully democratic.[4] In this milieu, a contradiction has become apparent; while Hong Kong courts are prepared to strike down unreasonable restrictions on voting and candidacy, sometimes with significant consequences, they have done very little to impact the most unfair and illegitimate aspects of Hong Kong's electoral systems. These aspects include the functional constituencies that have returned at least half of all legislators since 1985,[5] the 1200 member election committee that nominates and elects the chief executive, and the practice of corporate voting used in both the election committee and functional constituency elections.

From a critical examination of the relevant judicial review case law, this chapter explains how the contradiction came about and what sustains it. It then reflects on how the contradiction might be resolved going forwards, particularly after the 2015 failed attempt to introduce universal suffrage of the chief executive.[6] Two opposite paths of resolution are discussed. One sees courts applying political rights even more robustly to chip away at those illegitimate aspects mentioned above. The other sees courts becoming even more deferential, declining judicial review of electoral laws on the ground that they are matters best left for political negotiations and legislative review. The chapter notes that the impact of the political reform exercise of 2013 to 2015, which was overshadowed by a more assertive role played by the Chinese central government, may influence a more deferential approach in the future. However, arguments are made for why courts should resist taking such a path.

The making of a contradiction

Article 21 of the Hong Kong Bill of Rights (HKBOR) guarantees that every permanent resident has the

> right and the opportunity … (a) to take part in the conduct of public affairs, directly or through freely chosen representatives; [and] (b) to vote and to be

> elected at genuine periodic elections which shall be by universal and equal suffrage and shall be held by secret ballot, guaranteeing the free expression of the will of the electors.

As it is based on Article 25 of the International Covenant on Civil and Political Rights (ICCPR), Hong Kong courts have made reference to the United Nations (UN) Human Rights Committee's General Comment 25 in interpreting the rights in Article 21.[7] The rights can be restricted so long as the restrictions are not 'unreasonable' and do not make distinctions based on 'race, colour, sex, language, religion, political or other opinion, national or social origin, property, birth or other status' (non-discrimination clause).

From 1991 to 2015, there have been approximately 16 judicial review cases in which electoral rights in Article 21 (and/or Article 26 of the Basic Law) have been considered. The courts have been robust in striking down residency requirements for candidacy, exclusions in village elections, and criminal law related disqualifications for voting and candidacy. The courts have been far more reluctant, however, to address systemic inequalities and unfairness in core electoral institutions and practices. These institutions deny a vast part of the voting population an equal opportunity to take part in the conduct of public affairs and condone breaches of the 'one person, one vote' principle and significant disparities in voting power; but, the courts have found that these practices are not unreasonable or do not engage the guaranteed political right. This apparent contradictory approach to judicial review of elections begs the questions of whether the courts have been inconsistent in their approach or whether other reasons can be offered as an explanation.

Strong review of restrictions

Ten-year residency requirement

In the first Article 21 judicial review, Lau San Ching persuaded the High Court to strike down a requirement of being ordinarily resident for ten years preceding the date of nomination for District Board candidacy.[8] He won his case on two grounds: first, he met the ten-year requirement even though for a good part of that period he was imprisoned in a mainland jail for sedition; second, the ten-year requirement violated the right to be elected and was neither rationally connected nor proportionate to a legitimate aim. To assess the reasonableness of the restriction, Justice Peter Cheung applied a rigorous three-step restrictions test modelled on the approach applied in Canada, by the European Court of Human Rights (ECtHR) and the UN Human Rights Committee.[9] He found the 'clearest indication' of irrationality in the differential treatment of voters: permanent residents did not have to satisfy an additional residency requirement in order to vote.[10] His response to an argument for judicial deference to Hong Kong's unique circumstance was sharp: 'Even taken into account the political situation of Hong Kong ... and the historical context in which the Electoral Provisions

Ordinance was enacted, by no means of imagination can it be said that [the requirement] is consistent with Article 21.'[11] He referred to significantly shorter residency requirements in Canada, Australia, and New Zealand as examples of ways of achieving the aims of having local connection and knowledge by less restrictive means.[12] A Legislative Council (LegCo) select committee may have conducted periodic reviews of the residency requirement, but the judge pointed out the absence of evidence that those reviews took into account the implications of Article 21.[13] The government did not appeal. The case set a liberal tone for Article 21 review.

Village representative elections

The same robust approach resonated in the first Article 21 case before the Court of Final Appeal after 1997. The case of *Secretary for Justice* v. *Chan Wah* concerned the election of village representatives for over 600 villages in the New Territories.[14] The two applicants were born, raised, and had resided in their respective villages, but could not vote or stand as a candidate in their village election. This was because they were not indigenous villagers, i.e. they were not descendants through the male line of a person who resided in an established village in 1898.[15] No legislation governed village elections but the practice was that only indigenous villagers could serve as village representatives. Since approval by the Secretary for Home Affairs resulted in the elected person serving as village representative and possibly other roles in different statutory bodies, this conferred sufficient government connection for bringing the challenge under Article 21(a).[16]

The Court found that village representatives engaged in the 'conduct of public affairs' and to exclude villagers like the applicants from voting or running in village elections was an unreasonable restriction on the right and opportunity to take part in the conduct of public affairs.[17] Whether a restriction was reasonable had to be 'considered objectively' and the question might be answered differently from one era to another.[18] Chief Justice Andrew Li reasoned simply. Since a village representative was someone who

> is to and in fact does represent the village as a whole (comprising both the indigenous and non-indigenous villagers) and further has a role to play beyond the village level, the restriction on the ground of not being indigenous cannot be considered a reasonable restriction.[19]

Arguments based on the 'principle of gradual and orderly progress' in Article 68 of the Basic Law and the opportunities provided by District Councils for the conduct of public affairs were dismissed shortly as being irrelevant.[20] The decision had transformative consequences, since the government had to devise a new scheme of village elections, consult extensively on the new scheme, and enact the necessary legislation; the whole process from the Court's decision until the first village elections under the new legislation took approximately two-and-a-half years.[21]

Prisoner disqualification cases

A final set of cases to illustrate the courts' strong review of restrictions on voting and candidacy is the prisoners or criminal law related disqualification cases. Prisoner disenfranchisement cases have been politically controversial in many places. In the United Kingdom, despite more than a decade after the ECtHR (Grand Chamber)'s 2005 judgment in *Hirst* v. *The United Kingdom*, there has yet to be legislative reform to remove or minimise the ban on prisoners' voting.[22] The experience in Hong Kong has been very different.

In *Chan Kin Sum* v. *Secretary for Justice*, the three applicants (a legislator and two prisoners serving terms of imprisonment for offences of robbery) applied to the Court to have struck down the blanket bans on persons sentenced to or serving a term of imprisonment of any length from voting and registering to vote in LegCo elections.[23] Remanded persons awaiting trial were also barred from voting, not by law, but simply because no arrangements had been made to allow them to vote while detained. The Court found the bans on voting and registering violated the prisoners' right to vote as protected by Article 21 of the HKBOR and Article 26 of the Basic Law. It also declared that the Electoral Affairs Commission had a statutory duty to make all necessary arrangements to enable registered remanded persons held in custody to vote on an election day.[24]

In identifying the proper restrictions test to be applied, Justice Andrew Cheung followed *Lau San Ching*'s proportionality test and rejected less rigorous approaches, such as a *Wednesbury* reasonableness test.[25] He stated: 'In a society governed by the rule of law, the courts must be vigilant in the protection of fundamental rights and must vigorously examine any restriction that may be placed on them.'[26] The judge noted the breadth of the restriction, which applied not only to imprisoned convicted persons, but also to those on bail pending appeal, those serving a suspended sentence, and parolees. Citing authorities from Canada, Australia, the ECtHR, and South Africa, all of which upheld similar challenges, the judge noted, 'the modern trend is against disenfranchisement'.[27] The statement in *Chan Wah* that determinations of reasonableness may vary from era to era was used to reason that the position at the time of the decision in 2009 'may well be very different from that in 1997 when [the law was passed] in the infancy of the HKSAR'.[28] The Court was critical of the absence of evidence from government on the rational connection between the restriction and the legitimate aims of crime prevention, and enhancing civic responsibility and respect for the rule of law.[29] The Court concluded: 'the general, automatic and indiscriminate restrictions on the right to vote and the right to register as an elector cannot be justified under the proportionality test'.[30]

The Court's treatment of arguments for deference is noteworthy. The argument for deference due to Hong Kong's unique context and gradual development towards full democracy was turned on its head. The judge stated, 'where only 50% of the LegCo members are elected by universal suffrage, that makes the right to vote doubly important and precious'.[31] The argument for deference because the matter concerned questions of 'penal philosophy and policy' was brushed aside since the Court recognised that it was not being asked to draw the line of reasonableness, which is for the legislature and executive, but to examine the restrictions and decide whether they are unreasonable.[32] An argument for deference or a margin of appreciation was also made on the basis that LegCo had considered relaxing the restrictions on previous occasions but rejected it. The Court accepted that due respect and deference should be paid to these legislative choices; however, this did not immunise the provisions from scrutiny and the Court still had to exercise its constitutional role of examining 'the choices, as made, closely and see whether the restrictions on voting rights ... can be justified'.[33] After paying due respect and deference, it made no difference in the result.[34]

The Court made clear it was not saying no restrictions could be imposed on prisoners' voting, but where to draw the line was a matter for government.[35] In order to give the government time and space to consult the public and pass new legislation, the judge, on the government's application, ordered a temporary suspension of its declarations for approximately seven-and-a-half months.[36] The temporary suspension meant that the status quo would effectively continue and government could not be found in contempt for non-compliance during the period of suspension.[37] In effect the temporary suspension served as a catalyst for government action. In contrast to events in the UK, the Hong Kong government consulted the public and passed legislation not to impose any restrictions, in accordance with public opinion and the Court's judgment, all within the suspension period.[38]

The other two cases concern criminal law related disqualifications for candidacy. In *Tse Hung Hing* v. *The Medical Council of Hong Kong*, the applicant was a doctor who wanted to be elected to serve as a member of the Medical Council, a public body whose affairs came within the meaning of 'public affairs' in Article 21(a).[39] But since he had a conviction for careless driving, for which he was fined HK$1000, he was disqualified from being nominated because he had been convicted in Hong Kong of any offence punishable with imprisonment (careless driving being punishable up to six months' imprisonment). On the heels of the *Chan Kin Sum* decision, the judge, in a short judgment, accepted the parties' agreed position that the restriction violated Article 21(a).[40] While the aim of the restriction to ensure that Council members are trustworthy persons of high moral probity was legitimate, the indiscriminate means was disproportionate as exemplified by the facts of the case, where the conviction was minor and of 'no apparent relevance to the applicant's suitability to be a Council member'.[41]

Wong Hin Wai v. *Secretary for Justice* was heard and decided expeditiously, a few months before the September 2012 LegCo elections.[42] Both applicants wanted to be candidates in this election but were disqualified because they had been recently convicted of minor offences and sentenced to short terms of imprisonment.[43] Although granted bail pending appeal, the disqualification still applied to them because their sentence of imprisonment had yet to be served or pardoned. The Court held the restriction to be unconstitutional, finding no rational connection or proportionality between the restriction, when applied to persons on bail pending appeal and sentenced to less than three months' imprisonment, and the aim of maintaining public confidence in LegCo and the electoral process.[44]

While the Court's approach could be said to be rigorous, there are two important differences in Justice Johnson Lam's approach in this case when compared to that of Justice Cheung in *Chan Kin Sum*. First, Justice Lam was more influenced by recent ECtHR authorities that emphasised a wide margin of appreciation, which a court of supranational jurisdiction would be expected to adopt in respect of member states in cases concerning democratic rights.[45] This led Justice Lam to apply a different 'proportionality test' that does not assess whether the restriction was 'no more than necessary'.[46] Instead the restriction should not 'curtail the rights in question to such an extent as to impair their very essence or to deprive them of their effectiveness' – words taken from the ECtHR case law.[47] The Court 'must also have regard to the historical and current state of political development in Hong Kong'.[48] This suggests a more deferential test of proportionality, especially with the endorsement of what Lord Collins said in *R (Barclay)* v. *Lord Chancellor*, that electoral 'features which would be unacceptable in the context of one system may be justified in the context of another'.[49] The approach signals the end of comparative law assistance. Justice Lam did not address an important point made in *Chan Kin Sum* that the strong proportionality test (as applied in equality cases) would still need to be applied if the challenge was based on an Article 1(1) distinction, i.e. the non-discrimination clause.[50] In the by-election disqualification case, concerned with a newly enacted provision that disqualified LegCo members, who resign from office, from being a candidate in the by-election for the same seat within a six-month period from the date of resignation, Justice Thomas Au in *Kwok Cheuk Kin* v. *Secretary for Constitutional and Mainland Affairs* also applied the more deferential proportionality test: 'the court should only interfere if it finds that, upon scrutiny, the restriction is manifestly without justifiable foundation'.[51]

The second departure from what was said in *Chan Kin Sum* is in the treatment of legislative history and debates. Justice Cheung stated that deference should be accorded to the mere fact that the legislature had considered the matter without going too closely into what was actually said during the debates:

> one should be very slow, in a domestic context, to evaluate the quality of the legislative debate, particularly with a view to lowering the deference or respect that the courts should have, in a given case, for the choice made by the legislature. That is, generally speaking, no business of the courts.[52]

However, Justice Lam assessed the quality of the debates held in 1997 when he noted that legislators were 'unwittingly misled' by the administration on the purpose and effect of the amended restriction.[53] For Justice Lam, this meant that the legislature had not properly considered the implications of the Article 21 right and thus little if any weight could be attached to the 'judgment of the legislature'.[54] In conditioning deference to whether there had been legislative consideration of rights implications, the approach of Justice Lam was similar to that seen in *Lau San Ching*.[55] By contrast, in the by-election disqualification case, Justice Au held that the Court 'will be slow to interfere' when the challenged provision is the 'result of active and full debate in LegCo where competing interests were presented'.[56]

The government chose not to appeal *Wong Hin Wai* and, as with the first prisoners' right to vote case, they chose to conduct a public consultation in July 2014 on different options for reform.[57] Though *Wong Hin Wai* is counted as a strong review case, it shows the signs of a more deferential approach to review. It will need to be left to future cases to reach greater clarity on the two issues of the intensity of the proportionality test and the proper consideration of the quality of legislative debates in assessing weight to be accorded to legislative choices.

Weak review of institutional inequality

As a society transitioning to full democracy, there are a number of institutional aspects of the political system that appear unfair and illegitimate from the standpoint of the fundamental right to vote. Criticisms are typically directed at the functional constituencies, which were introduced by the British in 1985, retained by the Chinese government after 1997, and replicated in the system of sectors and subsectors in the election committee for the chief executive. The functional constituencies are criticised for privileging business, industry, and professional groups with additional political power and representation. These criticisms were voiced by many of the young protesters during the 79-day-long Occupy Central protests in the second half of 2014.[58] In its periodic review of Hong Kong's compliance with the ICCPR, the UN Human Rights Committee has criticised Hong Kong's political system for falling short of Article 21 requirements.[59]

Functional constituencies

When functional constituencies were introduced, they brought diversity to a legislature made up solely of appointed and official members.[60] Members returned by functional constituencies and a new electoral college made up 42 per cent of all legislators in 1985.[61] It was not until 1991 with the introduction of 18 directly elected seats (to replace the electoral college seats) that unfairness with the functional seats became apparent. While all registered voters had one vote to elect a geographical constituency member, some 69,825 registered voters (consisting of individuals and corporate bodies) had a second vote in the functional constituencies and thus a second representative in the legislature.[62]

The proportion of registered voters that had a second vote/representative widened to over one million in 1995, with Governor Chris Patten's controversial reforms, but this expansion was short lived and rolled back to 138,984 (127,075 individuals and 11,909 bodies) in the 1998 election.[63] The inequality of some having two votes continued in this extreme form in the 2000, 2004, and 2008 elections.[64] But for the 2012 election, as a result of a successful, but controversial, tri-partite negotiation, the inequality was removed by giving excluded voters a second vote in a new functional constituency in which only elected district council members could be nominated.[65] The five seats in this new district council functional constituency were known as 'super seats' because they had an electorate base of 3.2 million voters without any geographical delimitation.[66] China required functional and geographical seats to be in equal proportion,[67] but this reform in substance increased the proportion of popularly elected legislators to 57 per cent.

Even with the 2012 reform to extend a functional vote to all voters, there remains the problem of the gross disparity in voting power as between voters in differently sized functional constituencies. There are 12 traditional functional constituencies with fewer than 1000 registered voters.[68] The smallest is Insurance, which consists of 135 authorised insurance companies. The other 11 also comprise companies in different sectors of business, trade, and industry. These small constituencies do not typically hold contested elections since leadership can be decided by consultation and consensus.[69] The largest amongst the traditional functional constituencies has always been Education (comprising teachers) whose size was 92,957 in 2012.[70] Other large constituencies tend to consist of individuals practising different professions.[71] With the new District Council (second) constituency, the largest functional constituency now has 643,951 registered voters per legislator.[72]

There has only been one judicial review (*Lee Miu Ling* v. *Attorney General*) directed at the functional constituencies.[73] In 1994, two applicants brought an Article 21 challenge to the Patten reformed functional constituencies, which had over a million registered functional voters and no corporate voters. As neither applicant had a functional vote, they challenged the functional constituencies for being in breach of the 'one person, one vote' principle and for disparities in voting power (if indeed they had a functional vote). The High Court and Court of Appeal dismissed their challenge, and petition for leave to appeal to the Privy Council was refused.[74]

In respect of the 'one person, one vote' challenge, Justice Bokhary in the Court of Appeal found that paragraph (3) of Article VII of the Letters Patent was a specific provision that insulated functional constituencies from Article 21(b) review.[75] The paragraph provided that nothing in Article VII

> shall be construed as precluding the making of laws which, as regards the election of the Members of the Legislative Council, confer on persons generally or persons of a particular description any entitlement to vote which is in addition to a vote in respect of a geographical constituency.[76]

It was intended to qualify paragraph (5) of that same article, which entrenched the HKBOR and repealed laws made after 1991 that were inconsistent with the ICCPR as applied to Hong Kong.[77] Thus the Court found the Article 21 rights were not engaged and no question of reasonable restriction had to be addressed. After the 2012 reform, which conferred both functional and geographical votes on all voters, this issue has now become academic.

As for the unequal voting power challenge, the Court addressed the issue of whether the disparity was an unreasonable restriction. Justice Bokhary reduced the test to a question of would 'sensible and fair-minded people condemn [the] arrangement as irrational or disproportionate'.[78] This is a high threshold, implying a light approach to proportionality, less rigorous than what was applied in *Lau San Ching* and *Chan Kin Sum*, although similar to the test articulated in *Wong Hin Wai* and *Kwok Cheuk Kin*. As it was in the 'very nature' of functional constituencies 'to vary in size', they could not be faulted from the standpoint of 'sensible and fair-minded people'.[79] The Court was not interested in assessing whether it was possible to allocate seats to the constituencies in a fairer manner; as Justice Godfrey remarked, 'that … is a matter with which this court can have nothing to do'.[80] This is true if what his Lordship meant was that the Court should not attempt to redraw the constituency lines (like attempting to draw the line by which prisoners could be lawfully disenfranchised). As with the prisoners' right to vote cases, if, by applying a rigorous proportionality test, it was found reasonably practicable to devise a more rights compliant arrangement then the ball could be thrown back to government to come up with a better scheme.[81] This would be the beginning of a judicial–government dialogue that would lead to a position consistent with human rights requirements yet reflective of societal interests.[82]

It is interesting to note that the Court was not prepared to show deference to government simply because of Hong Kong's 'embryonic stage' of democratic development.[83] However, the Court noted the drastic political consequences of declaring functional constituencies unconstitutional, before putting the concern to one side.[84] It would invalidate the legislature and, as Justice Bokhary remarked light-heartedly, 'so much for local democracy' since English legislation would be needed to pass the new legislature law.[85] These consequences would be of less concern today. In 2006, the Court of Final Appeal held that when a court is prepared to strike down legislation for unconstitutionality it also has the power to suspend the declaration of invalidity for a fixed period.[86] This remedy was ordered in *Chan Kin Sum* with positive consequences for law-making.[87] However, given the need to have complete confidence in the legality of the legislature and its actions pending corrective legislation, it would probably be necessary to seek a temporary validity order to protect the legislature in the interim period.[88] It remains unsettled, however, whether Hong Kong courts have the power to make such an order.[89]

Corporate voting

Corporate voting was an original feature of the functional constituencies. In delineating these constituencies, well-established trade and business organisations were used as reference points for conferring votes on the membership of such organisations. Naturally many of these umbrella organisations had corporate members. For example, the Hong Kong General Chamber of Commerce's corporate members constitute the electors of the Commercial (First) constituency, the Chinese General Chamber of Commerce's corporate members constitute the electors of the Commercial (Second) constituency, the Federation of Hong Kong Industries' corporate members constitute the electors of the Industrial (First) constituency, and so on.[90] In 1998, functional constituencies, such as Transport and Agriculture and Fisheries, were added and given corporate electors by directly listing them in a schedule within primary legislation.[91]

Hong Kong is probably the only place that allows companies and other bodies to vote, alongside individual voters, in the election of its legislative members. As mentioned earlier, the corporate voters tend to populate the smaller sized constituencies, which do not typically hold contested elections.[92] Their representatives tend to put their respective sector's interest before the interest of the general public, even though they have constitutional responsibilities as legislators that go beyond the interests of their sector.[93] They are said by government to provide balanced participation in the legislature and contribute to sustaining Hong Kong's capitalist system.[94] They are also typically known as 'pro-establishment legislators' given their tendency to support both the Hong Kong and central governments on policy matters.[95]

Corporate voting in LegCo has often been criticised. To give functional constituencies more credibility, Governor Patten abolished corporate voting for the 1995 election, giving the votes to the directors of the previously enfranchised companies.[96] There are two main criticisms generally directed at corporate voting. First, as a result of inadequate safeguards, one corporate voter through the vehicle of subsidiaries and other controlled entities can effectively have more than one vote in breach of the 'one person, one vote' principle.[97] It is well known that this already happens with many large conglomerates.[98] In constituencies with only corporate electors, the potential unfairness of this lapse is mitigated somewhat by the fact that each corporate voter has the same chance to pack the constituency with their own controlled entities. But some constituencies have mixed corporate and individual voters and the ability of individuals to pack constituencies with controlled corporate entities will be much less than that of large enterprises.[99]

The second criticism is that the qualifying conditions for corporate voting are less strict than those for individual voting.[100] Corporate bodies vote by authorising a person to vote on its behalf and that authorised representative can be any employee or member of the body.[101] The problem arises because the qualifying conditions for voting apply only to the authorised representative and not to the corporate body itself. Take the permanent residency requirement as an example. Individuals must be permanent residents before they can qualify to vote. For corporate voters the authorised representatives must be a permanent resident, but the corporate body itself need not have any ties to Hong Kong.[102] So foreign consular posts, international organisations, agencies of foreign government, through their membership in commerce and trade umbrella organisations, could register to vote, until these loopholes were closed by amendments made in 2011 and 2012.[103]

In a judicial review challenging the constitutionality of corporate voting (*Chan Yu Nam* v. *Secretary for Justice*),[104] the applicants were a taxi driver and renovation worker who did not have the right to vote in any functional constituency.[105] Their main argument was that conferring the vote in LegCo elections on corporate bodies, which are incapable of having permanent residency status, was inconsistent with Article 26 of the Basic Law and Article 21 of the HKBOR, which only allow the right to vote to be given to individual permanent residents. It was also argued that corporate voting discriminated against individuals who lacked the financial means to form companies and thereby enjoy the additional political rights of corporate electors. The Court of First Instance and Court of Appeal rejected the challenge,[106] and both the Court of Appeal and Court of Final Appeal refused leave to appeal.[107] In the brief reasons of the appeal committee of the final court, the Court of Appeal's conclusion that Article 26 did not preclude corporate voting was found to be supported by the references to 'corporate bodies' in the annexes of the Basic Law, the 'history of legislative constitutional development in Hong Kong' and relevant extrinsic materials used as an aid to constitutional interpretation.[108]

The case raised an important question about the scope of application of the rights protected in Articles 26 and 21, specifically whether they applied to functional constituency elections. The first instance judge, Justice Cheung (surprisingly the same judge in *Chan Kin Sum*) held that the rights did not apply to this type of election; but, if they did, he accepted the applicants' submission that the right was engaged and the issue would be whether the restriction could be justified.[109] In the Court of Appeal, Vice-President Frank Stock, without deciding the correctness of Justice Cheung's decision on this point, postulated an 'alternative and tenable view' to reaching the same result.[110] His alternative view was that Article 26 'inalienably accorded to permanent residents ... the right, through elections, to take part in the conduct of public affairs of the Region', but without precluding government from conferring the right on anyone else.[111] Although not explicitly stated, his Lordship was apparently attempting to read the rights in Article 26 harmoniously with the rights in Article 21(a) and (b) of the HKBOR. He summarised his view in the following passage, which was emphasised in his subsequent leave decision and endorsed in the Court of Final Appeal:[112]

> What is clear is that art. 26 is part of a mosaic which includes arts. 45, 68 and Annexes I and II of the Basic Law the effect of which is that in the early years of Hong Kong's new constitutional dispensation, there is room for participation through election in public affairs by all permanent residents but for a simultaneous continuation beyond 1997 of corporate participation in such affairs by or through major organizations and associations at elections.[113]

While Vice-President Stock was reluctant to reject outright Justice Cheung's approach, which effectively immunises functional constituencies from Article 26 (and Article 21 of the HKBOR) review, the reference in the above passage to 'room for participation through election in public affairs' implies a broader interpretation of Article 26. According to this view, Article 26 applies to functional constituency and other elections, but, based on textual and contextual considerations, cannot be construed to preclude the continuity of corporate voting as originally conceived in the functional constituency system. This must be the better view since Justice Cheung's holding significantly narrows the scope of political rights, an approach inconsistent with giving fundamental rights a generous and purposive interpretation.

Vice-President Stock's approach to Article 26 is also more aligned with the Court of Appeal's approach in *Lee Miu Ling*, which did not categorically hold the non-application of Article 21 to functional constituencies. This approach gives effect to the rights in Article 26 'in accordance with law', that law by virtue of Article 39 of the Basic Law includes the ICCPR as applied to Hong Kong, taking into account Justice Brian Keith's approach in *Lee Miu Ling* to the election reservation to the ICCPR.[114] Justice Keith held that the reservation no longer had relevance after the Letters Patent was amended in 1995 to provide for an 'elected' LegCo.[115] However, Justice Cheung in *Chan Yu Nam* noted that under Justice Keith's approach (assuming it was correct) the reservation would be spent only from 1995, but of importance was that in 1990 when the Basic Law was promulgated, the election reservation had full effect in limiting the scope of the ICCPR political rights applicable to Hong Kong.[116] But, with respect, to freeze the meaning of fundamental rights to a snapshot of the legal position on the date of promulgation is to ignore the living tree principle of interpretation.[117] Article 26 rights are exercised in accordance with a dynamic law, which in this instance removes any constraint imposed by the election reservation once LegCo has become 'elected' (which has been the case since 1995). What this achieves is the same scope of protection afforded by electoral rights in the Basic Law and HKBOR.

Swati Jhaveri notes that both courts 'relied heavily on a historical approach to interpreting the provision'.[118] However there is a subtle but important difference to how each made use of the historical context. Vice-President Stock relied upon historical context to test the applicants' submission that the words of Article 26 intended to bring about a new state of affairs in which the right to vote in LegCo elections could only be conferred on individual permanent residents. He found this context to provide no logical or realistic support for this position.[119] Justice Cheung, on the other hand, referred to historical context to find that the drafters of the Basic Law and the National People's Congress intended the pre-1995 practice of corporate voting to continue after 1997.[120] From this finding, he leaped to the conclusion that Article 26 was never intended to apply to functional constituency elections.[121] This leap, not found in Vice-President Stock's alternative view, goes too far and was unnecessary to decide the issue.

The applicant's challenge based on permanent residency faced a steep hill from the outset, but it was regrettable the judges did not treat the challenge based on discrimination more seriously, having found shortcomings in the standing of the applicants (not being functional voters) to bring the challenge and in the terms of relief sought.[122] As Jhaveri writes, the case 'undermines the possibility of a more robust role for the various provisions in the Basic Law as tools for reducing the inequalities and anomalies in electoral rights'.[123]

Election committee for the chief executive

The election committee system for nominating and electing the chief executive is the least democratic electoral institution in Hong Kong, but also the most resistant to judicial review. It is criticised in the Chinese and English media as holding 'small circle elections', since the committee was as small as 400 individuals in 1996, grew to and stayed at 800 from 1998 to 2011, and reached its present size of 1200 for the 2012 chief executive election.[124] Critics of the chief executive, Leung Chun-ying, gave him the pejorative nickname '689' to highlight the total number of votes he obtained to be elected.[125] The 250,000-odd voters who elect committee members are delineated in an intricate arrangement of sectors and subsectors that reflect an expanded version of the functional constituencies; hence the system shares the problems and criticisms of functional constituencies and corporate voting.[126] Elections in subsectors, when they are held, are unpopular; they have the lowest voter turnout rates of all elections in Hong Kong.[127] Over 90 per cent of registered voters have no opportunity to participate in chief executive elections.[128]

It is a small improvement from the colonial era when the local population had no input on the selection of Hong Kong's governor. But the balance of interests amongst election committee members is such that the central government can decisively influence the final election result. What gave people hope was that Article 45 of the Basic Law stated that the 'ultimate aim is the selection of the Chief Executive by universal suffrage upon nomination by a broadly representative nominating committee in accordance with democratic procedures'. In December 2007, these hopes grew stronger when the Standing Committee of the National People's Congress (NPCSC) gave Hong Kong a timetable for universal suffrage: 2017 for the chief executive and, if this was implemented, 2020 for LegCo.[129] Pan-democrat legislators, who tend to make up almost 40 per cent of all legislators, are typically the first to attack the legitimacy of chief executive elections, yet with the aim of universal suffrage in sight they fielded candidates in both the 2007 and 2012 elections.[130] With the relatively low nomination threshold of 12.5 per cent, both candidates were nominated but with no chance of winning the election.

To everyone's disappointment, all hopes of realising universal suffrage in 2017 were extinguished on 18 June 2015 when the pan-democrat legislators vetoed the government's proposal for reform by precluding the two-thirds legislative majority needed to pass the proposal.[131] The apparent irony of pan-democrat legislators vetoing democracy belies their principled objections against the nomination restrictions imposed by the NPCSC on 31 August 2014. Those restrictions (i.e. the nominating committee, taking the same size and form as the

2011 election committee, would nominate two to three candidates, each of whom must have majority support from committee members) would continue to give the central government de facto control over nominations.[132] Pan-democrats could not accept this 'fake' system of universal suffrage, and the polls leading up to the vote showed that those who supported the veto had risen to more than 40 per cent.[133]

No attempt has been made to challenge the core inequalities of the system of electing the chief executive, including the election committee. From existing case law, the courts might follow three possible approaches to a judicial review of this system. First, the Court might hold that since the system (and change to the system) is so fully provided for in the Basic Law and the various decisions and interpretation of the NPCSC, no rights or other constitutional provisions could in any way be engaged by the operation of this system. This approach would be similar to the one followed by Justice Cheung in *Chan Yu Nam* in holding that Article 26 did not apply to functional constituencies.

The second more nuanced approach is to hold that while the system cannot be challenged for failing to provide for equal and universal suffrage (because this has been specifically excepted), political and other rights can still be engaged by the operation of the system. The focus would then be on justifying the reasonableness of any restriction. This approach was followed by the Court of Appeal in *Lee Miu Ling* and by Vice-President Stock in *Chan Yu Nam*. Similarly, in a case concerning whether judicial review was available to challenge the outcome of a chief executive election, Justice Lam held that, by virtue of Article 45, Annex I of the Basic Law and various NPCSC decisions and interpretation, the right to election by equal and universal suffrage was not engaged, but the 'concept of free election ("freely chosen representatives" and "free expression of the will of the electors") is applicable to an election pursuant to Article 45'; there was a need to ensure 'fundamental safeguards for free election'.[134]

The third approach is to follow the prisoner disqualification cases and treat the right to vote as being engaged by the system, whereupon the issue becomes one of reasonableness and proportionality. It is highly unlikely, however, that this approach will be followed. The second approach is to be preferred because it maintains a role for courts consistent with the dictates of the rule of law but has regard to constitutional realities.

With both the second and third approaches, there is still the issue of how rigorously will courts apply the justifications test. As mentioned earlier, there is uncertainty in both the scope of the proportionality test and approach to margin of appreciation. In *Leung Lai Kwok Yvonne* v. *The Chief Secretary for Administration*, one recent case that challenged not the system itself but the government's consultation and 2015 universal suffrage proposal, margin of appreciation was given as a reason for refusing leave to apply for judicial review on grounds of prematurity.[135] The applicant was a University of Hong Kong law student who argued that the government, in misapprehending the legal effect of the NPCSC's 31 August decision, conducted a tainted public consultation that also failed to take into account relevant considerations, namely the rights in Articles 26 and

21, and thus unreasonably restricted those rights. Justice Au refused leave on two grounds: immateriality (that the alleged correct understanding of the NPCSC's decision would not have affected the consultation or proposal) and prematurity (that the challenge could still be brought after LegCo approved the proposal). To buttress the latter point, Justice Au reasoned that since election law is an area, on which 'a due margin of appreciation' is accorded, citing Chief Justice Geoffrey Ma's judgment in *Leung Chun Ying* v. *Ho Chun Yan Albert*, the matter should be allowed to be debated in LegCo before it is reviewed by the Court.[136]

Explaining the contradiction

One way to begin to explain the contradiction in the Hong Kong courts' strong review of restrictions and weak review of institutional inequality is to consider the consequences and impact of the cases. The strong review cases addressed isolated disqualifying provisions that had limited policy support and could be struck down without too great an impact. The weak review cases, however, challenged systemic inequalities and would have had significant institutional and policy ramifications. But a distinction based only on the extent of the impact cannot account for the Court of Final Appeal's strong review decision in *Chan Wah*, which had significant and transformative institutional ramifications for village elections, albeit outside the spheres of chief executive and LegCo elections.

A better approach is to consider the nature of the potential consequence. Where the matter is of interest to the central government and within the scope of Hong Kong's political reform trajectory, courts are likely to be hands off even where fundamental rights are engaged. Village elections and disqualifying conditions, based on residency or conviction and punishment, are not reform issues along that trajectory, nor are they important enough to catch the central government's interest. However, functional constituencies, the election committee, the election of the chief executive, and corporate voting are all matters of great interest to both the central and Hong Kong governments and reserved for consideration in the reform exercises leading to universal suffrage. They are matters that go to the heart of the relationship between the central authorities and the Hong Kong Special Administrative Region and are of international importance. They concern China's authority over Hong Kong and, as stated in the 31 August decision, 'the long-term prosperity and stability of Hong Kong and the sovereignty, security and development interests of the country are at stake'.[137] Thus they are matters that courts tolerate, even to the extent of holding fundamental rights in abeyance, while giving time and space to governments, legislators, and the people to work out the proper way forward.

Hong Kong courts have adopted different strategies to tolerate and avoid confronting the institutional inequality in the political system. One is to narrow the ambit of rights making them wholly inapplicable to certain types of elections under the Basic Law (*Chan Yu Nam*, per Justice Cheung). Another is to refuse to extend the scope of the right unless that extension has support in legislative and historical contexts (*Chan Yu Nam*, per Vice-President Stock). A third is to find a derogation from a certain aspect of the right expressly condoned in another part of the constitution (*Lee Miu Ling*; *Leung Chun Ying* v. *Ho Chun Yan Albert*, per Justice Lam). A fourth is to apply a deferential proportionality test to find that the restriction on the right is justified (*Lee Miu Ling*; *Kwok Cheuk Kin*). Whatever strategy is applied, the upshot is the appearance of a contradiction, that while rights matter, rights matter less when the issue lies along Hong Kong's political reform trajectory, over which Beijing has great interest.

Getting beyond the contradiction

There are two ways for the contradiction to be resolved; each takes an opposite path. The first path is for courts to take a robust approach to political rights in all cases and confront institutional inequality head on. As Jhaveri argues, it would involve courts drawing and upholding baselines even in hard cases.[138] Yasmin Dawood has argued that courts can apply a structural rights approach to address structural deficiencies of the political system.[139] This would involve recognition of a new democratic right, the right to a fair and legitimate democratic process.[140] However conceptualised, the courts on this path would adopt a more critical approach to deference and conduct a rigorous proportionality review to assess whether any restriction is no more than necessary. Courts will be more inclined to question whether societal circumstances have changed so as to render past restrictions no longer reasonable. Where it is reasonably practicable for government to devise a better scheme to achieve legislative aims, i.e. one that impairs rights less, then governments should be given a fair opportunity to achieve a new scheme after the legislation is struck down. Constitutional remedies of temporary suspension or temporary validity will help further a dialogue between courts and government that aims to realise a new legal position informed by constitutional values and reasonable public policy.[141]

The other path sees courts becoming even more deferential, moving to a complete disengagement with entrenched political rights. Functional constituencies and corporate voting have already been constitutionalised by courts or made immune from scrutiny. Other areas, e.g. chief executive and election committee elections, will also become untouchable by courts. This process is already occurring with the application of the margin of appreciation in recent cases. In an almost automatic manner it has been said that since election law involves 'political and policy considerations', a 'due margin of appreciation' must be accorded even if drawing a line may result in a few 'hard cases' with 'detrimental effect on individuals'.[142] Where there has been active and full debate in the legislature, it was said, in the by-election disqualification case, 'the proper place to resolve this political issue is LegCo and not the court'.[143] Thus, on this path, all judicial reviews of elections become 'political issues' requiring a hands-off approach by the courts. The only possible exception is if a core right was engaged, but political rights would not be regarded as core rights.

The 2014 Occupy Central protests and the 2015 failed political reform vote impacted people's political awareness, expectations, and perceptions of Hong Kong's relationship with the mainland. Will these events have any impact on the approach of courts to future judicial review of election cases? The statements and actions of the central and Hong Kong governments may influence judges to take a more deferential path. Unlike previous reform exercises, the central government played a prominent and assertive role in the reform debate. Foreign governments were told not to interfere with this internal matter.[144] Both the central and Hong Kong governments asserted that there were no international standards relevant to the reform issue and, in any case, the election reservation rendered the ICCPR irrelevant.[145] The central government made clear that it wanted to control the nominations process in order to keep the vote outcome predictable and manageable. Functional constituencies, corporate voting, the election committee structure, the restriction on the chief executive from being a member of a political party, and other aspects of the status quo, would remain intact even after the chief executive was elected by universal suffrage.[146] No concessions would be made in response to public protests or to gain the support of pan-democrat legislators.[147] These actions send a loud message to courts not to interfere under the guise of fundamental rights with an internal political matter in which the central government has a strong interest.

But all of these political statements and gestures amount to no more than that; they do not translate into legal edicts, though they may appear in legal submissions. In remaining independent, courts apply the law and safeguard rights and freedoms of individuals.[148] Granted there will be occasions when Hong Kong judges may need to consider if their decisions will trigger a constitutional crisis, such as the one in 1999 when the NPCSC interpreted the Basic Law to reverse part of the Court of Final Appeal's interpretation in the first right of abode case.[149] But these occasions are rare and only of concern to the final court. Experience has since been gained on how these controversial issues can be addressed in an orderly manner through the reference mechanism in Article 158 of the Basic Law.[150] Mindful of a strong public reaction and the detrimental effect on the rule of law, the Hong Kong government has not tried again to request an NPCSC interpretation to reverse a Court of Final Appeal interpretation.

Deference on grounds that the matter comes within Hong Kong's political reform trajectory may need to be reconsidered if the path of that trajectory hits a hard wall. If the relevant political actors are unable to realise the aim of universal suffrage, why should courts continue to hold rights in abeyance and tolerate deficient institutions while waiting for a political process that may never bear fruit? While courts cannot, on their own, bring about universal suffrage, they can give effect to political rights in ways conducive to the gradual and orderly progress and development towards universal suffrage. This would be consistent with the constitutional ambitions of Articles 45 and 68 of the Basic Law.

If the political reform trajectory hits a wall or diverts on an unknown course, courts need to move away from deference and to consider more carefully the relevant legal principles. Recognised in Hong Kong law though rarely applied in the election cases, is the interpretive principle of conformity with binding international law.[151] As Bennion puts it, 'It is a principle of legal policy that the municipal law ... should conform to public international law.'[152] In relation to incorporating statutes like the HKBOR, Shaheed Fatima describes them as 'portals through which treaties pass to be received into the corpus of domestic law'.[153] By virtue of this principle, international standards do matter in judicial review, and they have contributed to the results seen in the village elections and prisoners' disqualification cases. The relevant international legal obligations are Articles 1 and 25 of the ICCPR, which are binding on China in relation to Hong Kong, by virtue of China's acceptance of ICCPR obligations in the Sino-British Joint Declaration and notification to the UN at the time of the handover.[154] The only exception to these obligations is the election reservation, which applies to Article 25(b).[155] The precise effect and scope of this reservation remains unsettled in Hong Kong law. Since a reservation's effect is to restrict a right, the accepted approach on restrictions is to construe them narrowly.[156] The narrow construction, accepted by the UN Human Rights Committee and Justice Keith in *Lee Miu Ling*, is that the reservation is spent once an election of any form is used to elect legislators and the chief executive.[157] A less narrow interpretation, which would allow it to still have substantive effect, is to reserve against the whole of Article 25 any rights to elect the chief executive, members of the executive council, and members of LegCo by universal suffrage. This would be consistent with the letter and spirit of Articles 45, 55, and 68 of the Basic Law. However, the rights in Article 25 can still be engaged by unfairness or inequality in the electoral system so long as the complaint does not seek substantively to realise universal suffrage.

Another aspect of deference which higher courts will need to review in the near future is the knee-jerk reaction to defer because the election law context is said to involve 'political and policy considerations'. Recent judgments exhibiting this tendency have tried to find support from the Court of Final Appeal's decisions in *Fok Chun Wa* v. *The Hospital Authority* and *Leung Chun Ying* v. *Ho Chun Yan Albert*.[158] However, on a close reading of both judgments, neither provides support for the knee-jerk reaction, which has had the effect of devaluing political rights in Hong Kong's constitutional framework. *Fok Chun Wa* was concerned with whether it was discriminatory to charge non-resident women from the mainland, who were awaiting residency status, higher fees than those charged to Hong Kong residents for delivering a child in a Hong Kong public hospital. In its analysis the Court considered how much deference should be accorded when the justification issue concerned socio-economic policy and the distribution of public funds. Chief Justice Geoffrey Ma noted that courts should allow more leeway when the context concerned 'socio-economic or other general policy matters'.[159] But courts would be more stringent in the application of the justification test in two categories of cases: (1) if the government's socio-economic or general policy has 'disregard for core-values'; or (2) if the subject matter of the challenge is concerned with 'fundamental concepts, in contradistinction to rights associated with social and economic policies'.[160] In relation to the first category, core-values relate 'to personal or human characteristics (such as race, colour, gender, sexual orientation, religion, politics, or social origin)'; they involve 'the respect and dignity that society accords to a human being' and are 'fundamental societal values'.[161] In relation to the second category, fundamental concepts are 'those which go to the heart of any society' and include 'the right to life, the right not to be tortured, the right not to be held in slavery, the freedom of expression and opinion, freedom of religion (among others)'.[162] The right to a fair trial and presumption of innocence was also mentioned. Although political rights were not expressly mentioned by the Chief Justice, core-values can be triggered in right to vote cases by virtue of the non-discrimination clause in Article 21 of the HKBOR, and political rights are closely connected to freedoms of expression and opinion, which were expressly mentioned.

The Court revisited the concept of margin of appreciation in *Leung Chun Ying* v. *Ho Chun Yan Albert*, a case concerned with election law but not political rights. At issue was whether the seven-day time limit to lodge an election petition with the Court to question a chief executive election infringed the right of access to the courts protected by Article 35 of the Basic Law. There was no discretion to extend the time limit. The Court found the inflexible time limit to be a justified restriction on the access right. It noted that election petitions were made as of right, that it was important to have these challenges dealt with speedily, that the overall scheme also allowed for limited judicial review within 30 days, that persons likely to file the petition would be intimately involved in the election and could be expected to comply with the time limit, and that other jurisdictions had comparable limits.[163] All of these reasons were stated in the Chief Justice's judgment before he addressed margin of appreciation in a short paragraph.[164] He referred to his decision in *Fok Chun Wa* and found that a due margin of appreciation should be accorded because elections 'involve political and policy considerations and it is in these areas where the legislature is involved' and the determination of the seven-day limit 'is one that does involve considerations other than legal ones'.[165] As to whether the issue concerned core-values or fundamental concepts, the Chief Justice did not address the question directly, noting only that 'the right of access to the courts is not an unlimited one, particularly in the present context';[166] this suggests a difficulty with conditioning the margin on the nature or type of right or issue involved. The case did not comment on the value or importance of political rights.

Neither of these two decisions can be read as authority for judicial deference in every case concerning political rights, which can hardly be said to be 'rights associated with purely social and economic policies'.[167] Relating to political and policy considerations may be one reason to allow the legislature some leeway, but the crucial prior question is whether the political right engaged is a 'fundamental concept', in which case courts should be more vigilant in protecting the fundamental right at stake. In considering this question, courts should bear in mind the following three aspects of political rights. First, it is often said that political rights serve to guarantee and protect other human rights.[168] 'It figures in the International Covenant as a right so fundamental that the realisation of many others depends upon it.'[169] Second, political rights are inextricably tied to other fundamental freedoms such that their restriction inevitably impacts on those other freedoms.

> [T]he expressive rights to free speech, press, assembly and association must in some way inform any theory of participation. Their prominence in the International Covenant reminds us that Article 25 should not be approached as an isolated provision, detached from the larger structure of rights in the Covenant.[170]

Third, in the context of one country, two systems, the political rights exemplify Hong Kong's 'separate system', and Hong Kong courts, following the approach in *Ng Ka Ling*, should give a 'generous interpretation' to such rights.[171] The wide expression of views from the community during the 2013–2015 reform exercise, whether in support of or against the government's proposal, is validation of the great importance of political rights and democratic institutions to Hong Kong people.

Conclusion

Like Hong Kong's journey on the road to democracy, the judicial review of elections has also experienced a bumpy ride. Its current state of contradiction reflects a broader tension between Hong Kong's robust and international approach to constitutional rights review and China's authoritative approach to Hong Kong's political development. After the 2015 reform veto, there has been no official indication of when the universal suffrage reform process will begin again. Before too long, those frustrated with the deadlock in the political process will turn to the courts to seek a consideration (or reconsideration) of the long-standing institutional inequalities in the political system. A dismissive response would render political rights under the Basic Law illusory and bring the two systems closer together, instead of marking their separateness. A too robust approach might provoke undesirable interference from the central government. The best way is to give Hong Kong permanent residents the full measure of their political rights by considering rights challenges with the same intensive scrutiny applied in previous cases concerned with the fundamental freedoms of expression, assembly, and association.[172] Under this approach, courts need not attempt to design or redesign political institutions. The articulation of legal principles that reflect the underlying purposes of Article 21 can serve as a catalyst for gradual progress in the direction of universal suffrage.

Notes

1 I thank Po Jen Yap, Gladys Li, Ernest Ng, Swati Jhaveri, Cora Chan, and Kareem Crayton for their comments on an earlier draft of this chapter.

2 Direct elections to District Boards began only in 1982 (see Miners (1998) 170; Young (1997) 656–658) and to the Legislative Council (LegCo) in 1991 (see Kwok *et al.* (1992) ch. 1). See also Chan and Lim (2011) ch. 8.

3 Hong Kong Bill of Rights Ordinance (Cap 383), s. 8, art 21 (HKBORO); The Basic Law of the Hong Kong Special Administrative Region of the People's Republic of China, 3rd Sess., 7th National People's Congress, 4 April 1990, reprinted in 29 ILM 1519, art 26 (Basic Law).

4 Articles 45 and 68 of the Basic Law, ibid., provide that the methods for selecting the chief executive and electing legislators is to be specified in light of the actual situation and in accordance with the principle of gradual and orderly progress; the ultimate aim is universal suffrage.

5 Loh and Civic Exchange (2006) chs 1 and 2.

6 Realising universal suffrage requires amendment of annex I (chief executive) or annex II (LegCo) of the Basic Law (n. 2), which in both cases requires two-thirds support of all legislators, the consent of the chief executive, and approval by the Standing Committee of the National Peoples Congress (NPCSC). Annex II was amended in 2010, though the first attempt in 2005 failed. See Interpretation by the Standing Committee of the National People's Congress of Article 7 of Annex I and Article III of Annex II of the Basic Law of the Hong Kong Special Administrative Region of the People's Republic of China, 8th Sess., 10th National People's Congress, 6 April 2004; Chen (2010); Lim (2011) 861–875.

7 UN Human Rights Committee (UNHRC), 'General Comment No. 25: the right to participate in public affairs, voting rights and the right of equal access to public service (Art. 25)', adopted 12 July 1996, UN Doc. CCPR/C/21/Rev.1/Add.7.

8 *Lau San Ching* v. *Apollonia Liu* (1995) 5 HKPLR 23 (HC).

9 Ibid. 49–50.

10 Ibid. 66.

11 Ibid.

12 Ibid. 65.

13 Ibid. 67.

14 *Secretary for Justice* v. *Chan Wah* (2000) 3 HKCFAR 459.

15 Ibid. 465.

16 Ibid. 467–471.

17 Ibid. 472–473.

18 Ibid. 474.

19 Ibid.

20 Ibid.

21 See Village Representative Election Ordinance (Cap. 576); *Lai Tak Shing* v. *The Secretary for Home Affairs* (2007) 10 HKCFAR 655, [7]–[10]; Jhaveri and Scully-Hill (2015) 517–519.

22 *Hirst* v. *The United Kingdom* (2006) 42 EHRR 41; Alexander Home and Isobel White, 'Prisoners' voting rights', UK House of Commons Library, Standard Note SN/PC/01764, 11 February 2015.

23 *Chan Kin Sum* v. *Secretary for Justice* [2009] 2 HKLRD 166 (CFI).

24 *Chan Kin Sum Simon* v. *Secretary for Justice*, unreported judgment on relief, HCAL79/2008, 11 March 2009, CFI, [32]; *Associated Provincial Picture Houses Ltd* v. *Wednesbury Corp* [1948] 1 KB 223, 230 and 234 (HL).

25 *Chan Kin Sum* (n. 23) [72]–[73].

26 Ibid. [81].

27 Ibid. [110].

28 Ibid. [111].
29 Ibid. [139]–[140].
30 Ibid. [164].
31 Ibid. [106].
32 Ibid. [148]–[149].
33 Ibid. [156].
34 See analysis by Chan (2010) 11.
35 *Chan Kin Sum Simon* (relief) (n. 24) [165].
36 Ibid. [87].
37 *Koo Sze Yiu* v. *Chief Executive of the Hong Kong Special Administrative Region* (2006) 9 HKCFAR 441, [33].
38 See Voting by Imprisoned Persons Ordinance, Ord. 7 of 2009, partially in force on 3 July 2009 (LN 162 of 2009), fully on 30 October 2009 (LN 216 of 2009); LegCo Secretariat, 'Voting rights of prisoners', paper for Panel on Constitutional Affairs meeting on 18 May 2009, LC Paper No. CB(2)1539/08-09(01); 'Voting by imprisoned persons ordinance fully begins today', HKSAR Government Press Release (30 October 2009), accessible at www.info.gov.hk/gia/general/200910/30/P200910300146.htm accessed August 2015; Jhaveri and Scully-Hill (2015) 519–522.
39 *Tse Hung Hing* v. *The Medical Council of Hong Kong* [2010] 1 HKLRD 111, [7] (CFI).
40 Ibid. [8].
41 Ibid.
42 *Wong Hin Wai* v. *Secretary for Justice* [2012] 4 HKLRD 70 (CFI).
43 Wong Hin Wai later had his conviction quashed in the Court of Final Appeal; see *HKSAR* v. *Wong Hin Wai* (2013) 16 HKCFAR 837.
44 *Wong Hin Wai* (n. 42) [95]–[96].
45 Ibid. [21]–[29] and [34].
46 Ibid. [34].
47 Ibid. [35].
48 Ibid.
49 Ibid., citing *R (Barclay)* v. *Lord Chancellor* [2010] 1 AC 464 [56] (UKSC).
50 *Chan Kin Sum* (n. 23) [74], now partially qualified by *Fok Chun Wa* v. *The Hospital Authority* (2012) 15 HKCFAR 409 [61]–[78].
51 *Kwok Cheuk Kin* v. *Secretary for Constitutional and Mainland Affairs* [2014] 2 HKLRD 283, [50] (CFI). Note the similarity to the *Wednesbury* unreasonableness test (n. 24).
52 *Chan Kin Sum* (n. 23) [154]. See criticisms in Chan (2010) 13; Lo (2014) 297–311.
53 *Wong Hin Wai* (n. 42) [57]–[62] and [79].
54 Ibid. [99].
55 *Lau San Ching* (n. 8).
56 *Kwok Cheuk Kin* (n. 51) [94(4)].
57 See Constitutional and Mainland Affairs Bureau (CMAB), *Consultation Paper on Disqualification of Candidates with Unserved Prison Sentences and other Related Matters*, 21 July 2014; CMAB, 'Results of the public consultation on disqualification of candidates with unserved prison sentences and other related matters and proposed way forward', paper for Panel on Constitutional Affairs, November 2014, LC Paper No. CB(2)267/14-15(03).
58 SCMP Editorial, 'Government must reach out to young to win their trust and support', *South China Morning Post* (Hong Kong, 10 November 2014); Chris Buckley and Michael Forsythe, 'Hong Kong's democracy supporters chafe at inequality and Beijing's sway' *International New York Times* (Hong Kong, 27 June 2014).
59 UNHRC, 'Concluding observations of the Human Rights Committee Hong Kong Special Administrative Region', 86 Sess., UN Doc. CCPR/CHKG/CO/2, 21 April

2006, [18]; UNHRC, 'Concluding observations on the third periodic report of Hong Kong, China, adopted by the Committee at its 107th session (11–28 March 2013)', UN Doc. CCPR/C/CHN-HKG/CO/3, 29 April 2013, [6].

60 Miners (1998) 114–117.

61 Ibid. 116.

62 Young (1997) 666.

63 Ibid. 667–668; Loh and Civic Exchange (2006) app. 5.

64 Loh and Civic Exchange (2006) app. 5; Electoral Affairs Commission (EAC), *Report on the 2008 Legislative Council Election Held on 7 September 2008*, Hong Kong, 4 December 2008, app. IV.

65 EAC, *Report on the 2012 Legislative Council Election Held on 9 September 2012*, Hong Kong, 22 November 2012, p. 2 ([1.4]).

66 Ibid. 2 and app. X(B).

67 Decision of the Standing Committee of the National People's Congress on Issues Relating to the Methods for Selecting the Chief Executive of the Hong Kong Special Administrative Region and for Forming the Legislative Council of the Hong Kong Special Administrative Region in the Year 2012 and on Issues Relating to Universal Suffrage, 35th Sess., 10th National People's Congress, 29 December 2007, [1].

68 EAC (n. 64) app. IV.

69 Young (2006) 133–134.

70 EAC (n. 64) app. IV.

71 Young and Law (2006) 80.

72 EAC (n. 64).

73 *Lee Miu Ling* v. *Attorney General* [1996] 1 HKC 124 (CA), affirming (1995) 5 HKPLR 181 (HC).

74 Leave to Privy Council was refused 6 June 1996 (Lords Goff, Steyn, and Hoffmann).

75 *Lee Miu Ling* (CA) (n. 73).

76 Ibid. 133.

77 Ibid. 132.

78 Ibid. 130.

79 Ibid. 131.

80 Ibid. 134.

81 See Young (1997) 719–720.

82 See generally Yap (2015).

83 *Lee Miu Ling* (CA) (n. 73) 129.

84 Ibid. 128.

85 Ibid.

86 *Koo Sze Yiu* (n. 37).

87 *Chan Kin Sum Simon* (relief) (n. 24).

88 See the similar state of necessity in *Re Manitoba Language Rights* [1985] 1 SCR 721.

89 *Koo Sze Yiu* (n. 37) [32]–[33]; ibid. [89]–[91]; *Vallejos Evangeline Banao* v. *Commissioner of Registration* [2011] 6 HKC 469, [9] (CFI).

90 Loh and Civic Exchange (2006) apps 2 and 3.

91 Ibid.

92 Ibid. apps 9 and 26.

93 See *Mandy Tam Heung Man* v. *The Hong Kong Institute of Certified Public Accountants* [2008] 1 HKLRD 238, [97] (CFI): the elected representative from the Accountancy functional constituency 'has a number of constitutional responsibilities, primarily set out in Article 73 of the Basic Law. These constitutional responsibilities plainly extend beyond the scope of matters affecting the professional interests of the accountancy profession.'

94 HKSAR Government, *Green Paper on Constitutional Development* (Hong Kong, July 2007) 10 and 36, but see Jake van der Kamp, 'Functional constituencies undermine our economy', *South China Morning Post* (Hong Kong, 9 February 2014).
95 Loh and Civic Exchange (2006) 4–5.
96 Young and Law (2006) 71–72; Young (1997) 667–668.
97 Young and Law (2006) 98–99.
98 Loh and Civic Exchange (2006) app. 13.
99 Young and Law (2006) 99.
100 Ibid. 95–98.
101 Ibid. 96.
102 Ibid. 101.
103 Legislative Council (Amendment) Ordinance 2011, Ord. 2 of 2011, s. 14; Electoral Legislation (Miscellaneous Amendments) Ordinance 2012, Ord. 11 of 2012, s. 34.
104 *Chan Yu Nam* v. *Secretary for Justice* [2010] 1 HKC 493 (CFI).
105 The Transport constituency only specified corporate bodies as voters; the second applicant had to be an individual or corporate voting member of the Real Estate Developers Association of Hong Kong, the Hong Kong Construction Association Ltd or the Hong Kong E&M Contractors' Association Ltd in order to have a vote in the Real Estate and Construction constituency.
106 *Chan Yu Nam* v. *Secretary for Justice* [2012] 3 HKC 38 (CA), affirming *Chan Yu Nam* (CFI) (n. 104).
107 *Chan Yu Nam* v. *Secretary for Justice*, unreported, FAMV39/2011, 18 January 2012, CFA AC; *Chan Yu Nam* v. *Secretary for Justice*, unreported, CACV3/2010, 21 October 2011, CA.
108 *Chan Yu Nam* (CFA AC) ibid. [5].
109 *Chan Yu Nam* (CFI) (n. 104) [61]–[65] and [88].
110 *Chan Yu Nam* (CA) (n. 106) [93].
111 Ibid.
112 *Chan Yu Nam* (CFA AC) (n. 107) [5]–[6]; *Chan Yu Nam* (CA) (n. 107) [7]–[9].
113 *Chan Yu Nam* (CA) (n. 106) [105].
114 At the time of ratification, the UK qualified the rights in Article 25(b) 'in so far as it may require the establishment of an elected Executive and Legislative Council in Hong Kong'. See Byrnes and Chan (1993) 215, 262.
115 *Lee Miu Ling* (HC) (n. 73) 197–198.
116 *Chan Yu Nam* (CFI) (n. 104) [115]–[116].
117 Recognised in *Ng Ka Ling* v. *The Director of Immigration* (1999) 2 HKCFAR 4, [73].
118 Jhaveri (2011) 232.
119 *Chan Yu Nam* (CA) (n. 106) [85].
120 *Chan Yu Nam* (CFI) (n. 104) [82] and [87].
121 Ibid. [83] and [88].
122 Ibid. [120]–[137]; *Chan Yu Nam* (CA) (n. 106) [109]–[115].
123 Jhaveri (2011) 232.
124 Young and Cullen (2010) app. 2; Amendment to Annex I to the Basic Law of the Hong Kong Special Administrative Region of the People's Republic of China Concerning the Method for the Selection of the Chief Executive of the Hong Kong Special Administrative Region, 16th Sess., 11th National People's Congress, 28 August 2010.
125 'Why are Hong Kong's protesters rallying around the number 689?' *Guardian* (London, 1 October 2014).
126 Young and Cullen (2010) 58–59.
127 Ibid. 71–74.
128 Ibid. 1.
129 Decision of the NPCSC (n. 67).

130 Young and Cullen (2010) 86–90; Suzanne Pepper, 'A chief executive election: pan-democrats and the election committee', *China Elections and Governance Blog* (16 January 2012), accessible at http://chinaelectionsblog.net/hkfocus/?p=327 accessed August 2015.
131 Young (2015).
132 Decision of the Standing Committee of the National People's Congress on Issues Relating to the Selection of the Chief Executive of the Hong Kong Special Administrative Region by Universal Suffrage and on the Method for Forming the Legislative Council of the Hong Kong Special Administrative Region in the Year 2016, 10th Sess., 12th National People's Congress, 31 August 2014; Young (2014).
133 Survey results from the Joint-University Rolling Survey on 2017 Chief Executive Election Proposal showed more than 40 per cent opposed from 1 to 13 June 2015, accessible at http://hkupop.hku.hk/english/features/jointUrollingSurvey/#3 accessed August 2015.
134 *Ho Chun Yan, Albert* v. *Leung Chun Ying* [2012] 5 HKLRD 149, [60]–[61] and fn 6 (CFI).
135 *Leung Lai Kwok Yvonne* v. *The Chief Secretary for Administration*, unreported, HCAL31/2015, 5 June 2015, CFI. See also *Kwok Cheuk Kin* v. *The Chief Executive of the HKSAR*, unreported, HCAL103/2014, 25 June 2015, CFI, where leave to challenge the fairness of the consultation process was also refused on the ground that it was academic after the NPCSC's decision.
136 *Leung Lai Kwok Yvonne* (n. 135) [57], applying *Leung Chun Ying* v. *Ho Chun Yan Albert* (2013) 16 HKCFAR 735, [45].
137 Li Fei, 'Explanations on the draft decision of the Standing Committee of the National People's Congress on issues relating to the selection of the Chief Executive of the Hong Kong Special Administrative Region by universal suffrage and on the method for forming the Legislative Council of the Hong Kong Special Administrative Region in the Year 2016', 10th Sess., 12th National People's Congress, 27 August 2014, 3 (English translation).
138 Jhaveri (2011) 233–234.
139 Dawood (2012).
140 Ibid. 553.
141 See Jhaveri and Scully-Hill (2015).
142 *Kwok Cheuk Kin* (n. 51) [52] and [90].
143 Ibid. [93].
144 Mo Hong'e, 'China urges UK to stop interference in Hong Kong's affairs', *Ecns.cn* (Beijing, 6 September 2014); 'China repeats opposition to foreign interference in HK affairs', *Xinhuanet* (Beijing, 4 December 2014); 'Back off HK, China tells other countries', *Xinhuanet* (Beijing, 27 February 2015).
145 'Civic nomination not a must for democracy', *news.gov.hk* (Hong Kong, 24 October 2014); CY Leung, 'On the record: reform must adhere to basic law', *news.gov.hk* (Hong Kong, 14 January 2015); Tang Danlu, 'China voice: an absurd Hong Kong report by UK MPs', *Xinhuanet* (Beijing, 6 March 2015).
146 HKSAR Government, *Consultation Report and Proposals on the Method for Selecting the Chief Executive by Universal Suffrage* (Hong Kong, April 2015) ch. 4.
147 Jeffie Lam, 'Beijing's reform plan for Hong Kong is final so don't expect last-minute changes, CY Leung says', *South China Morning Post* (Hong Kong, 2 June 2015).
148 Basic Law (n. 3) arts 4, 19, 35, 38, 84, and 85.
149 *Ng Ka Ling* (n. 117); Chief Executive, 'Report on seeking assistance from the central people's government in solving problems encountered in the implementation of the Basic Law of the Hong Kong Special Administrative Region of the People's Republic of China', 20 May 1999; Interpretation by the Standing Committee of the National People's Congress of Articles 22(4) and 24(2)(3) of the Basic Law of the

Hong Kong Special Administrative Region of the People's Republic of China, 10th Sess., 9th National People's Congress, 26 June 1999; Chan *et al.* (2000).

150 See *Democratic Republic of the Congo* v. *FG Hemisphere Associates LLC* (2011) 14 HKCFAR 95 (referral); (2011) 14 HKCFAR 395 (merits); *Vallejos Evangeline Banao* v. *Commissioner of Registration* (2013) 16 HKCFAR 45.

151 *Cheung Ng Sheong Steven* v. *Eastweek Publisher Ltd* [1995] 3 HKC 601, 610 and 623–624 (CA); *Solicitor (302/02)* v. *Law Society of Hong Kong* [2006] 2 HKC 40, [81] (CA), but see *Leung Lai Fong* v. *Ho Sin Ying* (2009) 12 HKCFAR 581, [41].

152 Jones (2013) 745 (s. 270). See also Waters (2007).

153 Fatima (2005) 65 ([3.11]).

154 Crawford (2005) 28–29; Xiao (2001) 196–218; Sino-British Joint Declaration on the Question of Hong Kong, 19 December 1984, UKTS 1984 No. 26, reprinted 23 ILM 1366, s. XIII of annex I.

155 See HKBORO (n. 3) s. 13, which incorporates the reservation against the whole of Article 21; compare with (n. 114).

156 *Ubamaka Edward Wilson* v. *Secretary for Security* (2012) 15 HKCFAR 743, [116].

157 UNHRC 2006 (n. 59); *Lee Miu Ling* (HC) (n. 73) 197–198; Lim (2015) 353; Seren S.T. Tang, 'Status of the reservation to the right to vote in Hong Kong', CCPL Occasional Paper No. 17, Faculty of Law, HKU, March 2008, 6; Lim (2011) 853–859.

158 *Fok Chun Wa* (n. 50); *Leung Chun Ying* (n. 136).

159 *Fok Chun Wa* (n. 50) [75(6)].

160 Ibid. [77] and [79].

161 Ibid. [77].

162 Ibid. [79].

163 *Leung Chun Ying* (n. 136) [41]–[44].

164 Ibid. [45].

165 Ibid.

166 Ibid.

167 *Fok Chun Wa* (n. 50) [79].

168 *Wesberry* v. *Sanders*, 376 US 1, 17 (1964); *Dixon* v. *British Columbia* (1989) 35 BCLR (2d) 273, 284; Young (1997) 697–699.

169 Steiner (1988) 131.

170 Ibid. 88; Steiner (2008) 446.

171 *Ng Ka Ling* (n. 117) [77].

172 See e.g. *Leung Kwok Hung* v. *HKSAR* (2005) 8 HKCFAR 229; *Dr Kwok-Hay Kwong* v. *The Medical Council of Hong Kong* [2008] 3 HKLRD 524 (CA).

References

Byrnes A. and Chan J.M.M. (eds), *Public Law and Human Rights: A Hong Kong Sourcebook* (Butterworths 1993).

Chan C., 'Judicial deference at work: some reflections on *Chan Kin Sum* and *Kong Yun Ming*' (2010) 40 *Hong Kong Law Journal* 1.

Chan J.M.M. and Lim C.L. (eds), *Law of the Hong Kong Constitution* (Sweet & Maxwell 2011).

Chan J.M.M., Fu H.L., and Ghai Y. (eds), *Hong Kong's Constitutional Debate: Conflict over Interpretation* (Hong Kong University Press 2000).

Chen A.H.Y., 'An unexpected breakthrough in Hong Kong's constitutional reform' (2010) 40 *Hong Kong Law Journal* 259.

Crawford J., *Rights in One Country: Hong Kong and China* (Faculty of Law, Hong Kong University 2005).

Dawood Y., 'Electoral fairness and the law of democracy: a structural rights approach to judicial review' (2012) 62 *University of Toronto Law Journal* 499.
Fatima S., *Using International Law in Domestic Courts* (Hart 2005).
Jhaveri S., 'Judicialising politics: a role for the courts in electoral reform in Hong Kong' (2011) *Public Law* 227.
Jhaveri S. and Scully-Hill A., 'Executive and legislative reactions to judicial declarations of constitutional invalidity in Hong Kong: engagement, acceptance or avoidance?' (2015) 13 *International Journal of Constitutional Law* 507.
Jones O., *Bennion on Statutory Interpretation: A Code* (6th edn, LexisNexis 2013).
Kwok R.Y.F., Leung J.Y.H., and Scott I. (eds), *Votes Without Power: The Hong Kong Legislative Council Elections 1991* (Hong Kong University Press 1992).
Lim C.L., 'Right to vote and right to political participation' in J.M.M. Chan and C.L. Lim (eds), *Law of the Hong Kong Constitution* (Sweet & Maxwell 2011).
Lim C.L., 'Britain's "treaty rights" in Hong Kong' (2015) 131 *Law Quarterly Review* 348.
Lo P.Y., *The Judicial Construction of Hong Kong's Basic Law* (Hong Kong University Press 2014).
Loh C. and Civic Exchange (eds), *Functional Constituencies: A Unique Feature of the Hong Kong Legislative Council* (Hong Kong University Press 2006).
Miners N., *The Government and Politics of Hong Kong* (5th edn, Oxford University Press 1998).
Steiner H.J., 'Political participation as a human right' (1988) 1 *Harvard Human Rights Yearbook* 77.
Steiner H.J., 'Two sides of the same coin? Democracy and international human rights' (2008) 41 *Israel Law Review* 445.
Waters M.A., 'Creeping monism: the judicial trend toward interpretive incorporation of human rights treaties' (2007) 107 *Columbia Law Review* 628.
Xiao W., *One Country, Two Systems: An Account of the Drafting of the Hong Kong Basic Law* (Peking University Press 2001).
Yap P.J., *Constitutional Dialogue in Common Law Asia* (Oxford University Press 2015).
Young S.N.M., 'The meaning of the right to vote in Hong Kong' (1997) 42 *McGill LJ* 650.
Young S.N.M., 'Elected by the elite: functional constituency legislators and elections' in C. Loh and Civic Exchange (eds), *Functional Constituencies: A Unique Feature of the Hong Kong Legislative Council* (Hong Kong University Press 2006).
Young S.N.M., 'Realising universal suffrage in Hong Kong after the Standing Committee's decision' (2014) 44 *Hong Kong Law Journal* 689.
Young S.N.M., 'Rethinking the process of political reform in Hong Kong' (2015) 45 *Hong Kong Law Journal* 381.
Young S.N.M. and Cullen R., *Electing Hong Kong's Chief Executive* (Hong Kong University Press 2010).
Young S.N.M. and Law A., 'Privileged to vote: inequalities and anomalies of the FC system' in C. Loh and Civic Exchange (eds), *Functional Constituencies: A Unique Feature of the Hong Kong Legislative Council* (Hong Kong University Press 2006).

3 Democracy and elections in India

Reviewing the role of the Election Commission and the courts

Surya Deva[1]

Backdrop

Elections in a democracy should be not only *periodic* but also *free and fair*. Barring one instance in the mid-1970s when an internal emergency was imposed in June 1975,[2] there have been no concerns about the regularity of elections in India, unlike many of its peers in Asia. To accomplish the objective of free and fair elections in the world's largest democracy,[3] the Indian Constitution employs two strategies. First, the Constitution establishes an independent Election Commission (EC), which under Article 324 of the Constitution has the power of 'superintendence, direction and control of the preparation of the electoral rolls for, and the conduct of' elections. Second, the judicial review power is conferred on higher courts – the High Courts and the Supreme Court – to deal with election disputes through election petitions.

Threats to free and fair elections in India have come from several sources such as the use of money-cum-muscle power, the involvement of people with criminal background, lack of transparency and internal democracy in political parties, political defections, and attempts to influence voters on religious grounds or through bribery. As discussed below, both the EC and the courts have had to intervene regularly to ensure that elections are free and fair. I will argue that considering the size of democracy and multiple challenges, the constitutional scheme has withstood the test of time to sustain a democracy in India which is far from perfect but is nevertheless vibrant and organic. An independent EC and a vigilant as well as powerful Supreme Court should be credited for this success, though the value of people's faith in democratic processes should not be underestimated.

I begin in the second section of this chapter by providing a brief overview of the Indian framework relating to democracy, elections and judicial review. This should allow readers unfamiliar with the Indian legal system to understand better the role played by the EC and the Supreme Court. The third section then offers an account of the structure, powers and the working of the EC. This examination should make it clear that the EC has been envisaged by the constitution makers as the 'first gatekeeper' to maintain a fair democratic process. In the fourth section, I analyse selected Supreme Court decisions in a thematic manner to demonstrate the nature and extent of judicial interventions aimed at ensuring that elections to both the Indian parliament and state legislatures are free and fair. In particular, the readers should note how the Court has initiated several good electoral practices through public interest litigation.

The term 'election' in this chapter is used in a wide sense, so as to cover the exercise of judicial review power in all election-related disputes and matters – from eligibility to contest elections to the powers of the EC, use of corrupt practices in elections and the practice of political defections.

Democracy, elections and judicial review: Indian framework

A dive into constitutional history would explain why India ended up as a democracy after breaking free from British colonial rule. During the first session of the Constituent Assembly debates, Jawaharlal Nehru – who later became the first Prime Minister of India – moved a resolution about the Declaration of Objectives on 13 December 1946.[4] This Objectives Resolution did not use the term 'democracy' at all, though it envisaged an independent India to be a 'republic' and stated that 'all power and authority of the Sovereign Independent India … are derived from the people'.[5] Nehru explained this omission as follows:

> Obviously we are aiming at democracy and nothing less than a democracy.… It will be for this House to determine what shape to give to that democracy, the fullest democracy, I hope. The House will notice that in this resolution, although we have not used the word 'democratic' because we thought it is obvious that the 'republic' contains that word … but we have done something much more than using the word. We have given the content of democracy in this Resolution.[6]

Apart from the above explanation, another historical fact was the lack of one single monarch that ruled the entire India – rather, there were many kings ruling different parts of India. Many attributes of the Objectives Resolution were enshrined in the Preamble of the Indian Constitution of 1950. It is worth noting that the constitution drafters ended up explicitly affirming India to be a 'democratic republic' in the Preamble.[7] Later, the Supreme Court held that 'democracy' is a 'basic feature' of the Constitution,[8] and hence India cannot be turned into an authoritarian regime even by a constitutional amendment. Furthermore, as democracy cannot be sustained without free and fair elections based on universal suffrage and multi-party contestations, these have also been held to be an integral part of democracy.[9]

Indian democracy faces multiple challenges: corruption, misuse of caste and religion to secure votes, opportunistic political defections, unparliamentary behaviour, (mis)use of official position and black money in election campaigns, lack of internal democracy within political parties, and the general lack of accountability of elected representatives.[10] Despite these shortcomings, India – unlike its peers in South Asia or the Global South generally – has been able to stay on the democracy road with the exception of a brief period during the mid-1970s.[11] It is no small achievement that regular elections, albeit not in perfect ways, took place at both federal and state levels with a significant voter turnout: ranging from about 45 per cent in the first general election of 1951 to more than 58 per cent in the general elections of 1999, 2004, 2009 and 2014.[12]

Drèze and Sen in their book, *An Uncertain Glory: India and its Contradictions*, offer the following assessment of Indian democracy:

> In India as in other democratic countries around the world, democracy in the full sense of the term (that of 'government of the people, by the people, for the people') has not been achieved, and there remain many gaps to fill in Indian democracy. Nevertheless, after more than sixty years of largely successful democratic governance, India has earned its status as a leading democratic country. The army has not moved to take over civilian affairs as has happened in many newly independent countries in the world – not least in South Asia. The country has also shown quite powerfully how democracy can flourish despite a multitude of languages, religions and ethnicities.[13]

There are several reasons why India has been able to sustain democracy continuously for more than six decades despite all the imperfections. The one reason that stands out is the holding of periodic elections which have given people hope that they have the power – even if symbolic and usable only at certain intervals – to change their destiny through peaceful political means.[14] 'We, the people of India' have invoked this power repeatedly to change governments at the central and state levels to send a political message against corruption, communalism or administrative inefficiency.

The Indian Constitution along with elections laws like the Representation of the People Act 1951 (RPA) provide a robust framework to ensure free and fair elections.[15] The Constitution provides for universal suffrage for all adults over the age of 18 years without any discrimination.[16] Any association or body of individual citizens of India can apply to the EC for registration as a political party under Section 29A of the RPA.[17] Allotment of symbols to political parties is governed by the Election Symbols (Reservation and Allotment) Order 1968 issued by the EC in exercise of its power under Article 324 of the Constitution. On acquiring a specified percentage of votes and considering the number of candidates returned, the EC recognises political parties as national, regional or state parties.[18] As discussed below, the Constitution establishes an independent EC to conduct free and fair elections. The RPA enumerates the grounds on which the validity of an election could be challenged before the High Court by way of an election petition.[19]

Granville Austin argues that the framers of the Indian Constitution envisaged 'the judiciary as a bastion of rights and justice'.[20] An independent judiciary armed with the power of judicial review was the constitutional device chosen to achieve this objective.[21] As the judiciary is the 'primary custodian' of the Constitution,[22] the same could be said about the role of courts in maintaining democratic governance, including ensuring that elections are free and fair.

The Indian judiciary has 'a single pyramidal structure with the lower or subordinate courts at the bottom, the High Courts in the middle, and the Supreme Court at the top'.[23] As India does not have a separate constitutional court, the higher judiciary – comprising the Supreme Court and 24 High Courts – deal with constitutional questions in exercise of their judicial review power. The Supreme Court has very wide original, appellate and advisory jurisdiction.[24] The law declared by the Court is binding on all courts in India, and all civil and judicial authorities are required to act in its aid.[25] Article 32 empowers the Supreme Court to issue directions, orders or writs to enforce any of the fundamental rights (FRs) enumerated in Part III of the Constitution. The remedy to approach the Apex Court under Article 32 is also a FR. Under Article 226 of the Constitution, the High Courts too have the power to issue directions, orders or writs to enforce any FR or for any other purpose.[26]

The power of judicial review in India could be traced to Article 13(2) of the Constitution, which provides that the state 'shall not make any law which takes away or abridges the rights conferred by' Part III of the Constitution and that 'any law made in contravention of this clause shall, to the extent of the contravention, be void'. However, it is pointed out that even in the absence of such a provision, Indian courts would have had the power of judicial review.[27]

The Supreme Court has been very vigilant in safeguarding its judicial review power. In fact, the Court has extended this power to the extent that it can review the constitutional validity of not only ordinary laws but also constitutional amendments.[28] It has achieved this feat by developing the doctrine of basic structure or basic features. As 'judicial review' has been held to be part of the basic structure, the power of judicial review cannot be excluded even by a constitutional amendment.[29]

Despite such an extensive *granted* as well as *self-acquired* judicial review power, the courts have limited jurisdiction over election matters. Article 329 of the Constitution provides that 'no election to either House of Parliament or to the House or either House of the Legislature of a State shall be called in question except by an election petition'. Such election petitions should be presented to the High Courts under the RPA.[30] The term 'election' in Article 329 has been given a wide interpretation to cover 'the entire procedure to be gone through to return a candidate to the legislature'.[31] For instance, disputes related to the rejection or acceptance of nominations papers have been held as part of the election process.[32]

As discussed below, the main reason for limiting the courts' judicial review power in election matters is because of the Constitution's vision of treating the EC as the first gatekeeper to ensuring that elections are free and fair.[33] Although recourse before the courts to redress any wrong done during the electoral process is available, 'it is postponed to the post-election stage', thus letting the EC be in charge during the entire election process.[34]

Election Commission: the first gatekeeper

The Indian Constitution establishes an independent institution in the form of the EC to ensure that elections are conducted in a free and fair manner. S.Y. Quraishi, the former Chief Election Commissioner (CEC) of India, outlines three basic requirements for free and fair elections: an independent electoral management body to conduct elections, a set of rules governing elections and an effective mechanism for resolving disputes related to elections.[35] It is arguable that the EC, as a 'non-party, quasi-judicial body',[36] has been conceived as the first gatekeeper – courts come into the picture only when there are election disputes or certain legal issues that require judicial interpretation or clarification.

Constitutional position and powers of the EC

The Constituent Assembly's Committee on Fundamental Rights had recommended that the independence of election should be regarded as a FR of every citizen.[37] Although the Assembly did not accept this recommendation, it did accept the rationale behind such a recommendation: Part XV of the Constitution establishes an independent EC with wide election-related powers.[38]

Article 324(2) of the Constitution provides that the EC 'shall consist of the Chief Election Commissioner and such number of other Election Commissioners, if any, as the President may from time to time fix'.[39] The CEC and other Election Commissioners are appointed by the President of India on the advice of the Council of Ministers headed by the Prime Minister.[40] If any other Election Commissioners are appointed, the CEC shall act as the chairman of the EC.[41]

In order to safeguard the independence of the EC, Article 324(5) provides that the CEC shall neither be removed from his or her office except in the like manner and on the like grounds as a Judge of the Supreme Court,[42] nor could the CEC's conditions of service be varied to his or her disadvantage after his or her appointment. The other Election Commissioners do not enjoy similar protection, though their removal too is not possible except on the recommendation of the CEC.[43] These differences led one past CEC, T.N. Seshan, to plead that the CEC's position is superior to other Election Commissioners. The Supreme Court clarified that the CEC is merely first among equals and that a law which creates a multi-member EC and requires that decisions are taken unanimously or by majority does not undermine the position or powers of the CEC vis-à-vis other Election Commissioners.[44]

The EC has three broad powers under the Constitution.[45] First, it exercises the power of 'superintendence, direction and control of the preparation of the electoral rolls' for all elections to the parliament, the legislature of every state and the offices of President and Vice-President.[46] Second, the EC has the responsibility to conduct all these elections.[47] Third, the EC advises the President of India (or the Governor of a state, as the case may be) on the question of disqualification of any member of the parliament or state legislature.[48] The Constitution specifies a number of grounds on which members of the central or state legislature could be disqualified, e.g. holding any office of profit, being declared insolvent or of unsound mind, acquiring citizenship of another country.[49] Although the legislators could also get disqualified on the ground of political defections,[50] the EC does not play any role in advising the President/Governor in such cases.

The Supreme Court has held that the EC's power under Article 324(1) is plenary in nature and that the terms used in the said provision – 'superintendence', 'direction' and 'control' of the electoral rolls and the 'conduct of all elections' – have wide meaning.[51] There are, however, at least two limitations on the EC's powers.[52] First, if a valid law has been enacted by the parliament in relation to elections, the EC should comply with the said law in exercising its powers. For example, in *AC Jose* v. *Sivan Pillai*,[53] the Supreme Court held that a defeated candidate could challenge the election on the ground of illegality when electronic machines were used for casting votes as per the EC's direction, but in breach of rules which stipulated only manual voting.

It is, therefore, suggested that Article 324 is more like a 'reservoir of power' to ensure free and fair elections:[54] by 'issuing necessary directions, [the] Commission can fill the vacuum till there is legislation on the subject'.[55] Using this leeway, the Supreme Court directed the EC to require all candidates to provide information about their educational qualifications as well as financial assets and the pending criminal cases against them.[56]

Second, the EC's decisions should be in conformity with the rule of law and the principles of natural justice.[57] In *Mohinder Singh Gill* v. *Chief Election Commissioner*,[58] the Supreme Court held that it was justified for the EC to cancel the poll and order a re-poll for the entire constituency on account of mob violence during the counting of votes, without giving a notice to all members of the public. The Court opined that it was sufficient if the EC heard the candidates before taking this decision.

EC's working in practice

Fali Nariman, a leading Indian jurist, notes that the Indian EC 'has now become one of the most significant constitutional institutions in our democracy. It is greatly respected because it acts independently and not in accordance with the wishes of the government for the time being.'[59]

The EC has been quite successful in conducting elections in a safe environment[60] and in implementing a voluntary model code of conduct adopted by political parties to self-regulate their conduct.[61] It has also adopted multiple strategies to counter the use of money power in elections.[62] Moreover, the EC has taken steps to be inclusive so that every voter – including those with disadvantaged backgrounds, like women, differently abled, transgender or those living in remote areas – are treated with equal respect in terms of their voting right.[63] For example, in 2009, the EC directed that the voter registration forms should have a column entitled 'others' to accommodate transgender and transsexual people.[64]

A former CEC, T.N. Seshan adopted an aggressive attitude, took on political heavyweights to stress the EC's independent status and enforced the EC's model code of conduct strictly.[65] While in some ways, this boded well for the EC's image of being an independent and powerful institution, to control Seshan's somewhat arrogant modus operandi, the government decided to make the CEC a multi-member body.[66] The Court upheld the constitutional validity of this law, and held that the CEC and other Election Commissioners enjoy an almost equal status.[67]

In short, the EC has performed its responsibilities quite well, despite enormous challenges inherent in managing elections in India. Drèze and Sen might perhaps have the EC as well in mind when they observed that 'the relatively healthy state – overall – of democratic institutions in the country provides significant opportunities for reasoned solutions to the problems that remain as well as for further extending the reach and quality of democratic practice'.[68]

Judicial review in election matters

Since the 1990s, the Indian Supreme Court has been playing a key role in promoting electoral reforms in India, e.g. enhancing transparency and accountability in election expenses, and facilitating access to information about the criminal record of candidates.[69] I examine below some key judgments in certain thematic areas that demonstrate the extent of judicial review power in election matters.

Attempt to exclude the Prime Minister's election from judicial review

Indira Gandhi v. *Raj Narain*[70] was a landmark decision illustrative of judicial determination to uphold the sanctity of free and fair elections for a number of reasons (e.g. the election of a Prime Minister was at stake, a constitutional amendment was introduced to protect the Prime Minister and the state of internal emergency was in force in the country at the time of this decision).[71] The Allahabad High Court set aside the election of Prime Minister Mrs Gandhi on the ground of corrupt practices.[72] While her appeal against this decision was pending before the Supreme Court, the parliament inserted Article 329A in the Constitution in 1975. The basic objective behind this constitutional amendment – which had stipulated that the elections of the Prime Minister and the Speaker to the parliament shall not be called into question before the courts like other elections – was to make the High Court decision inoperative. It is clear that the office of Speaker was added simply to avoid the impression that the Prime Minister's election to the parliament had been given special treatment.

It was argued before the Supreme Court that Article 329A was unconstitutional because it interfered with free and fair elections and excluded the power of judicial review, both of which attributes are basic features of the Constitution. *Raj Narain*, therefore, provided the Supreme Court with an opportunity to apply the basic structure doctrine propounded by it in the *Kesavananda Bharati* v. *State of Kerala*[73] just two years earlier. The Court unanimously held Article 329A to be unconstitutional, although the reasoning of judges varied, e.g. breach of the right to equality, the violation of the rule of law and separation of powers, and the infringement of the basic structure whether by exclusion of judicial review or by undermining free and fair elections.[74]

The Supreme Court through the *Raj Narain* decision sent a clear message that it will not hesitate to intervene in election disputes to protect the basic ethos of democracy, even if the threat paradoxically came from the people's representatives themselves and even if the Constitution was amended to undermine judicial powers.

Controlling the use of black money and/or excessive money

Campaigning in elections requires resources, especially if candidates have to reach a large number of potential voters.[75] Considering that no government funding is provided to candidates, uneven use of economic resources could potentially disadvantage candidates with access to limited funds. This situation in turn would undermine the idea of free and fair elections.[76] To overcome this problem, Section 77 of the RPA provides that every candidate contesting an election shall 'keep a separate and correct account of all expenditure in connection with the election incurred or authorised' by the candidate or his or her election agent. Moreover, a maximum limit on permissible expenditure has been statutorily fixed[77] and the EC has a comprehensive system in place to monitor the expenses by candidates.[78] The Supreme Court in *L R Shivaramagowde* v. *T M Chandrashekar*[79] held that the EC can go into the correctness of the account of election expenses filed by the candidate and disqualify a candidate under Section 10A of the RPA if the account is found to be false.

In several election petitions, an issue was raised whether the money spent by a candidate's political party or friends/relatives could be regarded as expenses incurred or authorised by the candidate.[80] The Supreme Court initially answered the question in the negative.[81] But later in *Kanwer Lal* v. *Amarnath*,[82] the Court held that if a political party sponsoring a candidate incurs expenditure in connection with his or her election (as opposed to the money spent on general party publicity), this could be regarded as implicitly authorised by the candidate. To overrule this decision, an Explanation was added to Section 77 to provide that any expenditure by a political party shall not be deemed to be expenditure in connection with the election incurred or authorised by the candidate or by his or her election agent for the purpose of this provision.[83]

The Court, however, did not take this statutory amendment lying down. Taking into account Section 293A of the erstwhile Companies Act 1956 (allowing companies to make donations to political parties) and Section 13A of the Income Tax Act 1961 (providing for tax exemption to political donations), the Supreme Court in *Common Cause* v. *Union of India*[84] ruled that a candidate who wants to take the benefit of Explanation 1 to Section 77 of the RPA must prove that the said expenditure was *in fact* incurred by the political party and not by him or her. Unless the candidate is able to show this, any expenditure in connection with the election of a candidate (including which has been incurred by his or her political party) shall be presumed to have been authorised by the candidate or his/her election agent.

The Court in *Common Cause* also directed all political parties – whether recognised as national parties or state parties or registered-unrecognised political parties – to maintain audited accounts and file a return of income with the tax authorities. Otherwise a political party will not be permitted to state that it has incurred or authorised expenditure in connection with the election of its candidates in terms of Explanation 1 to Section 77.

Corrupt practices

Section 123 of the RPA lists several conducts as 'corrupt practices' as a ground to challenge an election:

- bribery to induce any person to stand (or not stand) as a candidate or vote (or refrain from voting) at any election;
- any direct or indirect undue influence that interferes with the free exercise of any electoral rights;
- the appeal by a candidate or his or her agent to vote or refrain from voting for any person on the ground of his or her religion, race, caste, community or language or the use of, or appeal to, religious/national symbols;
- the promotion of feelings of enmity or hatred between different classes of the citizens of India on grounds of religion, race, caste, community, or language, by a candidate or his or her agent;
- the publication by a candidate or his or her agent of any statement of fact which is false, and which he or she either believes to be false or does not believe to be true, in relation to the personal character or conduct of any candidate;
- the hiring/procuring, whether on payment or otherwise, of any vehicle by a candidate or his or her agent or the use of such vehicle for the free conveyance of any elector to or from any polling station;
- incurring or authorising expenditure in contravention of Section 77 of the RPA; and
- booth capturing by a candidate or his or her agent or other person.

There have been many cases in which elections have been challenged on these grounds.[85] A few illustrative cases are discussed here to indicate the overall judicial approach in dealing with allegations of corrupt practices which undermine free and fair elections.[86] Indian courts have generally adopted a purposive and pro-active approach to weed out any attempts to influence fairness of the electoral process. For example, in *Rajendra Prasad* v. *Sheel Bhandra*,[87] the Supreme Court gave a wide meaning to the term 'offer' of money and held that even if no amount is specified, it might still constitute the corrupt practice of bribery.

Use of discretionary public funds by government ministers allegedly to influence voters often raises complex issues falling into grey areas, because money could be spent for bona fide development projects as well as for some quid pro quo bargain with the voters. In *Om Prabha Jain* v. *Abnash Chand*,[88] the issue was whether two discretionary grants made by a minister to build *dharamsalas* (rest houses) amounted to bribery to influence the voters of her constituency belonging to backward classes. The Court ruled that the minister's action done in the ordinary course of her duties could not be construed against her, as there was no evidence that it was part of a direct or indirect bargain with the voters. In fact, it was the beneficiaries of the discretionary grant who were anxious to lay hands on the money as soon as possible, as the grant might be cancelled later by a change of government after elections.

Building on *Om Prabha Jain* and *Ghasi Ram* v. *Dal Singh*,[89] the Supreme Court in *Bhanu Kumar Shastri* v. *Mohan Lal Sukhadia*[90] observed the following:

> Ordinarily amelioration of grievances of the public appears to be innocuous. If, however, there is evidence to indicate that any candidate at an election abuses his power and position as a Minister in the Government by utilising public revenues for conferring advantage or benefit on a particular group of people for the purpose of obtaining their votes, different considerations will arise.[91]

On the facts of the case, the Court in *Bhanu Kumar Shastri* did not set aside the election of a candidate, who was the Chief Minister of the state of Rajasthan at that time, to the state legislature, as the instances of alleged favour 'were long standing public grievances and the Government from time to time made suggestions and recommendations for redress of the grievances' and that it 'cannot be said that on the eve of the election there was any sudden or spontaneous outburst of public activity in the shape of diverting public money to win electors'.[92]

The publication of false statements in relation to the 'personal character or conduct' of any candidate will amount to corrupt practice under Section 123 of the RPA. The rationale behind targeting merely false personal attacks is that 'the electorate being politically educated and mature, would not be deceived by a false criticism against the public or political character of any candidate' and that

> even if any false statements are made about the political views of a candidate or his or her public conduct or character, the electorate would be able to judge on the merits and may not be misled the allegations by any false allegations in that behalf.[93]

However, the difficulty often arises in 'borderline' cases where the alleged statement may relate to both the public and personal life of a candidate. In *Inder Lal* v. *Lal Singh*,[94] the Supreme Court had to deal with such a situation. The Court set aside the election of a candidate to the state legislature of Rajasthan on account of the allegations made in the pamphlet that the respondent 'is a purchaser of the opponents of the Congress by means of money' constituted corrupt practice, as the false allegation of bribery related to the candidate's personal character as well.[95]

While false statements relating to a candidate's sexual life or misappropriation of public money will amount to corrupt practice under Section 123 of the

RPA, the same cannot be said about severe criticism of a person's past performance as an elected representative.[96] In *Kanhaiyalal* v. *Munnalal*,[97] the Supreme Court also held that the oral testimony in election-related matters should be judged with the greatest care, as an election dispute is not a private feud between two individuals; rather the whole constituency is intimately involved.

Misuse of religion in elections

Drèze and Sen note that 'the broad success of *secular democracy* in India' is 'a major accomplishment'.[98] Nevertheless, the backdrop of India's Partition on religious grounds in 1947 and the presence of rich religious diversity in an independent India continue to provide opportunities for the (mis)use of religion for political gains in elections. Over the years, the Supreme Court has issued several important pronouncements on the use of religion to influence voters.

In *Ram Dial* v. *Sant Lal*,[99] the issue before the Court was whether the poster issued by the head of a religious sect (Namdhari Sikhs) to his followers to vote for a particular candidate amounted to exerting 'undue influence' on the ground of religion.[100] While answering this question in the affirmative, the Court rejected the contention that a religious leader has as much the right to freedom of speech as any other citizen, and that, therefore, his exhortation in favour of a particular candidate should not have the result of vitiating the election. It reasoned:

> There cannot be the least doubt that a religious leader has the right freely to express his opinion on the comparative merits of the contesting candidate and to canvass for such of them as he considers worthy of the confidence of the electors.... Such a course of conduct on his part, will only be a use of his great influence amongst a particular section of the voters in the constituency; *but it will amount to an abuse of his great influence if the words he uses in a document, or utters in his speeches, leave no choice to the persons addressed by him, in the exercise of their electoral rights.*[101]

The Supreme Court also rejected the argument that Section 123(3)(3A) of the RPA, which bans using religion to influence voters, is a violation of the FR to profess, practise and propagate religion under Article 25 of the Constitution.[102] The Court ruled that Section 123(3) and 123(3A)

> only purport to curb the appeal on the ground of religion or propagating religion for creating feelings of enmity or hatred between different classes of citizens of India during the election campaign by the candidate or his agent or any person with his consent for furtherance of the prospects of the election of that candidate or for prejudicially affecting the election of any other candidate.[103]

In *R Y Prabhoo* v. *P K Kunte*,[104] the Court clarified that the scope of Section 123(3) is not limited to invoking one's own religion: this provision will also cover situations in which reference is made to the religion of another candidate with a request to refrain from voting for her. In this case, the allegation was that the voters were asked to vote for Prabhoo because he was a Hindu and that there were derogatory remarks made to Muslims. The Supreme Court declared void the election to the Maharashtra state legislature as the candidate and his agent appealed for votes on religious grounds or promoted enmity on religious grounds.[105] However, the *Prabhoo* decision – also known as the 'Hindutva judgment' – was quite controversial in that the Supreme Court held that Hindutva was a 'way of life' and could not be equated with 'narrow fundamentalist Hindu religious bigotry'.[106] As the Court invoked an ideal notion of Hinduism, it did not pay adequate attention to how the term was used in practice in political speeches to gain undue influence over voters.[107]

Criminalisation of politics

Section 8 of the RPA disqualifies anyone who has been convicted of a crime and sentenced for imprisonment of two years or more from contesting elections. However, as the trial process in India is very slow, many politicians continue to contest elections and remain members of the federal or state legislature. Moreover, Section 8(4) protects those who are already members of the legislature as long as they file an appeal against their conviction. The EC has been concerned about the misuse of these provisions and the role played by people with criminal records or backgrounds in politics generally.[108]

In a landmark judgment, the Supreme Court in *Lily Thomas* v. *Union of India*[109] declared Section 8(4) of the RPA unconstitutional, as the parliament lacked the legislative competence to enact this provision. The Court reasoned that the parliament

> does not have the power under Articles 102(1)(e) and 191(1)(e) of the Constitution to make different laws for a person to be *disqualified for being chosen* as a member and for a person to be *disqualified for continuing* as a member of Parliament or the State Legislature.[110]

In a public interest litigation case where the petitioner challenged the appointment of certain ministers in the central government on account of their alleged involvement in serious crimes, the Supreme Court declined to give any direction to the Prime Minister preventing him from recommending names of such ministers to the President for appointment.[111] However, one of the judges observed that

> the Prime Minister and the Chief Minister of the State … will be well advised to consider avoiding any person in the Council of Ministers, against whom charges have been framed by a criminal court in respect of offences involving moral turpitude and also offences specifically referred to in Chapter III [of the RPA].[112]

These decisions, along with previous decisions in which the Court directed all candidates to provide information about any pending criminal cases against them,[113] should to some extent discourage people with criminal background from entering politics. The Supreme Court also appears to be quite strict about ensuring compliance with its orders aimed at cleaning up politics. For instance, in *Krishnamoorthy* v. *Sivakumar*,[114] the Court held that if requisite information relating to criminal antecedents are not given during the filing of the nomination form, then this omission will be regarded as an attempt to suppress, misguide or keep the people in the dark; the said attempt undisputedly is undue influence and hence, will amount to a corrupt practice.

Disqualification on account of political defections

Several socio-political reasons have given rise to an era of political defections in India since the mid-1960s.[115] To discourage the practice of unprincipled political defections, the Tenth Schedule was inserted in the Constitution in 1985.[116] It provides that a member of a House belonging to any political party shall be disqualified if he or she (i) voluntarily gives up the membership of his or her party, or (ii) votes or abstains – without prior permission – from voting in such House contrary to any direction issued by the political party to which he or she belongs.[117] This disqualification provision shall not be attracted if there is a split in any political party (at least one-third members of the legislature party agree to form a new party or merge with another existing political party).[118]

Unlike other grounds of disqualification, the power to decide questions relating to disqualification on account of political defections has been vested in the Speaker of the concerned House.[119] It is notable that the Tenth Schedule tried to exclude the power of judicial review by stipulating that 'no court shall have any jurisdiction in respect of any matter connected with the disqualification of a member of a House under this Schedule'.[120] The Supreme Court in *Kihoto Hollohon* v. *Zachilhu*[121] upheld the constitutional validity of the Tenth Schedule. However, it declared the provision excluding the judicial review power unconstitutional, because it had the effect of amending the powers of the Supreme Court and High Court but without following the special procedure laid down in the proviso to Article 368(2), that is, ratification by the legislature of at least one-half of the states.[122]

Kihoto Hollohon was thus the first case in which part of a constitutional amendment was invalidated on procedural grounds. More importantly, however, the Supreme Court in a rare move trusted the institution of the Speaker and did not strike down a part of the amendment which excluded judicial review and thus violated the basic structure of the Constitution. The final outcome is that while the Speaker's power to decide questions relating to disqualification on account of political defections has been preserved, the courts could still exercise their judicial review power in appropriate cases.

Conclusion

This chapter reviews the role of the EC and courts in sustaining Indian democracy by ensuring that elections are free and fair. Based on the analysis undertaken in this chapter, several conclusions can be drawn. First, despite problems and imperfections in Indian democracy, the constitution makers deserve praise in conceiving a constitutional design which has sustained the world's largest democracy for over six decades.[123] If we look at the state of democracies in the peer countries in South Asia (or in the Global South generally), this achievement is no mean feat.[124]

Second, the EC has generally maintained its independence and performed well its role of ensuring that periodic elections are held in a free and fair manner. Since the early 1990s, the EC has been especially active in performing its constitutional or statutory duties. Keeping pace with changing technologies and the dynamic nature of electoral practices, the EC has employed innovative means to maintain people's faith in the electoral process.[125] The EC's pro-active role in monitoring all aspects of elections should have reduced the burden on Indian courts in addressing allegations of corrupt practices.

Third, it is evident that the Indian Supreme Court has been an active participant in upholding the fairness of the election process. In addition to dealing with specific elections disputes, it has also taken the lead in introducing electoral reforms by way of public interest litigation. I have already referred to some such cases. One may also refer to the Court's judgment in *People's Union for Civil Liberties* v. *Union of India*,[126] in which it directed the EC to create a 'none of the above option' (NOTA) in electronic voting machines. The rationale behind this decision was to put pressure on political parties to nominate *good* candidates. Although these efforts are praiseworthy, it also appears that such interventions might have released the pressure on the executive and the legislature to initiate electoral reforms. Judicial delay in disposing election petitions is another matter of concern,[127] because even if an election is set aside on grounds of corrupt practices, it might not be possible to declare elected a defeated candidate as fresh elections could have taken place since then.

Fourth, while the EC and the courts have been vigilant in safeguarding the sanctity of the election process, fundamental reforms are long overdue in India.[128] It is far from ideal to let the EC or courts deal with these problems in an ad-hoc manner.

Notes

1 I would like to thank Ms Jasmine Joseph for providing research assistance in writing this chapter.
2 See Kashyap (2010) 303–11.
3 For an excellent critical narrative of Indian democracy, see Guha (2007).
4 Lok Sabha Secretariat (1990) 15.
5 Ibid. 15 (paras 1 and 4).
6 Ibid. 19.
7 Constitution of India 1950, Preamble.

8 *Indira Gandhi* v. *Raj Narian* 1975 AIR SC 2299; *Kihoto Hollohan* v. *Zachillhu* 1993 AIR SC 412.
9 *People's Union for Civil Liberties* v. *Union of India* (2013) 10 SCC 1; *People's Union for Civil Liberties* v. *Union of India* (2003) 4 SCC 399; *Kuldip Nayar* v. *Union of India* (2006) 7 SCC 1.
10 Drèze and Sen (2013) 244–57; Guha (2007) 448–9, 463, 547–8; Nariman (2013) 267–341; Soutik Biswas, 'Why India is in Dire Need of Electoral Reform' *BBC News* (New Delhi, 28 June 2011) www.bbc.co.uk/news/world-south-asia-13692575.
11 On 26 June 1975, a national emergency, which lasted up to March 1977, was imposed. It is widely regarded as a black day for Indian democracy. See Austin (1999) 295–313.
12 See Election Commission of India, 'Election Results: Full Statistical Reports' http://eci.nic.in/eci_main1/ElectionStatistics.aspx.
13 Drèze and Sen (2013) 3.
14 Austin describes the Indian Constitution to be 'first and foremost a social document' aimed at bringing social revolution (Austin (1966) 50). 'Direct election was to be the pillar of the social revolution' (ibid. 46).
15 Sunny (2000) 210.
16 Article 326 provides that elections 'to the House of the People and to the Legislative Assembly of every State shall be on the basis on adult suffrage'. Article 325, on the other hand, stipulates that no person shall be ineligible for inclusion in any electoral roll 'on grounds only of religion, race, caste, sex or any of them'. The right to vote has been held to be merely a legal right and not a fundamental or constitutional right. *A C Pradhan* v. *Union of India* (1997) 6 SCC 1.
17 See, for the registration guidelines, Election Commission of India, 'Guidelines and Application Format for Registration of Political Parties' http://eci.nic.in/eci_main/ElectoralLaws/guidelinesandformat.pdf.
18 Centre for Indian Political Research and Analysis, 'Political Parties in India' www.cipra.in/paper/polparties.html.
19 Representation of the People Act 1951, Sections 100 and 101.
20 Austin (1966) 175.
21 Singh and Deva (2005) 671.
22 Austin (2000), 13.
23 Singh (2000) 251.
24 Constitution of India, Articles 32, 131–6 and 143. It can also review its decisions, and make such order as is necessary for doing complete justice in any cause or matter before it. Ibid. Articles 137 and 142.
25 Constitution of India, Articles 141 and 144.
26 For a discussion of the High Courts' power, see Singh (2013) 657–707.
27 Ibid. A-52.
28 *Kesavananda Bharati* v. *State of Kerala* (1973) 4 SCC 225; *Minerva Mills Ltd.* v. *Union of India* (1980) 3 SCC 625.
29 *S P Sampath Kumar* v. *Union of India* (1987) 1 SCC 124; *L Chandra Kumar* v. *Union of India* (1997) 3 SCC 261.
30 Representation of the People Act 1951, Sections 80 and 80A.
31 Singh (2013) 985.
32 *N P Ponnuswami* v. *Returning Officer* 1952 AIR SC 64.
33 For discussion of this issue in relation to Australia, see Orr (2012).
34 Singh (2013) 986.
35 Quraishi (2014), 31.
36 Austin (1966) 130.
37 Singh (2013) 979.
38 For rationale behind an independent EC, see Qurashi (2014) 27–30.

39 For controversies surrounding the appointment of Election Commissioners, see Quraishi (2014) 33–5.
40 Constitution of India, Article 324(2) read with Article 74.
41 Constitution of India, Article 324(3).
42 Article 124(4) lays down a cumbersome process to remove a Supreme Court judge: he or she could only be removed

> by an order of the President passed after an address by each House of Parliament supported by a majority of the total membership of that House and by a majority of not less than two-thirds of the members of that House present and voting has been presented to the President in the same session for such removal on the ground of proved misbehaviour or incapacity.

43 Constitution of India, Article 324(5).
44 *TN Seshan* v. *Union of India* (1995) 4 SCC 611.
45 For seven pillars that empower the EC, see Qurashi (2014) 50–60.
46 Constitution of India, Article 324(1).
47 Ibid.
48 Ibid. Articles 103(2) and 192(2).
49 Ibid. Articles 102 and 191.
50 Ibid. Articles 102(2) and 191(2) read with Tenth Schedule of the Constitution.
51 Singh (2013) 979–80. This will include the power to postpone elections in any state for legitimate reasons and the power to regulate the use of loudspeakers for campaigning. *Digvijay Mote* v. *Union of India* (1993) 4 SCC 175; *Election Commission of India* v. *AIDMK* (1994) Suppl 2 SCC 689.
52 Sunny (2000) 224–5.
53 (1984) 2 SCC 656.
54 Singh (2013) 980.
55 *Union of India* v. *Association for Democratic Reforms* (2002) 5 SCC 294.
56 *Union of India* v. *Association for Democratic Reforms* (2002) 5 SCC 294; *PUCL* v. *Union of India* (2003) 4 SCC 399. See also Election Commission of India, 'Order No. 3/ER/2003/JS-II', 27 March 2003, http://eci.nic.in/eci_main/ElectoralLaws/OrdersNotifications/Order_Assests_Affidavits.pdf; Mate (2014) 275–8.
57 Singh (2013) 980.
58 (1978) 1 SCC 405.
59 Nariman (2013) 158.
60 Quraishi (2014) 147–69.
61 Ibid. 237–58.
62 Ibid. 274–301.
63 Ibid. 92–111.
64 Ibid. 110.
65 Sanjoy Hazarika, 'India's Election Commissioner Gains a Following' *New York Times* (New Delhi, 30 January 1994) www.nytimes.com/1994/01/30/world/india-s-election-commissioner-gains-a-following.html; Ritesh Srivastava, 'Empowering the EC' *Zee News* (New Delhi, 5 March 2012) http://zeenews.india.com/blog/empowering-the-ec_658.html.
66 Singh (2013) 982.
67 S Mohan 'Chief Election Commissioner: equal or superior?' *Hindu* (New Delhi, 9 February 2009) www.thehindu.com/todays-paper/tp-opinion/chief-election-commissioner-equal-or-superior/article350740.ece.
68 Drèze and Sen (2013) 3.
69 Mate (2014) 271–8. In line with this progressive judicial thinking was perhaps the Court's decision in *Javed* v. *State of Haryana* 2003 AIR 3057. In this case, the Court upheld the constitutional validity of a law that disqualified persons having more than two children from contesting for, or holding, elective office in panchayats.

70 1975 AIR SC 2299.
71 For the Supreme Court's response to the impact of internal emergency on FRs, see Nariman (2010) 165–75.
72 For an insightful analysis of this case as well as the insertion of Article 329A, see Austin (1999) 314–25.
73 (1973) 4 SCC 225.
74 See Singh (2013) 1081–2.
75 The total number of electorates in certain parliament constituencies in India could be between two to three million. W.S.J. Staff, 'In Perspective: India's Smallest and Largest Constituencies' *Wall Street Journal* (New York, 31 March 2014) http://blogs.wsj.com/indiarealtime/2014/03/31/in-perspective-indias-smallest-and-largest-constituencies/.
76 See Quraishi (2014) 259–69.
77 Section 77(3) of the RPA read with Rule 90 of the Conduct of Elections Rules 1961.
78 Election Commission of India, 'Compendium of Instructions on Election Expenditure Monitoring' (January 2014) http://eci.nic.in/eci_main/ElectoralLaws/compendium/compendium2014_03022014.pdf.
79 1999 AIR SC 252.
80 Sunny (2000) 213.
81 Ibid.
82 1975 AIR SC 308, 315.
83 The Explanation was amended later to limit its scope: it now provides that the expenditure incurred by leaders of a political party on travel for propagating programme of a political party shall not be deemed to be expenditure in connection with the election incurred or authorised by a candidate.
84 (1996) 2 SCC 752.
85 See Election Commission of India, *Landmark Judgments on Election Law*, vols I and II (Election Commission of India 1999) http://eci.nic.in/eci_main/ElectoralLaws/Judgements/LandmarkJudgementsVOLI.pdf and http://eci.nic.in/eci_main/ElectoralLaws/Judgements/LandmarkJudgementsVOLII.pdf.
86 See Sunny (2000) 217–24.
87 1967 AIR SC 1445.
88 1968 AIR SC 1083.
89 1968 AIR SC 1191. In this case, the alleged corrupt practice was the grant of discretionary funds by the elected candidate to the legislature of the state of Haryana, who was a minister in the state government at that time, to village panchayats for building several public utility works.
90 1971 AIR SC 2015.
91 Ibid. 2039.
92 Ibid. In another case, the Kerala High Court held that the object of Model Code of Conduct was not to stop all governmental activities in states pending elections and that 'the policy decisions taken by the State prior to the issuance of the election notification could be implemented and necessary steps for the implementation of the same could be continued even during the subsistence of the election notification'. *Rajaji Mathew Thomas* v. *Election Commission of India* 2011 AIR Ker 109, [18].
93 *Inder Lal* v. *Lal Singh* (1968) 23 Election Law Reports 252, 256.
94 (1968) 23 Election Law Reports 252.
95 It should be noted that in many cases involving allegations of corrupt practices, the judicial delay in deciding election disputes may make the decision to set aside an election merely academic. For example, in *Inder Lal*, the election took place in 1957, but the Supreme Court judgment was delivered only in 1962, when fresh elections were about to take place. The Court did not, therefore, investigate whether the petitioner could be declared validly elected.
96 Sunny (2000) 223.

97 1976 AIR SC 1886.
98 Drèze and Sen (2013) 3 (emphasis added).
99 1959 AIR SC 855.
100 Ibid. The poster read:

> 'A command from Shri Sat Guru Sacha Padshah to the Namdharies of Halqa-Sirsa' Every Namdhari of this Halqa is commanded by Shri Sat Guru that he should make every effort for the success of Shri Ram Dayal Vaid, a candidate for the Punjab Vidhan Sabha, by giving his own vote and those of his friends and acquaintances, it being our primary duty to make him successful in the election.

101 Ibid. 860 (emphasis added).
102 *Subhas Desai* v. *Sharad J Rao* 1994 SC 2277.
103 Ibid.
104 1996 AIR SC 1113.
105 In this case, the candidate was declared elected in December 1987, while the Court set aside the election only in November 1995. As noted before, such judicial delay in disposing election petitions renders the decision to set aside an election merely of symbolic value.
106 Ibid. 1130.
107 For a critique, see Noorani (2002) 76–83.
108 Quraishi (2014) 362–6.
109 (2013) 7 SCC 653.
110 Ibid. [16] (emphasis added). In view of the finding of legislative incompetence, the Court did not go into the question whether Section 8(4) of the RPA also infringes the right to equality.
111 *Manoj Narula* v. *Union of India* (2014) 9 SCC 1.
112 Ibid. [12], per Justice Kurian Joseph.
113 *Union of India* v. *Association for Democratic Reforms* (2002) 5 SCC 294; *PUCL* v. *Union of India* (2003) 4 SCC 399. See also Election Commission of India (n. 56); Mate (2014) 275–8.
114 (2015) 3 SCC 467.
115 Kashyap (2010) 287, and generally 277–99. For some controversies related to defections and the application of the Tenth Schedule, see Noorani (2000) 173–93.
116 Constitution (Fifty-second Amendment) Act 1985.
117 Constitution of India, Tenth Schedule, para. 2.
118 Ibid. para. 4.
119 Ibid. para. 6.
120 Ibid. para. 7.
121 (1992) 1 SCC 309.
122 Singh (2013) 1072; Sunny (2000) 226–9.
123

> Constitutional experts regard the Election Commission as the greatest gift of the Constitution of India. The remarkable wisdom and foresight of the founding fathers ensured the formation of an institution that has stood the test of time as a powerful watchdog of democracy.
>
> (Quraishi (2014) 30)

124

> Most Indians seem to value the democratic structure of the country, including multi-party politics, systematic free elections, a largely uncensored media, a substantial guarantee of free speech, and the independent standing of the judiciary, among other characteristics of a lively democracy.
>
> (Drèze and Sen (2013) 12)

125 See, for example, the introduction of electronic voting machines. Nilekani (2009) 107. On use of technology generally, see Quraishi (2014) 170–205. For innovations just after independence, see Guha (2007) 134–5.

126 (2013) 10 SCC 1.

127 Although election petitions should be disposed of within six months, almost all High Courts have been taking four to five years in disposing of these petitions. Quraishi (2014) 411.

128 See Election Commission of India, 'Proposed Electoral Reforms', 2004, http://eci.nic.in/eci_main/PROPOSED_ELECTORAL_REFORMS.pdf; Election Commission of India, 'Important Electoral Reforms Proposed by the Election Commission' http://eci.nic.in/eci_main/electoral_ref.pdf; Law Commission of India, '170th Report on Reform of Electoral Laws', 1999, www.lawcommissionofindia.nic.in/lc170.htm.

References

Austin G., *The Indian Constitution: Cornerstone of a Nation* (Clarendon Press 1966).

Austin G., *Working a Democratic Constitution: The Indian Experience* (Oxford University Press 1999).

Austin G., 'The Supreme Court and the Struggle for Custody of the Constitution' in B.N. Kirpal, Ashok H. Desai, G. Subramaniam, R. Dhavan and R. Ramachandran (eds), *Supreme but not Infallible: Essays in Honour of the Supreme Court of India* (Oxford University Press 2000).

Drèze J. and Sen A., *An Uncertain Glory: India and its Contradictions* (Princeton University Press 2013).

Guha R., *India after Gandhi: The History of the World's Largest Democracy* (Picador 2007).

Kashyap S.C., *Indian Constitution: Conflicts and Controversies* (Vitasta Publishing Pvt. Ltd 2010).

Lok Sabha Secretariat, *The Constitution and the Constituent Assembly: Some Select Speeches* (Lok Sabha Secretariat 1990).

Mate M., 'High Court and Election Law Reform in the United States and India' (2014) 32 *Boston University International Law Journal* 267.

Nariman F.S., *Before Memory Fades….: An Autobiography* (Hay House 2010).

Nariman F.S., *The State of the Nation* (Hay House 2013).

Nilekani N., *Imagining India: The Idea of a Renewed Nation* (Penguin Books 2009).

Noorani A.G., *Constitutional Questions in India: The President, Parliament and the States* (Oxford University Press 2000).

Noorani A.G., *Citizens' Rights, Judges and State Accountability* (Oxford University Press 2002).

Orr G., 'Judicial Review of the Administration of Parliamentary Elections' (2012) 23 *Public Law Review* 110.

Quraishi S.Y., *An Undocumented Wonder: The Making of the Great Indian Election* (Rainlight Rupa 2014).

Singh M.P., 'Securing the Independence of the Judiciary: The Indian Experience' (2000) 10 *Indiana International and Comparative Law Review* 245.

Singh M.P., *VN Shukla's Constitution of India* (12th edn, Eastern Book Company 2013).

Singh M.P. and Deva S., 'The Constitution of India: Symbol of Unity in Diversity' (2005) 53 *Jahrbuch des Offentlichen Rechts der Gegenwart* (Yearbook of Public Law) 649.

Sunny K.C., 'Election Laws' in S.K. Verma and K. Kusum (eds), *Fifty Years of the Supreme Court of India: Its Grasp and Reach* (Oxford University Press 2000).

4 Judicial review of elections in Malaysia

Kevin Y.L. Tan

Introduction

Since 1955, the Federation of Malaya (and later the Federation of Malaysia) has had 13 general elections. Elections occur at both state and federal levels and while these elections are often simultaneously held, this has not always been the case as each state has a right to determine when its legislative assembly is to be dissolved.

The conduct of elections is overseen by the Election Commission or *Suruhanjaya Pilihan Raya Malaysia*, a body established under the Constitution. Over the past 60 years, the Malaysian courts have adjudicated on a number of issues involving elections, from the qualification and suitability of candidates to the validity of election results. This chapter provides an overview of the election controversies that have been brought to the courts and analyses the jurisprudence emerging from these judicial decisions.

Legal framework of elections[1]

The Federal Constitution

Malaysia operates a bi-cameral system of government at the federal level. The lower house, known as the *Dewan Rakyat* or House of Representatives (Parliament), is composed of 222 elected members from the various states and federal territories.[2] The upper house, known as the *Dewan Negara*, or Senate, has 70 Senators – two members from each state and federal territory, and 40 members appointed by the Yang di-Pertuan Agong (King).[3] The Senators are appointed for a fixed term of three years and their term of office may only be renewed once.[4] Part IV of the Federal Constitution lays down the rules relating to the composition of Parliament and the Senate, while Part VIII of the Constitution deals with the conduct of elections. The life of Parliament is five years but following British practice, the Prime Minister has the discretion of seeking an early dissolution of Parliament. The dissolution of Parliament does not in any way affect the term of the Senate.

The Election Commission

The conduct of elections is the responsibility of the Election Commission which is charged with conducting the 'elections to the House of Representatives and the Legislative Assemblies of the States' as well as preparing and revising the electoral rolls.[5] Members of the Electoral Commission are appointed by the Yang di-Pertuan Agong 'after consultation with the Conference of Rulers, and shall consist of a chairman, a deputy chairman and five other members'.[6] In addition to its function of conducting elections, the Commission is also charged with the review of the 'division of the Federation and the States into constituencies' and recommending 'such changes therein as they may think necessary'. This exercise is to be conducted at intervals of at least eight years[7] and must, in each instance, be completed within two years.[8] However, the Commission does not have the discretion to increase or decrease the number of seats in Parliament or the Senate since the composition of these bodies is constitutionally prescribed.

Other legislation

In addition to the constitutional provisions regulating the composition of the legislative branch of government and the electoral process, there are three other laws of great relevance: the Elections Act 1958, the Elections Offences Act 1954 and the Election Commission Act, 1957. The law on elections in Malaysia is highly technical and complex as many rules are found in subsidiary legislation such as: the Elections (Conduct of Elections) Regulations 1981, Elections (Registration of Electors) Regulations 1971, Elections (Registration of Electors) (Sabah) Regulations 1971, Elections (Postal Voting) Regulations 1968, Elections (Control of Motor Vehicles and Vessels) Regulations 1959 and Fees (Remission of Postage on Parliamentary and State Election Communications) Order 1959. Because of the multitude of rules and regulations, and the complexity of all the processes, hundreds of cases have arisen with respect to these provisions. This chapter does not attempt to consolidate and synthesise the case law on elections[9] but instead seeks to examine how the judicial review of elections is carried out.

The judiciary and the Election Judge

Judicial structure

Although Malaysia is a federation, its judicial structure is centralised at the federal level. There are no state-level superior courts. However, the political history that led to the establishment of the Federation of Malaysia in 1963 has resulted in the unusual nomenclature adopted in the description of the High Court system. Briefly, the Federation of Malaysia was created on 16 September 1963 through the amalgamation of four distinct former British colonies: the Federation of Malaya (independent since 1957), the State of Singapore (self-governing since 1959) and the North Borneo states of Sabah and Sarawak.

Geographically, Singapore and the Federation of Malaya are contiguously located at the southern-most tip of the Asian land mass while Sabah and Sarawak (located side-by-side with each other, with the independent state of Brunei sandwiched between them) are situated on the large island of Borneo. With Singapore's departure from the Federation in 1965, the old Federation of Malaya is often referred to as 'West Malaysia' or 'Peninsula Malaysia' while Sabah and Sarawak are referred to as 'East Malaysia'. Separating the two territories is the South China Sea, the largest body of water in the region. In Malaysia, the superior courts of record are: (a) the Federal Court, (b) the Court of Appeal and (c) the two High Courts – the High Court of Malaya and the High Court in Sabah and Sarawak. As one can observe from the nomenclature, the two High Courts – which are of coordinate jurisdiction and each headed by a Chief Justice – are named according to geographical locations.

Election petitions

Article 118 of the Federal Constitution provides for the process for challenging an election. The provision reads: '118. No election to the House of Representatives or to the Legislative Assembly of a State shall be called in question except by an election petition presented to the High Court having jurisdiction where the election was held.' Beyond this, the Constitution is conspicuously silent on how election petitions are heard. This is left to be governed by Part VII of the Election Offences Act. Section 33 of the Act states that '[e]very election petition shall be tried by the Chief Justice or by a Judge of any High Court nominated by the Chief Justice for the purpose'. The Chief Justice may not, however, nominate a Judge of a High Court of which he is not Chief Justice, without consulting with the Chief Justice of that Court.[10]

Election petitions may be presented to the High Court by a person 'who voted or had a right to vote at the election', or 'some person claiming to have had a right to be returned or elected at such an election' or 'some person alleging himself to have been a candidate at such election'.[11] Reliefs that may be sought are limited to: (a) a declaration that the election was void, (b) a declaration that the person was not elected or ought not to have been returned or (c) a 'scrutiny'[12] where the seat is claimed for an unsuccessful candidate on the ground that he had a majority of the lawful vote.[13] All petitions must be filed within 21 days of the election results being gazetted,[14] and be heard within six months of filing it.[15]

The Election Judge has 14 days to make a determination and 'certify his determination' to the Election Commission (in the case of federal elections) or the State Authority (in the case of state elections). A petitioner or candidate has the right to appeal against the decision of the Election Judge, and appeal lies to the Federal Court.[16] All appeals must be filed within 14 days from the date of the Election Judge's decision.[17] The Federal Court must hear and determine the appeal within six months of its presentation.[18] The decision of the Federal Court is final.[19] Prior to 2003, no appeals lay from the decision of the Election Judge and a number of cases were brought before the courts to determine if the decision of the Election Judge was final or subject to judicial review.

This issue was raised in the 1967 case of *C Devan Nair* v. *Yong Kuan Teik*[20] and went all the way up to the Privy Council. A key question in this appeal was whether the decision of the Election Judge was final or subject to appeal. Lord Upjohn, on behalf of the Privy Council observed:

> Constitutionally decisions on questions of contested elections are vested in the Assembly for which the contested election has been held, but in the course of the nineteenth century many countries, including this country and many of Her Majesty's possessions overseas, adopted the view that, as the deliberations of the Assembly itself were apt to be governed rather by political considerations than the justice of the case, it was right and proper that such questions should be entrusted to the courts. This required legislation in every case, and in many cases the right of appeal after the hearing of an election petition by an election tribunal to which those hearings was entrusted were severely limited clearly for the reason that it was essential that such matters should be determined as quickly as possible, so that the Assembly itself and the electors of the representatives thereto should know their rights at the earliest possible moment. But essentially the question whether there is any limitation upon the right of appeal must depend upon the terms of the enactment setting up the election tribunal. These are to be found in ss 33 and 36 of the Election Offences Ordinance.[21]

Section 33 of the Election Offences Act provides that every 'election petition shall be tried by the Chief Justice or by a Judge of any High Court nominated by the Chief Justice'. The Election Judge is, under section 36 of the Act, required to determine the petition and 'pronounce such determination in open court'. Lord Upjohn reasoned that as section 67 of the Malaysia Courts of Judicature Act 1964 made provision for appeals to be provided by 'other written law', the combined readings of sections 33 and 36 of the Election Offences Act precluded the Election Judge's decision from being appealed.[22]

The Malaysian courts have also held that the decision of an Election Judge is not subject to a writ of certiorari since it is not an inferior tribunal. In *Ignatius Stephen Malanjum* v. *Election Judge, Sabah & Anor*, the High Court had to decide if it could grant an application for certiorari against the decision of an Election Judge. Mohamad Noor J held:

> I have considered all the relevant features of the court in which the election judge sits including its constitution, jurisdiction and powers and its relationship with the High Court, in order to decide whether the court should properly be regarded as inferior to the High Court, so that its activities may appropriately be the subject of judicial review by the High Court. I am mindful, the fact that the High Court judge sits is not conclusive.

> Having regard to the aforesaid provisions of the law, I conclude that the election judge sits in the High Court exercising his powers relating to election petitions in accordance with the election law, which is a special law. And he exercises his powers in the same jurisdiction and holds coordinate jurisdiction. Therefore, the court in which the election judge sits is not an inferior court against which an order of certiorari or prohibition can be issued.[23]

This decision was followed in the High Court decision *Tengku Razaleigh bin Tengku Mohd Hamzah* v. *Election Judge for Election Petition No 33-6-1995 & Ors*,[24] and affirmed by the Court of Appeal in *Yong Teck Lee* v. *Harris Mohd Salleh & Ors*, and by the Federal Court in the 1998 case of *Wee Choo Keong* v. *Lee Chong Meng & Anor*.[25]

The 2002 Amendments to the Election Offences Act[26] created a right of appeal to the Federal Court and confirmed the status of the Election Court as part of the judicial hierarchy and made clear that it was not an inferior tribunal subject to judicial review.

Contentious issues

The right to vote

Article 119(1) of the Federal Constitution guarantees to every citizen above the age of 21 the right to vote 'in any election to the House of Representatives or the Legislative Assembly' unless he or she is disqualified under Article 119(3). Several cases relating to the right to vote have arisen over the years. Most of them pertain to the veracity and accuracy of the electoral rolls, or the ability of the voter actually to exercise his or her right to vote.

In 2004, an interesting issue was raised in relation to the right to vote in *Yazid bin Sufaat & Ors* v. *Suruhanjaya Pilihanraya Malaysia*.[27] The applicants were Malaysian citizens and were registered as voters in various different constituencies throughout Malaysia. They were also detainees at the Kamunting Detention Centre in Perak, having been detained under the Internal Security Act. When Parliament and the State Legislative Assemblies were dissolved on 4 March 2004 to pave the way for the eleventh general election, the appellants wrote two letters to the Election Commission, informing the latter of their right to vote and their intention to exercise their right to vote. They also asked the Commission to facilitate their casting of the vote. On the day of the election – 21 March 2004 – the appellants were unable to cast their votes. They then sought judicial review and declarations, *inter alia*, that the Commission had violated their fundamental right to vote in the election. The High Court dismissed the application, and the appellants appealed all the way to the Federal Court.

In the Court of Appeal, where the most detailed judgments were given, Low Hop Bing JCA held that while the appellants had the constitutional right to vote under Article 119 of the Federal Constitution, they could only exercise such rights under the prevailing law. In this case, they were regular 'walk in' voters and had to be physically present in their respective constituencies to vote. As the Election Commission had no control over the detaining authorities, they could not possibly arrange for the appellants to be released for the purpose of voting. Low JCA went further to suggest that the appellants had not exhausted their legal remedies before seeking judicial review because they could have, had they so wished, applied to be 'postal voters' under the Elections (Postal Voting) Regulations 2003. This judgment was approved and upheld in the Federal Court.

In a strong dissent, Zainun Ali JCA disagreed with Low JCA and held that the Election Commission had not done enough to facilitate the appellants' right to vote. The Commission clearly had powers under the Elections Act 1958 'to make alternative arrangements and provide facilities for electors by enacting rules and regulations for electors who for some reason are unable to vote in their respective constituencies' as in the appellants' case.[28]

Looking at the wording of the Elections (Postal Voting) Regulations, one is inclined to share the view of Zainun Ali JCA, rather than Low JCA's. Regulation 3(1) of the Regulations provides that any person

> who has registered as a Parliamentary or State elector under the Elections (Registration of Electors) Regulations 2002 and is referred to in an enumerated list, shall, on receipt of a postal ballot paper, be entitled to vote as a postal voter in an election.

The enumerated list that follows does not include detainees under the Internal Security Act. Low JCA had suggested that an application might have been made under Regulation 3(1)(f) which refers to 'a member of any category of persons designated as postal voters by the Election Commission from time to time by notification in the Gazette'. Regulation 3(2) provides that 'A person referred to in paragraphs (1)(b), (d), (e) and (f) desiring to vote by post shall apply to do so by using Form 1 in the Schedule.' It appears from a plain reading of this provision that anyone wishing to apply as a postal voter under the category of persons stipulated in Regulation 3(1)(f) should *already* have been designated as a postal voter by the Commission. In other words, Regulation 3(1)(f) is not intended to be a 'catch-all' category for persons not explicitly mentioned in the earlier paragraphs.

Questioning the electoral rolls

The power of the Election Judge to review the authenticity and accuracy of the electoral roll arose in the 2000 case of *Harris Mohd Salleh* v. *Ismail bin Majin, Returning Officer & Ors and Anor Application*.[29] In that case, Mohammad Kamil J, sitting as Election Judge in the High Court in Kota Kinabalu, had to consider if he had the power to review the electoral roll prepared by the Election Commission. In this case, the petitioners had alleged, *inter alia*, that the electoral rolls contained names of 'phantom voters'. The learned judge held:

> It is clear that under art 119 of the Constitution, only citizens, unless disqualified, have the right to vote. In other words, the right to vote is conferred by the Constitution only on citizens. This right is an exclusive right of citizens, which is non-alienable and cannot be bought or sold. In compiling an electoral roll, in Sabah it is governed by the Election (Registration of Electors) Regulations (Sabah) 1971, which is made pursuant to s 15 of the Election Act 1958, it is the primary duty of the Election Commission to see that only citizens are registered as voters and non-citizens, e.g. illegal immigrants and those who are not entitled to vote, must not be registered as voters or put on an electoral roll. An electoral roll which contains the names of non-citizens is wrong *ex necessitate legis*. If it is alleged that an electoral roll is illegal because it carries the names of non-citizens etc then the court may inquire into the alleged illegality within the spirit of the Constitution.
>
> ...The court, i.e. the High Court, may declare invalid any law enacted by Parliament or a State Legislature which is inconsistent with the Constitution, and an Election Court has no less the same jurisdiction. The Election Court has the jurisdiction to hear and determine the legality of an electoral roll and there is no law that prohibits the hearing of such challenges made against an electoral roll in an Election Court. An electoral roll is prima facie evidence that a person is entitled to vote in a constituency, vide regulation 14 of the Election (Conduct of Elections) Regulation 1981. If it should appear that there is evidence to show that non-citizens have been registered in an electoral roll as voters, that electoral roll is tainted by an illegality for the inclusion of non-citizens in an electoral roll, contrary to the law. In my view, an electoral roll which contravenes the provisions of the election laws and the Constitution, and admits non-citizens or those citizens who are disqualified by the law, may be challenged. Needless to say, an electoral roll may be challenged on the grounds of illegality in that non-citizens' names have inadvertently been entered into the roll, and the Election Court may make such a declaration that an electoral roll is illegal as contrary to federal law and therefore, is null and void.[30]

The stance taken by the Election Judge was consistent with the position taken by the Federal Court in respect of the status of an Election Judge when called upon to decide election petitions. But it was revealed that the learned judge had, in this instance, courageously 'resisted a telephone directive from the Chief Justice of the Federal Court to dismiss the petition'.[31]

An ongoing controversy over electoral rolls has been whether it has been regularly updated, and whether it accurately reflects the composition of the constituency. The Election Commission relies on data from the National Registration Department to update its electoral rolls. Complaints have arisen when names of deceased persons continue to appear on electoral rolls, and where 'phantom voters' turn up to take their place. Malaysia's opposition politicians have also accused the ruling Barisan Nasional of flying 'phantom voters' and 'instant citizens' to vote in tightly contested areas. This accusation was denied by Abdul

Aziz Mohd Yusof, Chairman of the Election Commission, who stated that there was nothing wrong with people sponsoring flights to ferry voters from one part of the country to another to cast their ballots.[32]

Electoral boundaries

One of the most problematic issues in relation to elections in Malaysia is the power of the Electoral Commission to delineate electoral boundaries. Article 113 requires the Commission to 'review the division of the Federation and the States into constituencies and recommend such changes therein as they may think necessary' at least once every eight years. At the time of Merdeka ('Independence') in 1957, Article 116 had three other clauses that were repealed in 1962. They read as follows:

> 116(3) Constituencies shall be allocated to the several States in such manner that the electoral quota of each State is as nearly equal to the electoral quota of the Federation as it can be without causing undue disparity between the population quota of that State and the population quota of the Federation.
>
> 116(4) Each State shall be divided into constituencies in such manner that each constituency contains a number of electors as nearly equal to the electoral quota of the State as may be after making due allowance for the distribution of the different communities and for differences in density of population and the means of communication; but the allowance so made shall not increase or reduce the number of electors in any constituency to a number differing from the electoral quota by more than fifteen per cent.
>
> 116(5) In this Article –
>
> (a) 'electoral quota' means the number obtained by dividing the number of electors in the Federation or a State by the total number of constituencies or, as the case may be, the number of constituencies in that State;
> (b) 'population quota' means the number obtained by dividing the population of the Federation of a State by the total number of constituencies or, as the case may be, the number of constituencies in that State;
>
> and for the purposes of this Article the number of electors shall be taken to be as shown on the current electoral rolls and the population as counted at the most recent census.

With the repeal of these provisions in 1962, Article 116(1) was amended to refer to a new Thirteenth Schedule to the Constitution which spells out the specific provisions relating to how electoral boundaries should be determined and delimited. Under this Schedule, the Commission is required to take into consideration four key 'principles':[33]

(a) while having regard to the desirability of giving all electors reasonably convenient opportunities of going to the polls, constituencies ought to be delimited so that they do not cross State boundaries and regard ought to be had to the inconveniences of State constituencies crossing the boundaries of federal constituencies;

(b) regard ought to be had to the administrative facilities available within the constituencies for the establishment of the necessary registration and polling machines;

(c) the number of electors within each constituency in a State ought to be approximately equal except that, having regard to the greater difficulty of reaching electors in the country districts and the other disadvantages facing rural constituencies, a measure of weightage for area ought to be given to such constituencies;

(d) regard ought to be had to the inconveniences attendant on alterations of constituencies, and to the maintenance of local ties.

The application of these principles would naturally require the Commission to favour larger representation for 'country districts' and 'rural constituencies' over more urban constituencies. Unfortunately, the terms 'rural constituency' and 'country district' are not defined anywhere and it falls on the Commission to determine what they mean. The question that arises is thus whether the Election Commission's decision in constituency delimitation is reviewable by a court of law. Just looking at the population statistics and the allocation of seats under Article 46 of the Federal Constitution, the discrepancies between the States in terms of population-per-representation ratio are quite stark. Table 4.1 is based on the official population figures of the Department of Statistics.[34]

Table 4.1 Malaysia

State	*Population*	*No. of representatives*	*Population per representative (to the nearest 1,000)*
Johor	3,348,283	26	129,000
Kedah	1,890,098	15	126,000
Kelantan	1,459,994	14	104,000
Malacca	788,706	6	131,000
Negeri Sembilan	997,071	8	125,000
Pahang	1,443,365	14	102,000
Penang	1,520,143	13	117,000
Perak	2,258,428	24	94,000
Perlis	227,025	3	76,000
Selangor	5,411,324	22	246,000
Teregganu	1,015,776	8	127,000
Sabah	3,117,405	25	125,000
Sarawak	2,420,009	31	78,000
Kuala Lumpur (FT)	1,627,172	11	148,000
Labuan (FT)	86,908	1	87,000
Putrajaya (FT)	67,964	1	68,000

The national average population-per-representation ratio is about 1 : 124,000, and states like Perlis and Sarawak are 'over-represented' while Selangor is seriously under-represented. Is it open to a Selangor voter to seek judicial review of the Election Commission's determination of the electoral boundaries on the grounds that it was unreasonable or that the Commission had failed to take into account relevant considerations?

No such case has yet come to the courts, but, if one does, the court will not, in all probability, pronounce the matter non-justiciable as this is not the usual practice of the High Court in past cases that have come before it. One of the first was the case of *Yusoff bin Abdul Latib* v. *Haji Adnan bin Haji Ramli & Anor*[35] where the applicant challenged the respondent Returning Officer's right to reject his objection to a nomination paper filed by his political opponent. Mohamed Dzaiddin J proceeded to examine the detailed provisions governing the Returning Officer's powers and discretion and concluded that he had not acted improperly or illegally. In *Teng Chang Kim* v. *Suruhanjaya Pilihanraya, Malaysia*,[36] the applicant sought a declaration that he had a right to be represented by an advocate and solicitor at the local enquiry held by the Election Commission in respect of the Seputeh Parliamentary Constituency P101. Wan Adnan J dismissed the application on the ground that there was no vested right to legal counsel in an appearance before the Election Commission and that the Commission had the discretion whether or not to allow the applicant to be so represented. In the course of his judgment, the learned judge noted that if this 'discretion has been properly exercised, the court will not interfere' and since the applicant did 'not allege improper exercise of discretion', the court would not interfere.[37]

More recently, in *Teo Hoon Seong & Ors* v. *Suruhanjaya Pilihan Raya*,[38] the applicants sought, *inter alia*, a declaration that they had a right, as Malaysian citizens living abroad, to be registered as 'absent voters', and a certiorari order to quash the Election Commission's refusal to register them as 'absent voters'. The High Court dismissed the application on the ground that the Election Commission was complying with Article 119(4) of the Constitution by adopting its narrow definition of 'absent voters' as a citizen who 'is registered as an absent voter' in his or her constituency; since the applicants were not accordingly registered as 'absent voters', the application was refused. In the course of her judgment, Rohana Yusuf J made it clear that the Election Commission was 'an entity constitutionally constituted under art 114 of the Federal Constitution' and that it was 'exercising power granted by law both under the Federal Constitution as well as the federal laws in particular the Elections Act'.[39]

Conclusion

Since its independence in 1957, Malaysia's electoral system has been the subject of much contention, with accusations of mal-apportionment and gerrymandering on the part of the Barisan Nasional – the coalition that has been in power since 1957 – to snuff out its political opponents. The Reid Commission had envisioned a fiercely independent Election Commission of three persons 'in whom all democratic parties and all communities have complete confidence', appointed by the Yang di-Pertuan Negara and whose members can only be removed 'in the same manner provided with regard to a Judge of the Supreme Court'.[40] And it was to this highly respected and constitutionally independent body that the Commission was entrusting the duties of conducting free and fair elections, as well as conducting regular reviews on the delimitation of constituencies in the Federation.

The system that was eventually created placed the Election Commission under the purview of the Prime Minister's Office, with the executive in the driver's seat. As Andrew Harding noted:

> The seven Commissioners are appointed by the *Yang di-Pertuan Agong* after consultation with the Conference of Rulers; since the former acts on the advice of the Government, it is effectively the Government that appoints the ECM [Election Commission, Malaysia]. All of the present Commissioners have had a career in the public service. The Chairman and Deputy Chairman and three ordinary members are Malay; one member is Chinese and one is Indian; one is from Sabah. The Commission reports directly to the Prime Minister with regard to the delineation of both Federal and State constituency boundaries, but the Prime Minister is required to submit the report to the *Dewan Rakyat* with a draft order which may amend the recommendations but has to be approved by the House before it can take effect.[41]

And although legislative endorsement is required for delimitation to be effective, this has never been a problem since the Barisan has almost always controlled the bulk of the seats in the Dewan Rakyat.

Up till 2002, it was unclear what the status of the Election Judge was, and whether his or her decision on election petitions was subject to judicial review or was amenable to appeal. The 2002 amendments to the Elections Act clarified the status of the Election Judge and equated the office to that of the High Court and provided for appeals to lie to the Federal Court. Traditionally, the courts have not shied away from reviewing either the decisions of the Election Commission or the manner in which it has exercised its discretion. However, even with the most independent of judicial benches, most of the rules governing the conduct of elections are still governed by laws enacted by Parliament and so long as the government in power is determined to manipulate an electoral system, there is little that the courts can do to stop them.

Notes

1 The law on Malaysia's electoral process has been admirably covered in Rachangan (1993). It remains a useful, albeit outdated book.
2 Article 46, Federal Constitution.
3 Ibid. Article 45.
4 Ibid. Article 45(3)(a).
5 Ibid. Article 113(1).
6 Ibid. Article 114.

7 Ibid. Article 113(2)(ii).
8 Ibid. Article 113(2)(iii).
9 This has been done by Tunku Sofiah Jewa (2003) in her two-volume work.
10 Section 33(1), Election Offences Act.
11 Ibid. Section 34.
12 A 'scrutiny' means a recount of the votes to determine which votes are valid and whether they were properly counted. The rules for the scrutiny are provided under Section 40, Election Offences Act.
13 Ibid. Section 35.
14 Ibid. Section 38.
15 Ibid. Section 35A.
16 Ibid. Section 36A.
17 Ibid. Section 36A(2).
18 Ibid. Section 36B.
19 Ibid. Section 36C.
20 [1967] AC 31.
21 Ibid. at 38.
22 Ibid. at 39.
23 [1989] 2 MLJ 433.
24 [1996] 4 MLJ 66.
25 [1998] 1 MLJ 434.
26 Elections Offences (Amendment) Act A1177 came into effect on 16 January 2003.
27 [2009] 6 MLJ 152.
28 [2009] 6 MLJ 221, at 255.
29 [2000] 3 MLJ 434.
30 *Wee Choo Keong* v. *Lee Chong Meng & Anor* [1998] 1 MLJ 434.
31 See Faruqi (2008) 609.
32 See 'Phantom voters? EC clears the air' *Straits Times* (4 May 2013).
33 Section 2, Thirteenth Schedule, Federal Constitution.
34 These figures are based on the official 2010 census figures issued by Malaysia's Department of Statistics, available at: www.statistics.gov.my/index.php?r=column/cthemeByCat&cat=117&bul_id=MDMxdHZjWTk1SjFzTzNkRXYzcVZjdz09&menu_id=L0pheU43NWJwRWVSZklWdzQ4TlhUUT09 (accessed 20 June 2015).
35 [1992] 1 MLJ 297.
36 [1994] 2 MLJ 241.
37 Ibid. at 245.
38 [2012] 4 MLJ 245.
39 [2012] 4 MLJ 245, at 249.
40 Report of the Federation of Malaya Constitutional Commission (HMSO 1957), para. 71.
41 Harding (2012) 90.

References

Faruqi S.S., *Document of Destiny: The Constitution of the Federation of Malaysia* (Star Publications 2008).

Harding A., *The Constitution of Malaysia: A Contextual Analysis* (Hart 2012).

Rachagan S.S., *Law and the Electoral Process in Malaysia* (University of Malay Press 1993).

Sofiah Jewa T., *Malaysian Election Law: Commentary, Cases and Materials on Election Petitions, Political Party Elections and Related Cases decided in Malaysia since pre-Independence* (Pacifica Publications 2003).

5 'Election disputes' or disputed elections?

Judicial (non-)review of the electoral process in Pakistan

Moeen H. Cheema

Introduction

The adjudication of regime change and electoral controversies is often considered the epitome of 'judicialisation of politics'.[1] Electoral politics is considered 'pure politics' and the courts' role in determining the validity of elections is thus fraught with danger. Even though many constitutions include provisions concerning the conduct of elections, judicial review of electoral matters presents courts with the risk of being seen as favouring one of the disputants, and judges may lose their credibility. Nonetheless, declining jurisdiction over a case is not a completely safe option either as courts risk being seen as irrelevant or supportive of the status quo. Beyond these precarious political dynamics, judicial review of electoral matters often presents courts with the challenge of engaging in large-scale and complex fact-finding, which is traditionally considered to be outside the core competence of the courts.

Pakistan presents a fascinating case study of the inherent politics of the judicial review of elections. The demand for the judicial scrutiny of elections, the Court's refusal, and a protest movement that nearly threatened to derail the democratic system, has dominated the country's political landscape since the last general elections held in May 2013. The Supreme Court's refusal to entertain demands for an inquiry into the conduct of elections stands in sharp contrast to the Court's earlier proclivity towards expansive judicial review during the tenure of former Chief Justice Iftikhar Muhammad Chaudhry. While the present controversy is on the verge of a resolution through the proceedings of a judicial commission composed of apex courts judges – constituted through an agreement reached between the government and the opposition – the larger questions concerning the role of courts in mediating electoral disputes are likely to remain or even re-emerge with a vengeance when the next elections come around.

Compelling a transition from military to civilian rule (2000–2008)

In October 1999, General Pervez Musharraf, Chief of the Army Staff, displaced Pakistan's elected Prime Minister, Mian Nawaz Sharif, who had commanded a two-thirds majority in parliament and had enjoyed seemingly unassailable power since the last elections held in 1996. General Musharraf was aboard a Pakistan International Airline flight returning from an official visit to Sri Lanka when the Prime Minister decided to sack him from the command of the military. The military's general cadre refused to accept the dismissal of General Musharraf and the appointment of his replacement, decided to take over Pakistan Television and other state installations, and placed the Prime Minister under house arrest. By the time military troops cleared Karachi airport for the landing of General Musharraf's plane, a bloodless coup d'état was well underway.

With General Musharraf's takeover, Pakistan entered its third extended cycle of direct military rule since it gained independence in 1947. Upon taking power, the military regime began to unveil a refined version of the constitutional blueprint of military rule developed by Pakistan's earlier military dictators – General Ayub Khan (1958–1968), General Yahya Khan (1968–1971), and General Zia ul Haq (1977–1988).[2] A Proclamation of Emergency was issued, the Constitution was put in abeyance, and a Provisional Constitution Order (PCO) was issued to provide a temporary governing framework.[3] However, this time around, martial law was not formally declared and General Musharraf assumed the self-styled office of the 'Chief Executive' of Pakistan. In January 2000 when the Supreme Court entertained a challenge to the validity of the military coup and the interim governance framework, concerted efforts to undermine the independence of the judiciary began in earnest. The judges of the superior courts were compelled to take a new oath of office pledging to serve under the PCO.[4] Six out of a total of thirteen judges of the Supreme Court refused to take the oath and resigned from the bench, including the then Chief Justice, Saeeduzzamman Siddiqui.[5]

A reconstituted Supreme Court decided the case of *Zafar Ali Shah v. General Pervez Musharraf* in May 2000 and validated the coup on the basis of the 'doctrine of state necessity'.[6] The Court granted virtually unlimited powers to the military regime, including the power to amend the Constitution. The Court, however, imposed one potentially meaningful restriction: the military regime had to hold general elections no later than three years from the date of the coup. Preparing for the elections for which a firm deadline had been set by the Supreme Court remained a key priority throughout the three-year period of direct military rule. In June 2001 General Musharraf dismissed the lame duck President and assumed that office through a decree.[7] In April 2002 he held a stage-managed referendum claiming to win 97 per cent of the votes cast and securing the office of the President for a five-year term that would end in October 2007. Many first- and second-tier leaders belonging to the major political parties, the Pakistan Muslim League of Nawaz Sharif (PML-N), and Pakistan Peoples Party (PPP) headed by Benazir Bhutto, were won over by the regime through a combination of threats of prosecution for corruption and incentives to cobble together a loyalist faction known as the Pakistan Muslim League (Q) (PML (Q)).

In August 2002, just prior to holding the general elections mandated by the Court, the Musharraf regime issued a Legal Framework Order (LFO), which consolidated a number of constitutional changes and revived the notorious

Article 58(2)(b) to the Constitution that empowered the President to dismiss the incoming parliament at will.[8] Despite the absence of key leaders from both political parties[9] and the efforts of the intelligence agencies, the so-called 'King's party', PML (Q) failed to win an outright majority in the national legislature.[10] An alliance of conservative religious parties, *Muttahida Majlis-e-Amal* (MMA), emerged as the prime beneficiary of the regime's efforts to undermine the mainstream political parties and won a substantial presence in the legislatures for the first time in the country's history. For over a year, the MMA and the other opposition parties succeeded in disrupting the business of parliament, thereby denying the military regime the façade of a stable elected government. Questions regarding the legal validity of the LFO, the referendum, and other actions taken during the three-year-long direct military rule, continued to hound the regime in this interregnum.

In December 2003, the regime finally reached an agreement with the MMA and, with its support, mustered the two-thirds majority in parliament necessary to pass the Seventeenth Amendment to the Constitution.[11] The Seventeenth Amendment validated almost all of the actions taken during the three-year interregnum, including the referendum and the revival of the presidential power to dismiss the parliament. In return, the MMA secured a promise from General Musharraf to give up his office as army chief by the end of 2004. The Seventeenth Amendment formalised that understanding by making the relevant disqualification clause in the Constitution applicable to the office of the President as of the first day of 2005.[12] Article 63(1)(d) of the Constitution mandates that a person is disqualified from becoming a member of parliament if 'he holds an office of profit in the service of Pakistan other than an office declared by law not to disqualify its holder'. Simply put, as of 1 January 2005, General Musharraf would be disqualified from holding the office of the President if he continued to remain as army chief.

In November 2004, the general reneged on his promise to give up the command of the armed forces and had parliament pass the President to Hold Another Office Act 2004 (PHAOA).[13] Without the support of the MMA, the regime could only muster a simple majority to pass an ordinary legislation, which stated that the office of the Chief of Army Staff (CoAS) was, under this law, declared to be an office that did not disqualify its holder from assuming the office of the President. This neat piece of legalism was made applicable to only one person, General Musharraf, and for one term of presidential office only. In the *Pakistan Lawyers Forum* case the Supreme Court was called upon to judge the validity of the Seventeenth Amendment as well as the PHAOA 2004.[14] The Court validated both the Amendment and the Act on a strictly positivist and literal reading of the constitutional provisions and the legislation in question. Earlier the Court had also refused to entertain any challenges to the LFO and Seventeenth Amendment,[15] or to General Musharraf's election as President through the referendum.[16]

The stability provided by the Seventeenth Amendment and the PHAOA lasted merely two years. As 2007 was scheduled to be the year of parliamentary and presidential elections, the regime was coming to its third term, a feat no previous military dictator had managed successfully to achieve in Pakistan. General Ayub Khan had been forced to resign after protests and General Zia had died in a plane crash before the end of their second terms. It would be much harder this time around to resist demands for more open and participatory elections. It was also inevitable that the question of 'dual office' would resurface with a vengeance. In an unexpected move the Musharraf regime suspended Iftikhar Chaudhry, Chief Justice of the Supreme Court, on charges of misconduct in March 2007. The Supreme Court had exhibited limited judicial activism under Chaudhry CJ, which clearly caused some nervousness amongst the military regime and its allied political parties about the outcome of any possible constitutional challenges. General Musharraf's action engendered a protest movement, which started with the lawyers but quickly began to attract wider support, especially amongst the cadres in the opposition parties.

In July 2007, a bench of the Supreme Court dismissed the charges against Chaudhry CJ and restored him to office. The regime reluctantly accepted the decision hoping to end the controversy. However, it appeared that the regime had precipitated what it feared at this time of transition – a relatively independent judiciary. General Musharraf's political future depended on securing another term in the office of President. Furthermore, he wanted to hold the presidential election before the general elections so that his supporters in the federal and provincial legislatures could muster the necessary number of votes required to achieve his re-election and also pass legislation sanctioning another term for him in the presidency while he concurrently held the office of military chief. Neither outcome could be guaranteed after the general elections which would be much harder to manipulate this time around. In October 2007, General Musharraf contested and won re-election to the presidency. The election was challenged before the Supreme Court, which allowed it to proceed subject to the condition that the election results may not be formally notified until the case was resolved in court.[17] As the hearings in the case proceeded and fearing an adverse outcome, General Musharraf imposed a state of emergency on 3 November 2007.[18]

The principal aim of the emergency was to bring about a compliant judiciary that would sanction General Musharraf's election as President and enable him to affect a transition to a third term in power.[19] Judges of superior courts were asked to take an oath under a PCO and an unprecedented number declined or were not invited to do so.[20] The regime thus effectively dismissed more than half of the judges of the superior courts including the Chief Justice of Pakistan for the second time in a year. The remaining Supreme Court judges validated the imposition of emergency and all actions taken pursuant to it. Nonetheless, widespread protests at home and rising international pressure seriously constrained General Musharraf's political space, and he was compelled to give up the office of military chief. In November, General (retired) Pervez Musharraf was sworn in as the President and announced that the state of emergency would be lifted on 15 December 2007.[21] Elections scheduled for early 2008 had to be initially postponed after the tragic assassination of Benazir Bhutto when she attended a political rally. Her party, the PPP, led by her widower Asif Zardari, nonetheless participated in the elections of February 2008.

The 'Chaudhry Court' and judicial review of electoral process (2009–2013)

Contrary to fears of massive rigging, the February 2008 elections were considered to be by and large fair. The PPP won the largest number of seats in the National Assembly but did not secure an outright majority and had to form a coalition government with a number of smaller parties.[22] For more than a year, the elected government refused to restore Chief Justice Chaudhry and many of the other judges of the superior courts who had been dismissed in the emergency. In September 2008, the PPP managed to oust President Musharraf under a threat of impeachment and succeeded in getting Asif Zardari elected as president. In March 2009, the issue of Chief Justice Chaudhry's reinstatement came to a boiling point as the lawyers and leading opposition parties organised a 'Long March' towards the capital Islamabad. Facing the threat of violent protest in the capital, and behind-the-scenes pressure from the military, the PPP government finally relented and reinstated Chief Justice Chaudhry to his office once again.

One of the first actions of the Supreme Court after Chief Justice Chaudhry's reinstatement was to invalidate the imposition of emergency and certain actions taken pursuant to it.[23] The Court did not, however, impugn the validity of the February 2008 elections, the formation of federal and provincial governments, and the presidential election of Asif Zardari. Nonetheless, the 'Chaudhry Court' progressively instituted a strong form of judicial review increasingly questioning legislative and executive actions of the PPP government. The Court began to take up allegations of governmental corruption and maladministration through petitions filed directly before the Court under its Original Jurisdiction. The Court also initiated a number of cases *suo motu*, that is of its own accord, based on media reports of corruption and illegalities. This created an atmosphere of tension between the Court and the elected executive that lasted until the end of the PPP government's tenure. In retaliation, the PPP government made a deliberate effort to resist the Court at every step, utilised all public forums available to it to politicise the Court's actions by portraying them as biased, and decried judicial overreach.

Amongst a range of matters taken up by the Court included cases concerning the disqualification of members of parliament. Amongst the most significant of such decisions was the disqualification of the incumbent Prime Minister for contempt of court. In a two-step process, the Supreme Court first charged and convicted Prime Minister Gilani for contempt of court in April 2012 for refusing to obey its instructions to lodge a mutual legal assistance request to Swiss prosecutors regarding a case implicating President Zardari, and imposed a nominal sentence on the Prime Minister.[24] The Prime Minister's legal team decided not to file an appeal against the conviction. A reference calling for the disqualification of the Prime Minister was sent to and disposed of by the Speaker of the National Assembly without furnishing adequate reasons. A three-member bench headed by the Chief Justice then agreed to hear a petition challenging the Speaker's decision and held that Article 63(1)(g) of the Constitution, which provides for the disqualification of a member of parliament if 'he has been convicted by a court of competent jurisdiction for propagating any opinion, or acting in any manner, prejudicial to … the integrity or independence of the judiciary of Pakistan, or which defames or brings into ridicule the judiciary' applied in this instance.[25] The Court thus disqualified and unseated an elected Prime Minister for his failure to obey its directions.[26]

In addition to Prime Minister Gilani, the Supreme Court disqualified several other members of parliament for submitting fake academic degrees in the 2008 elections and for possessing dual citizenship.[27] What was notable about all these decisions is that the Court appeared to be 'diluting' the text of relevant provisions of the Constitution, which vested the power to disqualify members of parliament (post-election) in the Election Commission.[28] The Court rationalised its actions by arguing that its *quo warranto* type powers under the Original Jurisdiction had to be read in harmony with the text of Article 63.[29] While discussing this particular issue in his concurring opinion in the *Prime Minister's disqualification* case, Khilji Arif Hussain J drew a parallel with Article 225 of the Constitution which, unlike Article 63, expressly vests a seemingly exclusive jurisdiction to decide election disputes in the Election Tribunals.[30] Hussain J also noted a long line of precedents in which the superior courts had exercised such *quo warranto* powers, albeit subject to certain limitations and conditions, despite Article 225.[31]

As the parliament neared the end of its term in 2013, the Chaudhry Court appeared to be playing a central but ambivalent role in the first ever transition from one elected government to another. On one hand, the Chaudhry Court's aggressive judicial review actions had undermined the electoral prospects of the PPP in the 2013 elections by painting a narrative of its corruption, maladministration, and incompetence. On the other hand, despite the increasing politicisation and criticism of its actions, the Court had presented itself for the first time in the country's history as an independent and somewhat credible arbiter of electoral process. As the 2013 elections approached, the Court took up a number of petitions overseeing the conduct of the electoral process, including matters such as demarcation of constituencies, preparation of electoral rolls, and overseeing the affairs of the Election Commission.

In *Imran Khan v. Election Commission of Pakistan*,[32] the Supreme Court set aside the Election Commission's objections that it was mandated by Article 219 of the Constitution to revise electoral rolls annually, and since it had recently prepared the electoral rolls for the metropolis of Karachi the same could not be redone for another year.[33] The Court held that the provision was an enabling one and the Election Commission's overarching obligation to conduct free and fair elections could not be fulfilled in the absence of an accurate preparation of the electoral rolls. Earlier, in *Watan Party v. Federation of Pakistan*,[34] the Supreme

Court had also issued directions regarding the delimitation of constituencies in Karachi while hearing a petition addressing the law and order situation in the metropolis. The Court took notice of concerns that constituencies had previously been gerrymandered by the Musharraf regime to favour the *Muttahida Qaumi Movement* (MQM), which was the dominant party in urban areas in southern Pakistan with largely ethnic appeal.[35] The bench headed by Chief Justice Chaudhry directed new delimitations to end ethnic enclaves and create multi-ethnic and diverse constituencies.

Most notably, in *Workers Party v. Federation*, the Court gave detailed instructions to the Election Commission regarding the conduct of the forthcoming elections.[36] After issuing notices to and eliciting responses from all major political parties, the Court issued directions to the Election Commission concerning the regulation of election expenses, of public gatherings, mode of canvassing, advertisements, banners, and billboards, amongst other matters. These directions were, however, of a general nature and amounted to little beyond an exhortation to the Election Commission to perform its constitutional and statutory duties. Nonetheless, the Court held itself out as the supervisor of electoral process and guarantor of its fairness. As Pakistan moved towards another general election in May 2013, there was considerable optimism for the holding of free and fair elections and a peaceful transfer of power to the next government. This optimism was further fuelled by the unanimous passing of the Twentieth Amendment to the Constitution by the major parties in parliament, which provided for an independent chairperson and provincial members of the Election Commission, and federal and provincial caretaker governments to be appointed with the agreement of the governments and the leader of opposition in each legislature.[37]

There was also a new dynamic in electoral politics of Pakistan as the 2013 elections approached. *Pakistan Tehreek-e-Insaaf* (PTI), led by famous cricketer-turned-politician Imran Khan, had finally emerged as a serious electoral contender in the months leading up to the elections and provided the electors with a third option beyond the PPP and the PML-N, which had dominated the political arena for the previous three decades.[38] The PTI was successful in energising hitherto depoliticised segments of Pakistan's population, especially the urban middle class youth, which had historically been disenchanted and detached from electoral politics. While the PTI expressed reservations over the neutrality of the caretaker set-ups and certain actions of the Election Commission, it decided to participate fully in the elections. The PTI appeared to invest considerable faith in the superior judiciary to act as guarantor of free and fair elections and even demanded that the vital roles of returning officers be entrusted to members of the lower judiciary rather than the bureaucracy, as had been the case in previous elections. The PTI was rightly concerned that both the PML-N and the PPP had successfully formed deep roots and cultivated loyal factions in the state's bureaucratic apparatuses.

While the PPP government bravely proclaimed its prospects of re-election on the basis of its broad-based coalition formation, continuing support in the rural and peri-urban areas on account of its farmer-friendly agricultural policies, and its backing amongst the poorest of the poor due to a generous cash grant scheme called the Benazir Income Support Programme (BISP) that it had instituted, independent observers doubted such an outcome. The PPP and its allies also campaigned under the threat of attacks on their rallies and leaders by the Taleban. The Taleban sought to penalise the nominally liberal and left-leaning PPP government for having facilitated US drone strikes in the territories occupied by them, while the right-leaning opposition parties were spared. Most importantly, during the previous four years, the Supreme Court appeared to have played a significant role in undermining the electoral prospects of the PPP by successfully shaping a narrative of corruption and bad governance at the highest levels. By the eve of the elections it appeared likely that the real contest would be between the PML-N and the PTI. The PML-N, which had effectively ruled the Punjab for more than two-thirds of the previous three decades, was the front runner. However, another hung parliament and a weak coalition government appeared to be the most likely outcome.

From an activist court to a reluctant arbitrator (2013–2015)

On 11 May 2013, the day of simultaneous polling for national and provincial assembly seats across Pakistan, reports of alleged rigging and irregularities in several constituencies became the talking point on private news outlets. When the unofficial results began pouring in later that evening and Nawaz Sharif, the leader of PML-N, made a somewhat premature victory speech just before midnight, the magnitude of the PML-N's electoral triumph had come as a surprise even to its supporters. Not only had the PML-N emerged as the largest party in the National Assembly, it was set to command an outright majority despite having garnered little support outside Punjab. The party had won the Punjab – Pakistan's largest province with more than 50 percent of the population and the corresponding constituencies in the National Assembly – with such a landslide that it would be able to form the federal government without the support of any other party. While the PPP lost the bulk of its presence in the National Assembly, it retained control over the provincial government in Sindh. The PTI, which emerged as the second largest party in terms of the number of votes polled but marginally third in number of seats in the National Assembly, was able to form a coalition government in Khyber Pakhtunkhwa.

Although all major political parties other than the PML-N complained about large-scale organised rigging in the election, all but the PTI agreed to accept the results. The PTI initially accepted the elections results under protest. In July 2013, the party began a concerted campaign to call in question the credibility of the elections, claiming widespread and systematic rigging in the elections. PTI candidates filed election petitions before the election tribunals in several constituencies. The party's central leadership demanded a thorough investigation into four constituencies as a means to test whether rigging had taken place and demanded that the Supreme Court take *suo motu* notice of and initiate an inquiry into the conduct of the elections.[39] Frustrated with the Supreme Court's refusal to initiate such a *suo motu* hearing, Imran Khan of the PTI criticised the 'shameful' role played by the judiciary, especially the judicial officers appointed as Returning Officers in the elections. Deeming the comments as scandalous and prejudicial to the prestige of the judiciary, the Supreme Court instead initiated contempt proceedings against the chairman of the PTI.[40]

The contempt proceedings were discharged as the Court accepted Imran Khan's argument that the comments were directed exclusively at the role of the members of the lower judiciary acting in an administrative capacity as the Returning Officers.[41] Nonetheless, implicitly relying on Article 225 of the Constitution which vests exclusive jurisdiction to determine election disputes in specially constituted election tribunals, the Supreme Court declined to initiate a *suo motu* investigation into the charges of large-scale electoral fraud. While arguably in accordance with the text of Article 225 and the established practice of the Court of not interfering in electoral matters, the Chief Justice's refusal to initiate a *suo motu* hearing appeared to be a departure from his more recent interventionist stance.[42] The rest of the Chaudhry Court's judicial review jurisprudence certainly weighed in favour of a systemic review of the conduct of the 2013 elections. As noted earlier, in Prime Minister Gilani's disqualification case, the bench had indicated in *obiter* that the exclusivity of Article 225 applied to individual single-constituency disputes and the Court could look at systemic issues especially concerning the role and conduct of the Election Commission.[43] Furthermore, in several high profile cases leading up to the 2013 elections the Supreme Court had adopted the practice of creating ad-hoc commissions to assist it in fact-finding.[44] In the notorious *Memogate* case, the Court had even created a commission comprising three senior judges of the High Courts to investigate allegations against Hussain Haqqani, then Ambassador of Pakistan to the US, that he had sent secret correspondence to US Chairman of the Joint Chiefs of Staff urging certain actions against the Pakistan military.[45]

The PTI attempted to highlight this contradiction between the Court's previously interventionist stance and the refusal to take up its demands of *suo motu* investigations into electoral misconduct. On its part, the PTI never formally filed a petition demanding such an investigation either. Instead, in an attempt to bypass the likely objection based on Article 225, it filed a civil miscellaneous application requesting the Court to take notice of the failure by the Election Commission to adhere to its directions in the *Workers Party* case.[46] With the end of the Chaudhry Court era in December 2013, the Supreme Court began to retreat from the strong-form judicial review it had developed. The Civil Miscellaneous Application remained undecided even though there had been eleven hearings under three different chief justices. The charge of judicial overreach against the Chaudhry Court had resonated to such an extent that the Court felt compelled to adopt a position of judicial restraint on a range of political questions that were raised before it. The *suo motu* and human rights jurisdictions dwindled and the Supreme Court progressively resettled to a more traditional judicial role.

The issue of election rigging simmered in the political domain as the Court repeatedly declined the call to act as the arbitrator in such disputes. In August

2014, more than a year after the conduct of elections and while the overwhelming majority of election petitions remained unresolved, the PTI launched a protest movement beginning with yet another Long March to the capital Islamabad. By December 2014, a protest sit-in continued in front of the Parliament house and the Supreme Court, while the PTI also organised public meetings, calls for strikes, and protest marches in various urban centres all over the country. The ghosts of eras past – speculations of or tacit support of the protesters by the military or even threat of direct military intervention – re-emerged to haunt Pakistan's political landscape.[47] All this while, the Supreme Court, the only institution seemingly capable of resolving this toxic political deadlock in a constitutional manner, sat quietly on the sidelines.

In January 2015, the PTI was forced to call off its protest movement, which appeared to be suffering from fatigue, especially after a gruesome terrorist attack on a military-run public school in Peshawar. In the interim, it was evident that the PML-N government had managed to survive the protests only because of the unconditional support it received from the other political parties and in return for having ceded the national security and foreign policy domains completely to a re-energised military command.[48] In March, the PML-N government finally relented and agreed to the formation of a judicial commission comprising judges of the Supreme Court to investigate the PTI's allegations of electoral fraud. The agreement was effected through the promulgation of a special ordinance by the President.[49] The same questions that formed the basis of a refusal by the Supreme Court to entertain a petition under its Original Jurisdiction lingered over the constitutionality of the commission: whether such a judicial investigation into election disputes contravened the exclusive jurisdiction of the election tribunals?[50] These questions were set aside when the incumbent Chief Justice Nasir-ul-Mulk constituted a judicial commission under his chairmanship in response to the request from the government. As a result, the judiciary was reluctantly thrusted back into the role of mediating a question of pure politics that could possibly lead to a change in government.

The terms of reference of the commission were to determine whether the 2013 elections had been:

- a organised and conducted impartially, honestly, fairly, justly and in accordance with law.
- b manipulated or influenced pursuant to a systematic effort by design by anyone; and
- c a true and fair reflection of the mandate given by the electorate.[51]

In July 2015, after extended hearings into the conduct of the 2013 elections, the judicial commission submitted its findings to the government. While the commission found that the Election Commission had exhibited severe lapses in its conduct of the elections and the electoral process had been marred by considerable irregularities, overall the elections had been conducted fairly and in accordance with the law. According to the commission, the PTI failed to present evidence of systematic rigging in favour of the PML-N government and the results were a true reflection of the mandate given by the electorate.

The findings of the commission's inquiry were a set-back to the PTI and were claimed as a vindication of the government's stance. Nonetheless, the PTI leadership accepted the commission's findings, subject to some reservations. As a result of the commission's proceedings, one of the most significant recent episodes of political uncertainty appears to have come to an end and the incumbent government seems secure in its position until the next general elections. However, this condition of political stability may not last. Important challenges to the government's and the electoral process' legitimacy are not far off in the future. The question of electoral reform still lingers. Given the commission's findings, the focus will inevitably shift to the identified issues in electoral process and the weaknesses in the Election Commission's operations. A parliamentary committee on electoral reform, constituted in July 2014 to deflect some of the political criticism emanating from the PTI, has not completed its work despite the passage of more than a year.[52] It is unclear how far-reaching the proposed reforms will be, and whether they will bring about a significant improvement in the electoral process.[53]

Conclusion

As Pakistan lurches through a protracted crisis relating to governance, economic stagnation, terrorism, and social discord towards another election year tentatively scheduled for 2018, the outcome of this belated judicial investigation will determine whether the country remains on a democratic trajectory or ends up with another episode of military rule. The military has emerged once again as the most popular institution in the country and has reclaimed a prominent role in national security. A successful year-long campaign against Taleban militants in the tribal areas in the north has helped the military regain much of the prestige it lost during the last years of Musharraf's rule. The military has also expanded its campaign against terrorism and militancy to the port city of Karachi, Pakistan's largest city and commercial hub. This has resulted in overt tensions between the military, the PPP government in Sindh, and the MQM. The support for the PML-N government that other opposition parties exhibited during the PTI's protests – fearing an imminent military coup – also appears to be crumbling in the aftermath of the federal government's support of the military's actions in Karachi.

With the fragmentation of the political landscape, another episode of political instability created by disputed elections may prove to be the end of the democratic system. As such, consensus-based electoral reforms and the conduct of free and fair elections are now vital to the continuation of democracy in Pakistan. Pakistan's superior judiciary has the capacity to act as a meaningful arbitrator of the conflicts that threaten the current political balance, but it has now retreated from a more activist role displayed during the Chaudhry era. This new inactivism has allowed potentially destabilising disputes to boil over in the political arena and allow for the military to re-emerge as the most powerful institutional player. Pakistan's courts invested with constitutional jurisdiction have, therefore, little choice but to embrace their function as the guarantors of democratic process and as arbitrators that can credibly defuse political tensions before they reach a point of no return.

Notes

1 See Hirschl (2006, 2008).
2 See Kennedy (2006).
3 Provisional Constitution Order, PLD 1999 Central Statutes 448.
4 Oath of Office (Judges) Order, 2000, PLD 2000 Central Statutes 38.
5 Five Supreme Court judges were removed for declining to take the oath under the PCO. The remaining twelve judges decided to challenge the constitutionality of the military takeover. See Haq (2005).
6 *Zafar Ali Shah* v. *General Pervez Musharraf*, PLD 2000 SC 869.
7 President's Succession Order 2001, PLD 2001 Central Statutes 392.
8 Legal Framework Order 2002, PLD 2002 Central Statutes (Supplement) 1604.
9 The LFO barred the leaders of PML-N and the PPP from contesting the elections held in October 2002. Nawaz Sharif, who had been charged with and convicted of terrorism and hijacking charges for directing the diversion of General Musharraf's aeroplane at the time of the coup had already been sent into exile in Saudi Arabia, pursuant to a deal brokered by the Saudi royals. Benazir Bhutto and Asif Zardari had also been in self-imposed exile since the late 1990s in order to avoid corruption charges.
10 See Khan (2009) 490.
11 Constitution (Seventeenth Amendment) Act, 2003 (Act No. 2 of 2003).
12 Section 2, Constitution (Seventeenth Amendment) Act, 2003.
13 Article 63(1)(d), Constitution of Pakistan.
14 See *Pakistan Lawyers Forum* v. *Federation of Pakistan*, PLD 2005 SC 719.
15 See *Watan Party* v. *Chief Executive*, PLD 2003 SC 74.
16 *Hussain Ahmed* v. *Pervez Musharraf*, PLD 2002 SC 853.
17 General Musharraf's election as President was challenged on the basis that he was not eligible to contest the election while occupying the office of military chief. Furthermore, it was argued that the practice of contesting election when parliament was nearing the end of its term was contrary to the democratic spirit of the Constitution. See Moeen Cheema, 'Supreme Challenge: Pakistan's Presidential Election Goes to Court' (*Jurist*, 18 October 2007) http://jurist.org/forum/2007/10/supreme-challenge-pakistans.php accessed 29 July 2015.
18 See Moeen Cheema, 'Martial Law by Another Name in Pakistan' (*Jurist*, 3 November 2007) http://jurist.law.pitt.edu/forumy/2007/11/martial-law-by-another-name-in-pakistan.php accessed 29 July 2015.
19 See Proclamation of Emergency, PLD 2008 Federal Statutes 108.
20 See Moeen Cheema, 'Pakistan: Mock Trials, Kangaroo Courts and Court Jesters' (*Jurist*, 9 November 2007) http://jurist.law.pitt.edu/forumy/2007/11/pakistan-mock-trials-kangaroo-courts.php accessed 29 July 2015. In total sixty-one judges of the superior courts were thus deposed: thirteen out of eighteen (seventeen permanent and one ad hoc) Supreme Court judges, including the Chief Justice; eighteen out of thirty-one judges of the Lahore High Court; twenty-four out of twenty-eight judges of Sindh High Court, including the Chief Justice; and six out of thirteen judges of Peshawar High Court, including the Chief Justice.

21 See Peter Lloyd, 'Musharraf Announces End to Emergency Rule in Pakistan' (*ABC News*, 30 November 2007) www.abc.net.au/news/2007-11-30/musharraf-announces-end-to-emergency-rule-in/973226 accessed 1 September 2015.

22 The PPP, founded by Zulfiqar Ali Bhutto and later led by his daughter Benazir Bhutto, had historically been an anti-establishment and leftist party in Pakistan's politics. Since the 1990s, however, the party learnt to reach a level of accommodation with the military and has gradually lost its leftist credentials.

23 *Tikka Iqbal Muhammad Khan* v. *General Pervez Musharraf Chief of Army Staff*, PLD 2008 SC 6.

24 See *Criminal Original Petition No. 06 of 2012, In Suo Motu Case No. 04 of 2010*, PLD 2012 SC 553. Earlier, in the so-called *NRO* case the Supreme Court had issued directions to the government to write a letter to the Attorney-General's office in Geneva effectively to restart prosecution for money laundering against President Zardari that had been pending in the Swiss courts since the late 1990s: see *Dr. Mobashir Hassan* v. *Federation of Pakistan*, PLD 2010 SC 1.

25 See Article 63 cl. 1(g), Constitution of Pakistan.

26 See *Muhammad Azhar Siddique* v. *Federation of Pakistan*, PLD 2012 SC 660. The author served as the Judges' Associate to the Supreme Court bench that decided the so-called Prime Minister's disqualification case.

27 See *Muhammad Rizwan Gill* v. *Nadia Aziz*, PLD 2010 SC 828; *Mian Najeeb-ud-Din Owaisi and another* v. *Amir Yar Waran and others*, PLD 2013 SC 482; *Syed Mehmood Akhtar Naqvi* v. *Federation of Pakistan*, PLD 2012 SC 1089.

28 See Article 63 cls 2 and 3, Constitution of Pakistan.

> 63. Disqualifications for membership of Majlis-e-Shoora (Parliament):
>
> (2) If any question arises whether a member of Majlis-e-Shoora (Parliament) has become disqualified from being a member, the Speaker or, as the case may be, the Chairman shall, unless he decides that no such question has arisen, refer the question to the Election Commission within thirty days and should he fail to do so within the aforesaid period it shall be deemed to have been referred to the Election Commission.
>
> (3) The Election Commission shall decide the question within ninety days from its receipt or deemed to have been received and if it is of the opinion that the member has become disqualified, he shall cease to be a member and his seat shall become vacant.

29 See concurring opinion of Khilji Arif Hussain J in *Muhammad Azhar Siddique* v. *Federation of Pakistan*, *supra* note 26.

30 See Article 225, Constitution of Pakistan:

> 225. Election dispute
>
> No election to a House or a Provincial Assembly shall be called in question except by an election petition presented to such tribunal and in such manner as presented to such tribunal and in such manner as may be determined by Act of Majlis-e-Shoora (Parliament).

31 In *Farzand Ali* v. *Province of West Pakistan*, PLD 1970 SC 98, the Supreme Court interpreted Article 171 of the 1962 Constitution which was the antecedent to Article 225 of the 1973 Constitution. The Court observed that:

> An election dispute is a dispute raised by a voter or a defeated candidate in his individual capacity under the Statute. It determines the private rights of two persons to the same office but a proceeding for an information in the nature of quo warranto is invoked in the public interest. The latter seeks to determine the title to the office and not the validity of the election. These are two distinct and

> independent remedies for enforcing independent rights, and the mere fact that the disqualification has been overlooked or what is worse, illegally condoned by the authorities who were responsible for properly scrutinising a person's right to be enrolled as a voter or his right to be validly nominated for election would not prevent a person from challenging in the public interest his right to sit in the house even after his election if that disqualification is still continuing.

Also, see *Niaz Ahmed* v. *Province of Sind*, PLD 1977 SC 604; *Muhammad Hayat Khan* v. *Imtiaz Ahmad Khan*, PLD 2008 SC 85; *Federation of Pakistan* v. *Muhammad Nawaz Sharif*, PLD 2009 SC 644.

32 *Imran Khan* v. *Election Commission of Pakistan*, Constitution Petition No. 31 of 2011, www.supremecourt.gov.pk/web/user_files/File/Const.P.31of2011etc.pdf accessed 29 July 2015.

33 See Article 219, Constitution of Pakistan:

> 219. Duties of Commissioner.
> The Commission shall be charged with the duty of:-
> (a) preparing electoral rolls for election to the National Assembly and the Provincial Assemblies, and revising such rolls annually,
> (b) organizing and conducting election to the Senate or to fill casual vacancies in a House or a Provincial Assembly; and
> (c) appointing Election Tribunals;
> (d) the holding of general elections to the National Assembly, Provincial Assemblies and the local governments; and
> (e) such other functions as may be specified by an Act of Majlis-e-Shoora (Parliament).

34 *Watan Party* v. *Federation of Pakistan*, PLD 2011 SC 997.

35 The MQM was founded as the representative party of the descendants of *mohajirs* or migrants from north-central India at the time of partition and who form the largest ethnic group in the urban areas of southern Pakistan, especially Karachi. General Musharraf was ethnically *mohajir*. The MQM allied itself with the Musharraf regime and enjoyed considerable power at the provincial and local level during his tenure.

36 *Workers Party* v. *Federation*, PLD 2012 SC 681.

37 See Constitution (Twentieth Amendment) Act, 2012 (Act No. V of 2012).

38 The PML-N, led by Nawaz Sharif, is the largest and most popular of the right-leaning factions of the Muslim League. PML-N originated in the late 1980s under the patronage of then military ruler General Zia ul Haq. In the 1990s the PML-N twice won general elections held in 1990 and 1996 and Nawaz Sharif served as the country's Prime Minister. On both occasions his tenure was cut short, first when he was forced to resign after a tussle with the President in 1993 and second as a result of General Musharraf's coup in 1999.

39 See Amir Jalil Bobra, 'General Elections 2013: Imran asks CJP to take suo motu on "Pre-planned Rigging"' (*Daily Times*, Islamabad, 3 May 2014) www.dailytimes.com.pk/national/03-May-2014/general-elections-2013-imran-asks-cjp-to-take-suo-motu-on-pre-planned-rigging accessed 29 July 2015.

40 See *Criminal Original petition No. 92 of 2013 (Contempt Proceedings against Imran Khan, Chairman PTI)*. The short order dated 2 August 2013 is available at www.supremecourt.gov.pk/web/user_files/File/Crl.O.P.92_2013_dt_02.08.2013.pdf accessed 29 July 2015.

41 See *Criminal Original petition No. 92 of 2013 (Contempt Proceedings against Imran Khan, Chairman PTI)*. The detailed judgment is available at www.supremecourt.gov.pk/web/user_files/File/Crl.O.P.92of2013-dt-9-10-2013.pdf accessed 29 July 2015.

42 Contrast from the cases disqualifying members of parliament for dual citizenship or fake degrees. See *supra* note 27. Likewise, in the Prime Minister's disqualification

case, *supra* note 26, where the Court similarly grappled with the question whether the qualifications and disqualifications of members of parliament were matters exclusively to be determined by the Election Commission.

43 See *supra* notes 25 and 26, and accompanying text.

44 See, for example, *Suo Motu Case No. 5 of 2012*, PLD 2012 SC 664, arising out of allegations of financial impropriety against the Chief Justice's son.

45 *Watan Party and others* v. *Federation of Pakistan*, PLD 2012 SC 292.

46 See *C.M.A. 7679 of 2013* in *C.R.P. No. 191 of 2012* in *Constitution Petition No. 87 of 2011 (Application on behalf of Mr. Saifullah Nyazee, Additional Secretary PTI for recount of votes in 4 constituencies, after verification of thumb impressions)* www.supremecourt.gov.pk/web/user_files/File/cma.7679_2013.pdf accessed 29 July 2015.

47 See Tim Craig and Shaiq Hussain, 'Protesters March towards Pakistan's Parliament in Sign of Deepening Crisis' (*Washington Post*, Islamabad, 19 August 2014) www.washingtonpost.com/world/asia_pacific/pakistans-sharif-enlists-army-to-secure-high-security-zone-ahead-of-protests/2014/08/19/1ea58938-27a9-11e4-8593-da634b334390_story.html accessed 29 July 2015; 'Rebutting Allegations: Army, ISI not Backing Protesting Parties, says ISPR' (*Express Tribune*, Islamabad, 2 September 2014) http://tribune.com.pk/story/756813/rebutting-allegations-army-isi-not-backing-protesting-parties-says-ispr/ accessed 29 July 2015; and Katharine Adeney, 'Shadow of Military Looms Large over Pakistan Street Protests' (*Conversation*, 2 September 2014) http://theconversation.com/shadow-of-military-looms-large-over-pakistan-street-protests-31132 accessed 29 July 2015.

48 A notable example of this arrangement is the broad agreement amongst the government and opposition in parliament to pass a constitutional amendment for the creation of military courts to try terrorism cases. See Constitution (Twenty-First Amendment) Act, 2015 (Act No. I of 2015).

49 General Elections 2013 Inquiry Commission Ordinance, 2015 (Ordinance No. VII of 2015).

50 See Khawar Ghumman, 'Is the Judicial Commission "Constitutional"?' (*Dawn*, Islamabad, 3 April 2015) www.dawn.com/news/1173648 accessed 29 July 2015.

51 Section 3, General Elections 2013 Inquiry Commission Ordinance, 2015.

52 See Irfan Haider, 'NA Speaker Constitutes Committee on Electoral Reforms' (*Dawn*, Islamabad, 26 July 2014) www.dawn.com/news/1121556 accessed 29 July 2015.

53 See Iftikhar A. Khan, 'Work Begins on 13 Constitutional Amendments: Dar' (*Dawn*, Islamabad, 29 July 2015) www.dawn.com/news/1197038/work-begins-on-13-constitutional-amendments-dar accessed 29 July 2015.

References

Haq A.Z., 'Mechanisms of Political Capture in Pakistan's Superior Courts' in Cotran E. and Lau M. (eds), *Yearbook of Islamic and Middle Eastern Law: Volume 10 (2003–2004)* (Brill 2005).

Hirschl R., 'The New Constitutionalism and the Judicialisation of Pure Politics Worldwide' (2006) 75 *Fordham Law Review* 721.

Hirschl R., 'The Judicialisation of Mega-Politics and the Rise of Political Courts' (2008) 11 *Annual Review of Political Science* 93.

Kennedy C.H., 'A User's Guide to Guided Democracy: Musharraf and the Pakistani Military Governance Paradigm' in Kennedy C.H. and Botteron C. (eds), *Pakistan: 2005* (Oxford University Press 2006).

Khan H., *Constitutional and Political History of Pakistan* (Oxford University Press 2009).

6 Judicial review of the electoral process in Singapore after *Vellama*

Po Jen Yap

Introduction

Vellama d/o Marie Muthu v. *Attorney General*[1] remains the first and the only occasion where the Singapore judiciary had the opportunity to review a challenge to the local electoral process. Specifically, the Singapore Court of Appeal held that the Prime Minister had a constitutional duty under Article 49[2] of the Constitution to call for a by-election when a casual vacancy arose. But, on the facts, the Court of Appeal also held that the applicant, a resident voter of the Hougang Single Member Constituency (SMC), had no standing to seek declaratory relief from the courts after a by-election to fill the vacancy at Hougang SMC had been carried out, and she thus incurred no 'special damage'[3] after that to seek judicial relief.

The facts and the procedural history of the case may be briefly stated. Following the vacancy of the Parliamentary Hougang SMC on 14 February 2012, a resident voter of the said SMC instituted judicial review proceedings for a mandatory order requiring the Prime Minister to advise the President to issue a writ of election for Hougang SMC and a declaration on the proper construction of Article 49 of the Constitution. On 2 March 2012, the Prime Minister announced that he intended to call for a by-election in Hougang SMC but had not decided on a time. On 3 April 2012, the High Court granted the applicant leave for a judicial review hearing. The by-election was subsequently held on 26 May 2012. The High Court dismissed the applicant's case on 1 August 2012 and the Court of Appeal dismissed her appeal on 5 July 2013.

In this chapter, I shall examine three core issues relating to the judicial review of the electoral process in Singapore that was raised in *Vellama*: (1) the *locus standi* of the Applicant; (2) the constitutional duty of the Prime Minster to call for a by-election when a vacancy arose; and (3) the determination of cost orders for such public interest litigations.

Locus standi

The Court of Appeal's dismissal of the Applicant's case was premised on the ground that she lacked standing to seek declaratory relief. After the by-election in Hougang SMC was held on 26 May 2012, the facts underpinning her original application was rendered moot and the Applicant could only assert 'a public right arising under Art 49, rendering her no different from any other citizen interested in the proper construction of Art 49'.[4] As observed by the Court: 'Where the applicant asserts no more than a public right which is shared in common with other citizens, however, standing accrues only if a nexus between the applicant and the desired remedy is established by demonstrating "special damage".'[5] If proof of 'special damage' was not required, the Court of Appeal expressed concern that the judiciary would be 'inundated by a multiplicity of actions, some raised by mere busybodies and social gadflies, to the detriment of good public administration'.[6]

It is also noteworthy that the Court of Appeal was unwilling to adopt the 'more expansive'[7] *locus standi* rules currently applied in the United Kingdom as the English rule on standing had been amended in 1977 to allow for an applicant merely to show that he or she has a 'sufficient interest in the matter to which the application relates'.[8] Therefore, the Court argued that, unlike Singapore, there was 'greater scope in the English courts to grant leave where there is public interest litigation of the matter even though the applicant is not personally affected'.[9] Hence, what would be of relevance to Singapore would be the pre-1977 English rules and the corresponding case-law as 'the English rules of court were then identical'[10] and the liberalised English law on standing established in 1982, following the landmark House of Lords decision in *Inland Revenue Commissioners* v. *National Federation of Self-Employed and Small Businesses*[11] (*National Federation*), was not endorsed.

In *National Federation,* the House of Lords faced a judicial review proceeding brought by the National Federation of Self Employed and Small Businesses. The National Federation argued that the Inland Revenue acted illegally in granting amnesty to casual workers in Fleet Street, who had been evading taxes for years, on condition that *inter alia* the workers' tax would in the future be deducted at source. For our purposes, the pertinent issue on appeal was whether the National Federation had sufficient interest to bring such a proceeding in the first place. In particular, a majority of the Law Lords took the view that the crux was whether the allegedly breached statute had granted the applicant a right to seek redress. However, they accepted that even if the legislation in question did not confer standing on the applicant, the courts may still grant leave where some 'exceptionally grave or widespread illegality'[12] was alleged, but this was not demonstrated on the facts.

In *Vellama*, the Court of Appeal's failure to adopt *National Federation*'s 'sufficient interest' test as good law is questionable for three reasons, and it is to these grounds I now turn.

First, the Court of Appeal in *Vellama* was not even consistent about rejecting all post-1977 English case-law development on *locus standi*. In fact, in *Vellama*, the Court of Appeal expressly endorsed *National Federation* insofar as the Law Lords unanimously held that the issue of standing, although determined as a preliminary issue, could be re-opened at the substantive hearing of the application for judicial review.[13] The Court in *Vellama* also noted that this proposition of law espoused in *National Federation* had been applied in subsequent English cases.[14] Therefore, the Singapore Court of Appeal, following 'such overwhelming authority'[15] decided that it could continue to review the applicant's standing 'until the courts have arrived at a final determination'.[16] But it is puzzling why the Court of Appeal was persuaded to adopt the 'overwhelming [English] authority'[17] on this specific point on *locus standi* but would not accept the *National Federation*'s liberalised test on 'sufficient interest'. Unfortunately, the Court of Appeal made no attempts to explain this inconsistency.

Second, while the Court of Appeal was not wrong to be concerned about preventing busybodies from clogging up the judicial process, the imposition of this 'special damage' requirement may have unfortunate consequences. By denying all individuals the right to challenge a public body's action, solely because the grievance suffered is shared between all members of society, a grave lacuna would be left in Singapore's public laws as no remedy may be granted when *everyone* is injured. This, in turn, would provide public authorities with perverse incentives to make any public wrongs more prevalent and widespread. Taking *Vellama* to its logical conclusion, the more pervasive the alleged violation of a public right is, the more the public authorities can be insulated from any judicial challenge, such that a gravely unlawful act may be left uncorrected indefinitely.

Third, the Court of Appeal in *Vellama* had drawn support for its 'special damage' test on the basis that this was also consistent with the positions taken by the Malaysian and Australian courts.[18] But it is noteworthy that in Malaysia and Australia, their courts of final resort have now both departed from their past restrictive *locus standi* rules.

The Federal Court of Malaysia in *Malaysian Trade Union Congress* v. *Menteri Tenaga*[19] (*MTUC*) held that an applicant, in the context of a public interest litigation (PIL), merely had to show that he or she had a 'real and genuine interest in the subject matter'[20] and it was 'not necessary for the applicant to establish infringement of a private right or the suffering of special damage'.[21] In particular, the 'special damage' test laid out in *Lim Kit Siang*, which was endorsed by the Court of Appeal in *Vellama*, was distinguished on the basis that in *Lim Kit Siang* the applicant's claim was brought in private law.[22] On the facts in *MTUC*, the Malaysian federal government, the Selangor state government, and a consortium had entered into a tri-partite Agreement, which allowed the consortium to raise the tariffs of the water it was supplying by 15 per cent if certain performance targets were met. The Malaysian Trade Union Congress, a society of trade unions, was granted standing to apply for judicial review when the government refused to disclose a copy of the said Agreement and the Audit Report that justified the increase in water tariffs, though their judicial review action was unsuccessful on the facts.

Similarly, the High Court of Australia no longer applies the restrictive 'special damage' or 'special interest' test articulated in *Australian Conservation Foundation* v. *Commonwealth of Australia*.[23] In that case, the Australian

Conservation Foundation, a well-known Australian environmental group, was denied standing to contest a proposed tourist development in Farnborough, Queensland because the foundation failed to establish any special interest in the preservation of the locality. According to Justice Gibbs:

> I would not deny that a person might have a special interest in the preservation of a particular environment. However, an interest, for present purposes, does not mean a mere intellectual or emotional concern. A person is not interested within the meaning of the rule, unless he is likely to gain some advantage, other than the satisfaction of righting a wrong... if his action succeeds or to suffer some disadvantage, other than a sense of grievance or a debt for costs, if his action fails.[24]

But one must note that *Australian Conservation Foundation* is not the High Court of Australia's last word on *locus standi.* Since then, a majority on the High Court of Australia in *Bateman's Bay* declared, by way of dicta, that the public interest may also be vindicated 'at the suit of a party with a *sufficient material interest* in the subject matter'.[25] Unfortunately, the Australian judges did not explain therein what they meant by this terminological change or whether they were lowering the standing threshold for a public-interested claimant.

More importantly, in *Ronald Williams* v. *Commonwealth of Australia*,[26] a majority on the High Court of Australia held that a father of four children had standing to challenge the validity of a Funding Agreement reached between the federal government and a religious organisation, Scripture Union Queensland, for the provision of funding for chaplaincy services, and the relevant payments made under the Funding Agreement, to the school his children were enrolled in. It is noteworthy that the majority only looked at whether there was 'the existence of a sufficient interest in the plaintiff'[27] and that the plaintiff was found to have standing even though he was challenging expenditures incurred by the federal government when his children had not begun attending the school in question.[28]

Fortunately for Singapore, after *Vellama*, the Court of Appeal has begun to reconsider its restrictive rules on *locus standi.* In *Jeyeretnam Kenneth Andrew* v. *Attorney General*,[29] a private individual and opposition politician had sought to bring judicial review proceedings against the Singapore Government on the basis that its contingent financial loan to the International Monetary Fund was in violation of Article 144(1) of the Singapore Constitution.[30] The Court ultimately rejected the applicant's claim on the basis that he had no *locus standi* to bring suit in the first place as he, a mere private individual, was 'unable to assert any rights – private or public – to the alleged breach of duty,... his claim is brought in the public interest'.[31]

Nevertheless, in *obiter*, the Court of Appeal made the following new concessions:

> [I]t seems to us that 'special damage' might also possibly encompass those rare and exceptional situations where a public body has breached its public

> duties in such an egregious manner that the courts are satisfied that it would be in the public interest to hear it.[32]

While this exception was inapplicable on the facts, the Court held that it would be unthinkable that citizens would have no recourse when 'there has been an obvious and flagrant disregard for the law'[33] by the public authorities. *National Federation* is thus now good law in Singapore.

Equally important is the Court of Appeal's second concession in *Jeyeretnam*:

> [I]t is crucial to note that the law on standing … is not statute-based, but is a judge-made doctrine based on the common law which has, over the centuries, undergone enormous changes, not just in Singapore, but in many other common law jurisdictions.[34]

In other words, the Court of Appeal has openly acknowledged that it can, on its own accord, modify or liberalise the rules on standing as circumstances may necessitate in the future.

Constitutional duty to fill a casual vacancy

Even though the Court of Appeal held that the Applicant did not have the standing to bring this judicial review action, it nevertheless went on to examine the substantive issues raised by the Applicant.

Very laudably, the Court of Appeal rejected the government's argument that the Prime Minister had an unfettered discretion to decide whether to call for a by-election when a casual vacancy arose, and instead imposed a constitutional duty on the Prime Minister to fill a casual vacancy within a 'reasonable time'.[35]

In view that Article 49 of the Singapore Constitution states that a 'vacancy *shall* be filled by election', the Court of Appeal held that there was a constitutional imperative on the Prime Minister to fill a vacancy. As observed by the Court: 'The implication of a less definitive and directory rather than mandatory verb where the word "shall" is used, and where its ordinary sense is not open to question, is simply unwarranted.'[36] In so doing, the Court of Appeal overruled the High Court's conclusion that the Prime Minister had an unfettered discretion as 'the phrase "shall be filled by election" in Art 49(1) refers to the process whereby vacated seats of elected Members are to be filled … and not the event of election'.[37]

Moreover, according to the Court of Appeal, the absence of a time-limit clause governing a by-election in the Constitution does not mean that 'the Prime Minister is thereby completely free to do as he pleases'[38] because Section 52 of the Interpretation Act provides that 'where no time is prescribed … that thing shall be done with all convenient speed'; and in the Court's view, this statutory provision basically enshrines the 'common law concept of a reasonable time'.[39]

A fortiori, the Prime Minister has a constitutional duty to call for a by-election when a vacancy arose within a reasonable time.

Unfortunately, the Court went on to take the wind out of this decision by conceding that the Prime Minister

> could justifiably take into account matters relating to policy ... [and] it is impossible to lay down the specific considerations or factors which would have a bearing on the question as to whether the Prime Minister had acted unreasonably for not, to date, calling a by-election to fill a vacancy,[40]

such that 'no pre-determination of the Prime Minister's considerations would be warranted.'[41] Therefore, so long as the Prime Minister does not openly reject the possibility of a by-election, it would appear that there are no other constitutional limits laid down by the Court on the Prime Minister's exercise of this discretion.

This deferential stance taken by the Court of Appeal is emblematic of the judicial ethos in Singapore that 'matters of public policy are the proper remit of the Executive'[42] and that courts should not be seen as 'the first line of defence against administrative abuses of power: instead, control can and should come internally from Parliament and the Executive itself in upholding high standards of public administration and policy'.[43] If so, as admitted by the Court, judicial intervention in election cases in Singapore would only occur in the most 'exceptional cases';[44] and in almost all cases, any such review would only be a mere chimera.

Cost order

Finally, another central and interesting development arising from the *Vellama* litigation was the judicial determination of the appropriate cost order in such proceedings. After the High Court ruled against the Applicant on substantive grounds on 1 August 2012, it subsequently decided on 1 November 2012 that it would make no order as to costs for all applications leading to its substantive judgment (and the cost hearing), even though the general rule in Singapore is that costs follow the event and the Applicant had been unsuccessful in her suit.

According to the High Court, this dispute raised 'public law issues of general importance'[45] and it was appropriate for the Court to exercise its discretion and *not* order a cost order against the unsuccessful private litigant.

This was certainly a landmark judgment in Singapore as, prior to *Vellama*, the Singapore courts had never exercised this discretion in favour of an unsuccessful private litigant. The Singapore judiciary had only done so in favour of unsuccessful *public bodies* performing regulatory functions.[46] Nevertheless, the High Court of Singapore drew support from English, Australian, and New Zealand case-law and decided that private litigants raising such matters of public interest may also benefit from the exercise of the judicial discretion on costs.[47]

It is also noteworthy that the Court of Appeal on 2 November 2014, just one day after the High Court's judgment on cost was handed down, issued its decision on whether the Attorney General should pay the Applicant's costs when the former withdrew its appeal against the High Court's decision on 3 April 2012 to grant the Applicant leave to bring judicial review proceedings. The Court of Appeal therein had addressed a separate, uncontroversial, and very narrow issue on cost. But what was of particular significance was that the Court of Appeal on 2 November 2014 expressly noted the High Court's judgment on 1 November 2014, even though it was wholly irrelevant to its appeal, and the Court of Appeal also made the following observation: 'The general rule is that costs follow the event, but that rule applies only if the court in exercise of its discretion sees fit to make any order of or incidental to the proceedings.'[48] In other words, the general rule on costs is not really a rule at all, as it applies only if the judge sees fit. Naturally, one can only speculate on the reasons for and the timing of the Court of Appeal's judgment. But, arguably, in expressly referencing the High Court's judgment on costs, and insofar as the Court of Appeal emphasised that the general rule on costs applies '*only if* the court in exercise of its *discretion* sees fit to make any order', the Court of Appeal may have obliquely endorsed the High Court's decision of not making a cost order even if the private litigant was unsuccessful on the facts. It is also noteworthy that when the Court of Appeal dismissed the Applicant's substantive appeal on 5 July 2013, it also held that 'each party is to bear his or her costs',[49] though this was justified on the basis that the Court was in the main with the Applicant on the substantive issue relating to the construction of Article 49 of the Singapore Constitution.

Conclusion

While the Singapore Court of Appeal may not have been as bold in *Vellama* as it could have, this groundbreaking case remains a watershed decision for Singapore. Insofar as the Court of Appeal recognised that there was a constitutional duty on the Prime Minister to call for an election when a vacancy arose, it has once again reaffirmed the 'basic proposition of the rule of law that all discretionary power is subject to legal limits'.[50] Furthermore, the High Court's refusal to award costs against the unsuccessful private litigant, on the basis that she had raised a 'legal question of genuine public concern',[51] is to be welcomed as this judicial innovation removes a key obstacle to the future development of PIL in Singapore.

In a most interesting post-script, the Court of Appeal in *Yong Vui Kong* v. *Public Prosecutor*[52] made a couple of fascinating observations about the citizenry's right to vote in a completely unrelated constitutional challenge to the legality of the judicial corporal punishment regime in Singapore. While upholding the constitutionality of judicial caning *inter alia* on the basis that the prohibition against torture does not form part of the basic structure of the Singapore Constitution, the Court nevertheless suggested that the right to vote could 'possibly'[53] form part of the 'basic structure of the Constitution',[54] and thus 'may not be amended even by a validly passed constitutional amendment'.[55] In short, even though the right to vote is not expressly enshrined in the Singapore Constitution, it nevertheless forms part of the basic structure of the Constitution such that it may not even be abrogated by a constitutional amendment. It remains unclear why the judges decided to make such an observation, especially since voting rights were in no way engaged in *Yong Vui Kong*, but Singapore is better for it. Only time will tell whether this liberalising trend would continue in Singapore.[56]

Notes

1 *Vellama d/o Marie Muthu* v. *Attorney General* [2013] 4 SLR 1 (Singapore Court of Appeal); *Vellama d/o Marie Muthu* v. *Attorney General* [2012] 4 SLR 698 (Singapore High Court).
2 Article 49(1) of the Singapore Constitution reads: 'Whenever the seat of a Member, not being a non-constituency Member, has become vacant for any reason other than a dissolution of Parliament, the vacancy shall be filled by election.'
3 *Vellama d/o Marie Muthu* v. *Attorney General* [2013] 4 SLR 1 [33].
4 *Vellama* (n. 3) [43].
5 Ibid. [33].
6 Ibid.
7 Ibid. [18].
8 See O. 53 r. 3(5) of the English Rules of the Supreme Court (Amendment No. 3) 1977 (SI 1977 No. 1955) (United Kingdom) and s. 31(3) of the Senior Courts Act 1981 (c. 54) (United Kingdom).
9 *Vellama* (n. 3) [17].
10 Ibid. [31].
11 *Inland Revenue Commissioners* v. *National Federation of Self-Employed and Small Businesses* [1982] AC 617 (House of Lords).
12 Ibid. [647].
13 *Vellama* (n. 3) [14].
14 Ibid.
15 Ibid.
16 Ibid.
17 Ibid.
18 Ibid. [28], [43].
19 *Malaysian Trade Union Congress* v. *Menteri Tenaga* [2014] MLJU 92 (Malaysia Federal Court).
20 Ibid. [58].
21 Ibid.
22 *Government of Malaysia* v. *Lim Kit Siang* [1988] 2 MLJ 12 (Malaysia Federal Court).
23 *Australian Conservation Foundation* v. *Commonwealth of Australia* (1980) 146 CLR 493.
24 Ibid. [530].
25 See *Bateman's Bay Local Aboriginal Land Council* v. *Aboriginal Community Benefit Fund* [1998] 194 CLR 247. In this case, the Aboriginal Community Benefit Fund was granted standing to challenge the Bateman's Bay Local Aboriginal Land Council's statutory right to conduct a contributory funeral benefit fund for all Aboriginal persons.
26 *Ronald Williams* v. *Commonwealth of Australia* [2012] HCA 23.
27 Ibid. [117].
28 A majority on the High Court of Australia eventually held that the Funding Agreement, and the payments made under the Agreement, was unlawful as it was beyond the executive power of the Commonwealth under Section 61 of the Australian Constitution.

29 *Jeyeretnam Kenneth Andrew* v. *Attorney General* [2014] 1 SLR 345 (Singapore Court of Appeal).

30 Article 144 of the Singapore Constitution reads:

> (1) No guarantee or loan shall be given or raised by the Government –
> (a) except under the authority of any resolution of Parliament with which the President concurs;
> (b) under the authority of any law to which this paragraph applies unless the President concurs with the giving or raising of such guarantee or loan; or
> (c) except under the authority of any other written law.

31 *Jeyeretnam Kenneth Andrew* (n. 29) [51].
32 Ibid. [62].
33 Ibid. [60].
34 Ibid. [33].
35 *Vellama* (n. 3) [84].
36 Ibid. [77].
37 *Vellama* v. *Attorney General* [2012] 4 SLR 698 [80].
38 *Vellama* (n. 3) [78].
39 Ibid. [84].
40 Ibid. [85].
41 Ibid.
42 Ibid. [34].
43 Chan (2010) 480.
44 Ibid.
45 *Vellama d/o Marie Muthu* v. *Attorney General* [2013] 1 SLR 797 at [44].
46 *Law Society of Society* v. *Top Ten Entertainment* [2011] 2 SLR 1279 (Court of Appeal).
47 *Vellama d/o Marie Muthu* v. *Attorney General* [2013] 1 SLR 797 at [42].
48 *Attorney General* v. *Vellama d/o Marie Muthu* [2013] 1 SLR 439 at [15].
49 *Vellama* (n. 3) [93].
50 Ibid. [85].
51 *Vellama d/o Marie Muthu* v. *Attorney General* [2013] 1 SLR 797 at [43].
52 *Yong Vui Kong* v. *Public Prosecutor* [2015] SGCA 11.
53 Ibid. [69].
54 Ibid.
55 Ibid. [72].
56 See Yap (2015).

References

Chan S.K. CJ, 'Judicial Review: From Angst to Empathy' (2010) 22 *Singapore Academy of Law Journal* 469.

Yap P.J., *Constitutional Dialogue in Common Law Asia* (Oxford, Oxford University Press 2015).

Part II

Civil Law Asia

7 The curious case of quasi-weak-form review

Judicial review of electoral process in Indonesia

Stefanus Hendrianto

Introduction

On August 21, 2014, the Indonesian Constitutional Court issued the decision on the 2014 presidential election results dispute, and it rejected all grounds of challenge raised by the losing presidential candidate Prabowo Subianto and officially declaring Joko Widodo as the president-elect.[1] The international media and observers gave high praise for the Court's decision, especially for its ability to deliver justice in a fair and democratic manner.[2]

But the narrative of the Indonesian Constitutional Court's decisions on the election issues is far more complex than the Court's decision in that presidential election dispute last summer. In the last decade, the Court has decided many cases that relate to the electoral process, ranging from voting rights[3] to a statutory regulation governing the open lists system.[4] In the first decade since its inception, the Constitutional Court has created some new constitutional rules on electoral process through judicial construction. This chapter examines the role of the Indonesian Constitutional Court in interpreting electoral law during the first decade since its inception. Before I move to analyse the Court's decisions on electoral issues, some clarifications are necessary. First, this chapter will focus primarily (though not exclusively) on how the Court dealt with judicial review of the electoral process of national legislative elections and it will not explore the regional head elections (*Pemilihan Kepala Daerah* – PILKADA), which include the election of Governors, Bupatis (Head of District) and Mayors. Nonetheless, it will also consider a few cases that involve the presidential election law and the election of the Regional Representative Council (*Dewan Perwakilan Daerah* – DPD).

The second point of clarification is that although this chapter focuses on the judicial review of electoral process, it has some implication for the study of institutional design. Some legal scholars and political scientists have tried to explain the Indonesian Constitutional Court through its institutional design. Marcus Mietzner of Australian National University argues that the Indonesian Constitutional Court was designed to be a 'negative legislator' that can annul but cannot enact legislation.[5] Mietzner argues further that in some electoral related cases, the Court entered new legal territory by moving beyond its traditional role as negative legislator into the role of positive judicial lawmaking.[6] Similarly, Professor Donald Horowitz of Duke Law School explained that Indonesian politicians crafted the law[7] to limit the Court's authority over constitutional cases to only after the enactment of a challenged statute and only upon a challenge by a party adversely affected by the statute;[8] moreover, the said law prohibited the court from rendering advisory opinions.[9]

This chapter argues that the design of the Indonesian Constitutional Court is more complex than a simple classification as a positive or negative legislator. As Professor Horowitz noted, the Court only has authority to pronounce on the consistency of statutes with the Constitution. In other words, the Court only has authority to review a constitutional question in an abstract way and not to resolve a concrete constitutional case. The Court's abstract review does not aim to resolve the injury that is suffered by the claimant; rather, it would simply pronounce on the constitutionality of the challenged statute. The impact of the court's decision would rest on its moral authority and the willingness of the other political branches to abide by its decision.

The original purpose behind the analysis of the judicial review electoral process in Indonesia is meant to be descriptive, not normative. This chapter makes no claims that judicial review of the electoral process in Indonesia can be a model for other courts. This chapter presents an interesting phenomenon unique to the Indonesian Constitutional Court. Under the leadership of the first Chief Justice Jimly Asshiddiqie, the Court began to adopt a technique called 'conditionally constitutional', under which it allowed the challenged law to remain valid as long as it was applied or implemented in the way the Court interpreted it.[10] In the last ten years, the Court has frequently employed the 'conditionally constitutional' technique in dealing with the judicial review of the electoral process.

In order to understand the relation between the judicial review of the electoral process in Indonesia and the 'conditionally constitutional' technique, I would like briefly to review the notion of weak-form review. Mark Tushnet and Rosalind Dixon explain that there are many different models of 'weak-form review' in Asian constitutional design[11] and posit that the closest model of weak-form review exists in Mongolia.[12] The Mongolian model has two components of review: first, a three-person panel of judges will consider constitutional challenges to legislation. If the panel finds the legislation unconstitutional, its decision will be sent to the nation's parliament. In the second stage of review, the parliament will consider whether to accept or reject the Court's interpretation.[13]

Tushnet and Dixon also posit the notion of quasi-weak-form review, under which the Court may wholly defer to the legislature's interpretation of the Constitution, persist in its own interpretation but acknowledge the legislature's power to disagree, or defer to the legislature's interpretation as displacing its own.[14] Tushnet and Dixon point out that the model of quasi-weak-form review exists in Japan and India. The Japanese Supreme Court is usually described as 'conservative' as the Court rarely exercises its power of constitutional review to invalidate legislation.[15] In India, the constitutional amendment process provides a vehicle for the legislatures or politicians to engage in a dialogue with the courts by generating new interpretations of the Constitution.[16]

This chapter argues that the experience of judicial review of the electoral process in Indonesia suggests that there is a kind of 'quasi-weak-form review' insofar as the Court only issues advisory remedies without involving itself in complex political decision-making. With the issuance of an advisory remedy, a claimant has little to gain in asking the Court to declare a law unconstitutional. At the end of the day, a favourable Court decision would not be able to remedy the claimant's injury. Furthermore, the Court has also developed a new technique, in which it refuses to declare a statute unconstitutional and instead asks the government to interpret the statute in a certain way or prescribes some directives for the government to interpret the statute. This chapter further argues that this kind of quasi-weak-form of review is a product of the structural limitation on the Constitutional Court instead of a judicial innovation by the Constitutional Court Justices.[17]

Judicial review of electoral process under the chairmanship of Jimly Asshiddiqie

Prelude

On November 9, 2001, the Third General Assembly Session of the People Consultative Assembly (*Majelis Permusyawaratan Rakyat* – MPR) voted in favour of a Constitutional Amendment that conferred the Constitutional Court with the authority to review impeachment motions against the President and/or Vice President. Moreover, the Constitutional Amendment also equipped the new Court with the authority to review the constitutionality of statutes, to resolve disputes over the powers of state institutions, to review petitions for the dissolution of a political party, and to solve electoral disputes.[18]

The Constitution mandated that the government erect the new Constitutional Court by August 17, 2003 at the latest.[19] The government and the House of Representatives (*Dewan Perwakilan Rakyat* – DPR), however, did not approve the bill establishing the Constitutional Court until August 6, 2003. The Constitution provides that the Constitutional Court shall be composed of nine constitutional court justices, in which three shall be nominated by the President, three nominated by the People Representative Council (*Dewan Perwakilan Rakyat* – DPR) and three nominated by the Supreme Court.[20] Following the approval, the government, the DPR, and the Supreme Court (*Mahkamah Agung*) rushed to select judges for the Court before the Court opened its doors on August 13, 2003.

Soon after the Constitutional Court Justices were inaugurated, their first meeting was to elect the Chief Justice and Deputy Chief Justice. Jimly Asshiddiqie was elected as the Chief Justice after he garnered five out of eight votes.[21] An academic-cum-bureaucrat, Asshiddiqie is a notable constitutional law professor at the prestigious University of Indonesia and he spent many years in government service.

The **Communist Party** *case: planting the seed*

The first high profile case that involved the electoral process was the *Communist Party* case in 2003.[22] The claimants were thirty-five political activists who filed a petition challenging the constitutionality of the General Election Law, which barred former members of the Indonesian Communist Party and/or its affiliates from running for office as national or regional legislators.[23] The event that triggered the ban was the mysterious coup on September 30, 1965, in which six generals and a lieutenant were kidnapped by a group of leftist officers. The Army maintained that the coup was plotted and carried out by the Indonesian Communist Party (*Partai Komunis Indonesia* – PKI). Afterwards, the Indonesian Communist Party was dissolved and its members were banned from public office.[24] After the fall of the military government, especially since the 1999 general election, former members of the Communist Party were only allowed to vote and could not be elected as legislators. The Constitutional Court struck down the provision in the General Election Law, and held that 'individual members of the Communist Party and its affiliates should be treated equally as citizens without discrimination'.[25]

In the days following the Constitutional Court decision, however, Chief Justice Asshiddiqie announced that the decision would not have immediate effect, as it would only be implemented for the 2009 general elections.[26] In addition, Chief Justice Asshiddiqie stated that the decision should not be implemented because the deadline for submitting legislative candidates for the 2004 election had passed by the time the Court announced its decision on February 24, 2004.[27] This announcement was shocking for many people, first, because the Court never mentioned such holding in its decision, and second, as the Chief Justice signified that the claimants would not enjoy any benefit from winning in the Court.

There are two plausible explanations for why the Court's decision could not be applied immediately. First, the Court was constrained by a statutory limitation which provides that the effects of the Court's decision only begins the day of the announcement of the decision.[28] This statutory regulation meant that the Court's decision will only be applied prospectively and not retroactively. The second explanation is that the nature of judicial review in Indonesia is basically an abstract review. In the *Communist Party* case,[29] the Court was actually dealing with an abstract constitutional question on the statutory prohibition of the former Communists to run as legislators. The Court did not review the decision of the Electoral Commission to reject the candidacy of the former Communists. Therefore, the Court's decision did not aim to restore the right of former Communists who had been rejected as legislative candidates by the Electoral Commission, but rather to resolve the question on the constitutionality of the General Election Law. The bottom line was that the Court could only issue declaratory relief, that is, to pronounce on the consistency of the statute with the Constitution. The Court could not issue a remedy that would redress the injuries suffered by the claimants.

The 'conditionally constitutional' electoral law

Mark Tushnet in his analysis on judicial review explained that there are two kinds of remedies, namely strong and weak remedies.[30] The weak remedies may come in a number of forms. First and foremost is the declaratory remedy, in which the Court only has authority to issue a declaratory judgment on the constitutionality of a statute.[31] The second type of weak remedy occurs whenever the court requires government officials to develop plans that hold out some promise of eliminating the constitutional violation within a reasonably short time period.[32] Based on Tushnet's analysis, the decisions of the Indonesian Constitutional Court basically fall under the category of weak remedies. The Court can only provide a declaratory remedy and cannot resolve the injury that was suffered by the claimant. Apart from the weak remedies in the form of declaratory remedies, the Court has further defined a different kind of weak remedy – declaring a legislation to be 'conditionally constitutional'.

The notion of 'conditionally constitutional' legislation is not peculiar to Indonesia. For instance, in almost two decades of its existence, the Korean Constitutional Court has employed different types of constitutional remedies.[33] The first type of remedy is when it declares the law 'unconformable to the Constitution', which means that the Court acknowledges a law as unconstitutional but it requests the National Assembly to revise it within a certain period while the law remains effective until that time.[34] The second type of remedy is called 'unconstitutional in certain contexts', which occurs whenever the court prohibits a particular way of interpretation of a law as unconstitutional, while upholding other interpretations as constitutional.[35] The third type of remedy is called 'constitutional in certain contexts', which means that a law is constitutional if it is interpreted in a certain way.[36] The Indonesian Constitutional Court seems to have followed the approach taken by the Korean Constitutional Court by developing a type of remedy called 'conditionally constitutional'. This notion of 'conditionally constitutional' is similar to the 'constitutional in certain contexts' in the Korean Constitutional Court, in which the law is constitutional if it is interpreted in a certain way.

Regarding the judicial review of the electoral process, the Asshiddiqie Court applied its 'conditionally constitutional' remedy in the *Political Crime* cases. In the *Political Crime I* case,[37] although the Court did not deal with the judicial review of legislative elections, the case was significant in laying the foundation for the judicial review of Legislative Election law in the *Political Crime II* case.[38] In the *Political Crime I* case, some political activists challenged the provision in the Presidential Election Law, which provided that a presidential candidate shall not be previously convicted of a crime that imposes a five-year imprisonment or more.[39] One of the claimants was Budiman Sudjatmiko, a former Chairman of the People's Democratic Party, a leading opposition group during the military dictatorship. Sudjatmiko was sentenced to thirteen years' imprisonment, but was released after the fall of the New Order military regime. Sudjatmiko argued that the law was unconstitutional because it prevented him from running as a presidential candidate. The Court, however, held that the law was constitutional as long as the prohibition did not include political crimes and minor offences.[40] The Court defined political crimes as political expression, which was contrary to the political view of the previous New Order military regime.[41]

In the *Political Crime II* case, the claimant challenged the Legislative Election Law, which provided that a candidate for national legislator shall not be previously convicted of a crime with a penalty of five years' imprisonment or more.[42] The Court re-affirmed its holding in the *Political Crime I* case that the law was constitutional so long as the prohibition did not include political crimes and minor offences. The Court, however, did not define the scope and meaning of minor offences, even though the claimant did not commit any political crime but was convicted of aggravated assault.[43]

In the *DPD Residence* case,[44] some members of the DPD[45] challenged the Electoral Law, which did not require a candidate for DPD to have domicile in the province where he/she was seeking election.[46] First, the Court held that the requirement of residence in a respected province for a DPD candidate was required by the Constitution and therefore it should be included explicitly in the requirement of the Electoral Law.[47] The Court, however, held that the law was conditionally constitutional, and should be read or interpreted to include the requirement of a DPD candidate to have a residence in the province where he/she seeks election.[48]

A brilliant innovation or structural limitation?

Since the *Communist Party* case, the Asshiddiqie Court had developed at least two techniques in dealing with the Electoral Laws. First, the Court declared that a law is unconstitutional but its invalidity will only apply in the future. In the *Communist Party* case, the invalidation of the law would only take place in the next general election. In other words, the claimant could not immediately receive the benefit of the Court's favourable decision. The second technique was to declare a challenged statute to be 'conditionally constitutional' – a statute was consistent with the Constitution as long as it was interpreted or read according to the guideline or interpretation of the Constitutional Court.

Simon Butt of the University of Sydney noted that the Court's jurisprudential techniques, such as declaring statutes to be 'conditionally constitutional', are pragmatism in disguise and those techniques might even be considered as hidden activism.[49] Butt observed that the Court employed these techniques to make its decisions more politically palatable to the legislature.[50] It might be true that the Court was trying to be strategic, but I would argue that the Court's decisions concerning the electoral process were not the product of a brilliant jurisprudential innovation, but were instead conditioned by the Court's structural limitation.

As I mentioned earlier in this chapter, the Court's authority is limited to reviewing a constitutional question in an abstract way and not to solve any concrete constitutional cases. Consequently, the Court could only provide an abstract remedy to some abstract constitutional question that was presented before it. The most telling example is the *DPD Residence* case, where the claimants basically presented a constitutional question as to whether or not the Constitution requires a DPD candidate to have a residence in the province where he/she was seeking election. In this case, the Court did not deal with the validity of the application of a DPD candidate; rather, it dealt with the interpretation of the requirement of residency for a DPD candidate as required by the Constitution. The Court then answered that the Constitution explicitly required a candidate to have a domicile in the province where he/she sought election; and, therefore, the Electoral Law should be interpreted in a certain way.

Chief Justice Jimly Asshiddiqie only stayed in the Court for five years. Due to an internal power struggle within the Court, he was ousted as the Chief Justice and subsequently resigned in disgrace.[51] Nonetheless, Chief Justice Asshiddiqie had planted this jurisprudential technique as a seed to address future issues relating to the electoral process, which would be applied further by his successor, Mohammad Mahfud.

Judicial review of electoral process under the chairmanship of Mohammad Mahfud

Mohammad Mahfud was a professor of constitutional law at the Islamic University of Indonesia (*Universitas Islam Indonesia*). Prior to his appointment as the second Chief Justice of the Constitutional Court, Mahfud had a successful political career as the Minister of Defence, the Minister of Justice, and a member of the House Judiciary Committee.[52]

Not long after Mahfud took over the position of the Chief Justice, the Court issued its first electoral law decision in the *Mohammad Sholeh* case.[53] Mohammad Sholeh was a legislative candidate from the Indonesian Democratic Party of Struggle (PDI-P). He challenged the constitutionality of Law No. 10 of 2008 on Legislative Election on two different grounds. First, he challenged the provision that required at least one in every three candidates on the list to be a female.[54] Sholeh argued that the provision made it easier for women to win seats, because the voters will easily spot a female candidate.[55] Thus, he argued that the provision was discriminatory.

Second, Sholeh made a link between the provision on female candidates with the requirement on the electability of a candidate. To be elected, a candidate must achieve at least 30 per cent of the Voting Division Number (*Bilangan Pembagi Pemilihan* – BPP).[56] The BPP was calculated by dividing the total number of valid votes of all political parties that pass the threshold of 2.5 per cent of the vote in a district by the number of seats available in that district.[57] If no candidate achieved 30 per cent of the BPP, a seat would be assigned to a candidate listed in the highest ranking on the ballot of the political party that gained the most votes in a district. Consequently, a candidate with the highest-ranking position on the candidate list would most likely be elected as a legislator. Sholeh argued that it was extremely difficult for a male candidate like himself to be listed in the top ranking of the party list because the top ranking list was usually assigned to a senior party member.[58] Sholeh was ranked seventh in the candidate list, and he was unlikely to win the legislative seat based on that ranking. Sholeh argued that it would be easier for a female candidate to win a seat because a female candidate would always be included in the top three candidates of the party list.

The Court held that the female candidate provision was not unconstitutional because the provision was aimed to fulfil the international legal obligations to provide gender equality.[59] The Court, however, held that Article 214 of the Electoral Law, which required a candidate to obtain a minimum 30 per cent BPP or listed in the highest ranking of the party list, was unconstitutional. The Court considered that the law employed a double standard, under which a seat would be determined based on the highest votes and the ranking in the party's list. Second, the Court explained that the philosophy behind the representation system was to elect a candidate who obtains the most number of votes instead of the highest ranking in the party list.[60] The Court then ordered the General Election Commission to assign the seats to any candidate who won the most number of votes in a district.[61]

Donald Horowitz of Duke Law School both praised and criticised the Court's decision in the *Mohammad Sholeh* case. On one hand, Horowitz praised the Court's decision because the politicians' accountability to the electorate was enhanced by the decision. Aspiring candidates would rush to their districts to win over voters in ways that candidates on a closed list system did not have to do.[62] On the other hand, Horowitz argued that the Court had missed a critical point about the Electoral Law, that is, the 30 per cent BPP requirement was far more liberal and generous to individual candidates compared to the previous Electoral Law, which required a candidate to win votes equal to or greater than 100 per cent of the BPP.[63]

The Court's decision in the *Mohammad Sholeh* case seemed to be quite radical, not only because it enhanced the accountability of a candidate to the electorate but also because the Court invalidated the Electoral rule and prescribed a new directive for the General Election Commission. Nevertheless, five years after the Court issued the decision, Chief Justice Mahfud wrote an op-ed piece, in which he explained that the Court decision did not bring any radical change in the electoral system.[64] Mahfud explained that the Court only removed the BPP 30 per cent requirement and never intended to set a new rule that a seat shall be assigned to a candidate with the highest votes.[65] Mahfud argued that it was the legislatures who prescribed in the Electoral Law that a seat shall be allocated to a candidate who wins the most number of votes in a district, instead of the Court.[66] Mahfud's argument might seemed odd, but it may be understood from the perspective of weak-form review, in which the Court's decision in the *Mohammad Sholeh* case was never intended to change the electoral system, but rather to answer a constitutional question that was presented by the claimant to the Court. Moreover, for Mohammad Sholeh himself, there was little to be gained from the favourable Court decision, because his party considered his legal action as an act of insubordination and, therefore, he was removed from the party list entirely.[67]

The Mahfud Court continued to deal with judicial review of the electoral process in the *ID Card* case.[68] The case arose when poor election management left forty-seven million voters unregistered in the legislative elections.[69] Refli Harun was a political activist who was not registered as a voter. He filed a petition to the Court and challenged Law No. 42 of 2008 on Presidential Election, which required that in order to cast a vote, a voter must be registered in the Final Electoral Roll (*Daftar Pemilih Tetap* – DPT).[70]

The Court ruled that the challenged provision was conditionally constitutional, so long as it did not deprive the voting rights of citizens who were not registered in the Final Electoral Roll.[71] In other words, the Court did not declare the challenged statute as unconstitutional. But the Court held that it should provide a solution to remedy the defect in the final electoral roll. The Court held that 'all Indonesian citizens who were not registered on the final electoral roll could show their IDs in order to cast a vote and those who are living overseas can use their passports to cast a vote'.[72] The Court held further that 'voters using an ID card must also show their family card (*Kartu Keluarga*) and may only cast their ballot in their residential neighborhood'.[73] The Mahfud Court inherited the conditionally constitutional technique from the Asshiddiqie Court and continued to employ this technique in the *ID Card* case. The bottom line was that the Court refused to declare the challenged statute unconstitutional; instead the Court imposed a directive to remedy the defect in the Final Electoral Roll, and so the challenged statutory provision remained constitutional.

The Mahfud Court continued to deal with judicial review of the electoral process in the *Left over Votes* case.[74] In this case, the Court had to deal with the issue of how to determine 'left over' votes (*sisa suara*) in national legislative elections to allocate 'left over' seats (*sisa kursi*) in the parliament. As I explained earlier, Law No. 10 of 2008 stipulated that the number of votes required for each seat in the national legislatures is determined by the BPP. Once a party's votes meets the BPP, it obtains a seat. The issue is that not all seats can be filled in the 'first round' of seat allocation; some parties will not receive enough votes to obtain a seat, or other parties will obtain seats but their left over votes are insufficient to obtain left over seats. The law prescribed that there must be a 'second round' of seat allocation to fill the left over seats, under which the political parties' votes must meet at least 50 per cent of the BPP to obtain a seat.[75] The General Election Commission ruled that votes used to obtain a seat in the first round of seat allocation could not be used again in the second round.[76] In other words, the remaining seats would be allocated by reference to the left over vote alone.

Zainal Maarif, a legislature candidate from the Democratic Party (*Partai Demokrat*) and his colleagues challenged the General Election Commission decision to the Supreme Court,[77] arguing that the votes used to obtain a seat in the first round should be counted again for the second round allocation of seats.[78] The Supreme Court decided in favour of Zainal Maarif and ruled that the General Election Commission Decision was incompatible with Law No. 10 of

2008. The Supreme Court decision favoured some major political parties and it was predicted that the ruling Democratic Party would obtain thirty-one extra seats, the second finisher Golkar would also obtain thirty-one extra seats and the third finisher PDI-P would obtain six extra seats.[79]

Hanura (*Hati Nurani Rakyat – People's Conscience Party*) and Gerindra (*Gerakan Indonesia Raya – Greater Indonesian Movement*) were two new political parties that ran in the 2009 Legislative Election. Under the Supreme Court decision, both parties would have lost a significant number of seats.[80] Therefore, they went to the Constitutional Court and asked the Court to interpret the law on the second round seats allocation.[81] The Court held that the provision was conditionally constitutional. The Court considered that if all the votes, including those that had already been exhausted in obtaining a seat in the first round, would be re-used to determine the seats in the second round, then there will be a double calculation.[82] The Court held that such an interpretation was contrary to the proportional representation system as there would be a huge discrepancy between the total votes and the number of seats that can be obtained by a political party in one district.[83] Nevertheless, the Court held the provisions to be conditionally constitutional as long as they were interpreted according to the Court's interpretation. The Court held that parties that fulfil 50 per cent or more of the BPP would receive a seat in the second round of counting.[84] If any seats remained, those seats would be allocated in a third round of seat allocation. Finally the Court held that the law was conditionally constitutional as long as votes used to obtain a seat in the first round would be exhausted and could not be used again in the second round.[85]

As I explained earlier in this chapter, the Court was constrained by a statutory limitation that its decision can only applied prospectively. In the past, the Court did not really bother to address the issue because it had been operating under the framework that its decision only addressed a specific constitutional question instead of remedying any injury. Nonetheless, in the *Left over Votes* case, the Court realised that its decision should provide some remedy to those parties that would have lost seats. Otherwise, those parties could neither use the favourable Court decision to reclaim their seats, nor force the General Election Commission to undo its seats allocation. Thus, the Court presented a crucial statement at the end of its judgment that the principle of non-retroactivity was not absolute.[86] Although the law sets that the Court's decision can only be applied prospectively, the Court held that its decision should be applied retroactively with regard to the allocation of seats for the 2009 national legislative election.[87] The Court held further that the decision should be applied retroactively without any compensation or financial remedy to redress the injuries that were caused by the previous regulations.[88] The Court did not provide any reasoning on why there should be no compensation or financial remedy. Moreover, the Court did not provide a clear justification either on the retroactive application. The Court only provided a short explanation that an exception is necessary in order to achieve public order (*ketertiban umum*).[89] But the Court never specified the meaning of public order in the context of this retroactive application of its decision.

In the *Left over Votes* case, the Court basically invented a new technique; it refused to declare a challenged statute unconstitutional but asked the government to make further attempts at compliance by declaring that the decision would be applied retroactively. One plausible explanation for the invention of this new technique is that the Court realised that the government would simply ignore its recommendation otherwise. For instance, in the *Mohammad Sholeh* case, the General Election Commission refused to comply with the Court's decision that a seat should be determined by the most votes in one district. Chief Justice Mahfud then had to make a press statement and warned the Election Commission that there would be political and criminal consequences for all commissioners who refused to comply with the Court's decision.[90] He argued that the situation forced him to speak out to the media; otherwise the General Election Commission would have never abided by the Court's decision.[91]

In sum, the Mahfud Court continued to employ this 'conditionally constitutional' technique that was invented by the Asshiddiqie Court. The Mahfud Court also began to issue some directives for the government to follow. Moreover, the Mahfud Court gave its decision retrospective effect, so that the decision could be used to remedy certain harms that were suffered by the claimants. Although the Mahfud Court was aware that the Court had structural limitations and its decision did aim to remedy any immediate harm, the Court had no other choice but to give its decision retrospective effect because it had to deal with more complex cases than the Asshiddiqie Court. During the tenure of Chief Justice Jimly Asshiddiqie (2003–2008), Indonesia had just begun its democratic experiment and the 2004 general election took place a few months after the Court opened. Furthermore, the young Constitutional Court had not yet become an important player in Indonesian constitutional politics. During the tenure of Chief Justice Mahfud, the Court became an important veto player in Indonesian Constitutional politics. Moreover, by the time Mahfud assumed his position as Chief Justice, Indonesia had enjoyed democracy for a decade and more complex electoral process issues had begun to arise in this period.

Judicial review of electoral process under the chairmanship of Hamdan Zoelva

In November 2012, Mahfud told the People Representative Council (DPR) that he intended to leave his job in April 2013. Chief Justice Mahfud officially resigned from his position on April 1, 2013.[92] There had been rumours that Mahfud was a potential candidate for President in the 2014 election.[93] Therefore, some believe that his decision to resign was part of his bigger plan to run for President. Mahfud was succeeded by Chief Justice Akil Mochtar, but Mochtar only held the position of Chief Justice for six months. Mochtar was removed from the Court for corruption charges after the Anti-Corruption Commission confiscated approximately US$260,000 from his residence.[94] The money was connected to a dispute involving a regional election for the Head District (*Bupati*) of Gunung Mas in Central Kalimantan, which was being litigated in the

Constitutional Court. The money was allegedly given so that Mochtar would rule in favour of the incumbent candidate, Hambit Bintih.[95]

After the removal of Akil Mochtar, Deputy Chief Justice Hamdan Zoelva took over the leadership of the Constitutional Court, and was subsequently elected as the fourth Chief Justice of the Constitutional Court on November 1, 2013. When Hamdan Zoelva was inaugurated on November 6, 2013, he inherited a court in crisis. The biggest challenge for Zoelva was to restore public confidence to the Court after the tragic fall of his immediate predecessor.

The first test of Chief Justice Zoelva's leadership was in the *Presidential Threshold* case,[96] in which the Court had to decide the constitutionality of the presidential threshold. According to the Presidential Election Law, a presidential candidate shall be nominated by a political party or a coalition of political parties who hold at least 20 per cent seats in the House of Representatives or obtain at least 25 per cent of the popular vote in the legislative election.[97] On December 8, 2013, Yusril Ihza Mahendra, a seasoned politician from the Star and Crescent Party announced his candidacy for the presidency despite his party having no seats in the House and with little prospect of fulfilling either the seat or popular vote threshold in the 2014 legislative election.[98] A few days later, Mahendra launched a legal challenge in the Constitutional Court to enable him to run for President on his party's ticket, the Star and Crescent Party.

In his petition, Mahendra postulated that the Constitution did not specify any threshold for the presidential election. Mahendra referred to Article 6(2) of the Constitution, which stated that 'each ticket of presidential candidates shall be proposed prior to the holding of general elections by political parties or coalitions of political parties which are participants in the general elections'.[99] Mahendra asserted that there were twelve political parties in the 2014 election and, therefore, he urged the Court to declare that all of these parties had the right to nominate their candidates for President.[100]

The Court rejected Mahendra's petition and held that Mahendra had requested the Court to issue an advisory opinion in regards to the meaning of Article 6(2) of the Constitution. The Court held that it had no authority to issue an advisory opinion, and thus it could not grant Mahendra's petition.[101] Previously, under both the Asshiddiqie Court and the Mahfud Court, the Court had not been reluctant to issue opinions in similar cases.[102] The decision signalled that the Zoelva Court would prefer the Court to play a more minimal role in politically charged cases.

The Zoelva Court also handed down an important decision in the *General Election Schedule* case.[103] According to Law No. 42 of 2008 on the Presidential Election, a presidential candidate shall be nominated by a political party or a coalition of political parties who holds at least 20 per cent seats in the House of Representatives or obtain at least 25 per cent of the popular vote in the legislative election. The Presidential Election Law also states that the legislative and presidential elections must be held at least three months apart.[104] Under these conditions, only a few large parties will be likely to nominate a presidential candidate. Moreover, political parties cannot nominate a candidate until they find out the official result of the legislative election.

On January 10, 2013, a political activist, Effendi Ghazali, challenged Presidential Election Law No. 42 of 2008, which prescribed two separate election schedules for legislative and presidential elections. First, Ghazali argued that the current election mechanism had subverted the presidential system.[105] His concern was that a coalition of political parties that nominates a President will have too much leverage over a President-elect. In other words, Ghazali argued that a President-elect could be held hostage by the interest of a coalition of political parties that supports his nomination.

Second, Ghazali argued that the law had infringed upon his voting rights. Ghazali referred to his personal experience in the 2004 general election.[106] At that time, he was doing his doctoral research in the city of Nijmegen, Netherlands. Ghazali went back to Indonesia to cast his vote for the legislative election on April 5, 2004. Ghazali, however, could not cast his vote for the Presidential Election on July 5, 2004 because he had to go back to Netherlands earlier. Ghazali argued that his voting rights had been deprived by the law that set two separate election schedules.

If one reviews the case closely, there is a mismatch between the challenged statute and the injury claimed. On the one hand, Ghazali invoked an injury that was caused by the 2004 presidential election process, which was based on Law No. 23 of 2003 on the Presidential Election. On the other hand, he challenged Law No. 42 of 2008 on the Presidential Election, which was enacted by the House in 2008. Thus, the challenged statute did not cause any immediate harm to Ghazali's voting rights.

In its decision, the Court concurred with the claimant that a President-elect could be held hostage to the interest of the political parties that nominated him. As the Court stated: 'In the last two presidential elections (2004 and 2009), which occurred after the legislative election, a presidential candidate had to offer political compromises in order to secure his nomination.'[107] The Court agreed with the claimant that such political compromises would give political parties too much leverage over a President-elect and, consequently, would undermine the presidential system. The Court ruled that the legislative election and the presidential election should be held simultaneously.

Many people hoped that the decision would be applied to the 2014 general election; however, the Court ruled that the decision would only be applied in the upcoming 2019 general election. The Court held that the decision cannot be applied right away because it would likely disrupt the 2014 general election preparations. This decision was not a surprise because the Zoelva Court was not able to move beyond the institutional constraint that the Court can only render declaratory relief without granting any further remedy for the claimant's injury. In this case, the Court's decision did not aim to redress the claimant's injury on the violation of his voting rights, but only issued a judgment which declared that the presidential election and legislative election shall be held simultaneously in the future.

The *Presidential Threshold* and the *General Election Schedule* cases are two prominent cases that were decided by the Zoelva Court. Nonetheless, it is also important to explore two other important cases that were decided by the Zoelva Court on the electoral process in Indonesia. Both cases involved a challenge to Law No. 42 of 2008 on the presidential election. In the first case, the *Armed Forces Voting Right* case,[108] two political activists challenged a provision in the Presidential Election Law, which provided that 'in the Presidential Election of 2009, a member of the Indonesian Armed Forces and National Police shall not use its voting rights'.[109] The claimants argued that such prohibition should also be applied to the 2014 general election because there was still a necessity for the Armed Forces and National Police to maintain their neutrality during the general election. The Court accepted the claimants' argument and declared that the provision was conditionally unconstitutional, so long as it was not be interpreted to include the 2014 general election. Here the Court tried to frame its decision in a different language. Instead of declaring the law to be conditionally constitutional, it declared that the law was conditionally unconstitutional because it only applied to the 2009 general election. Nevertheless, if Law No. 42 of 2008 on Presidential Election was interpreted to include the 2014 general election, then it would be deemed constitutional.

In the second case, the *Presidential Candidate* case,[110] some political activists challenged a provision on how to determine a President-elect. The law stipulated that a President-elect is a presidential candidate who obtains more than 50 per cent of the total votes in the presidential election with at least 20 per cent of the votes in each province spread throughout more than half of the provinces in Indonesia.[111] The claimants argued that the provision was ambiguous because it did not specify whether the formula was to be applied when there were multiple presidential candidates or two candidates. The Court concurred with the claimants and declared that the law was conditionally unconstitutional, so long as it was applied when there were two presidential candidates.[112] Here again, the Zoelva Court framed its decision in negative and weak language, which can be confusing. Basically, the Court considered that the law shall not be applied if there are only two presidential candidates.[113] In other words, if there are only two presidential candidates in the presidential election, the candidate with the most votes will be declared as the winner.

Chief Justice Zoelva only stayed in his position for a little over a year. The new President Jokowi decided not to re-appoint him for the second term.[114] Furthermore, Chief Justice Zoelva had to endure a humiliating experience in his effort to cling to his position.[115] In his brief tenure as the Chief Justice, Hamdan Zoelva led the Court to re-affirm its weak-form of review, especially in regard to the judicial review of electoral process. Moreover, the Zoelva Court created more complications with its conditionally unconstitutional decisions that led to more confusion for the public.

Conclusion

Since the *Communist Party* case, the Indonesian Constitutional Court has adopted various techniques of quasi-weak-form review in dealing with the judicial review of electoral process. In a nutshell, the Court only has authority to issue an advisory remedy that can only be applied prospectively. In many instances, the Court refused to invalidate the statute but declared it as conditionally constitutional, under which the Court merely asked the government to follow the Court's interpretation or prescribed certain directives for the government to apply the law. Nevertheless, in one instance, the Court declared that its decision should be applied retroactively. The last technique is a declaration that a statute would be unconstitutional so long as it was interpreted in a certain way. All of these techniques are not products of a brilliant innovation by the Constitutional Court Justices, but rather are conditioned by the structural limitation of the Court. The Court has been designed with limited jurisdiction and can only conduct an abstract statutory review. Consequently, the Court can only perform quasi-weak-form review, especially with regards to the judicial review of the electoral process.

Notes

1 Constitutional Court Decision No. 1/PHPU-Pres-XII/2014 reviewing the Presidential Dispute between Prabowo Subianto and Joko Widodo.
2 Ben Otto and I Made Sentana, 'Indonesian Court Upholds Widodo's Electoral Win' *Wall Street Journal* (Jakarta, August 21, 2014) www.wsj.com/articles/indonesia-court-expected-to-clear-vote-results-1408595018 accessed May 14, 2015. Joe Cochrane, 'Indonesian Court Rejects Election Challenge, Clearing Way for Joko Presidency' *New York Times* (Jakarta, August 21, 2014) www.nytimes.com/2014/08/22/world/asia/indonesian-court-rejects-election-challenge-clearing-way-for-joko-presidency.html?_r=2 accessed May 14, 2015.
3 See Constitutional Court Decision No. 011–017/PUU-I/2003 (hereinafter the *Communist Party* case).
4 See Constitutional Court Decision No. 22–24/PUU-VI/2008 (hereinafter the *Mohammad Sholeh* case). An open list system describes a variant of party-list proportional representation where the number of votes will determine which party's candidates are elected. In other words, the number of votes each candidate receives fully determines seats allocation. This as opposed to a closed list system, in which seats would be awarded based on the order or ranking of the candidate on the parties' lists. A closed list system allows only party officials to determine the order or ranking of the candidates.
5 Mietzner (2010) 404.
6 Ibid. 411.
7 Law No. 23 of 2003 on the Constitutional Court (*Undang – Undang No. 23 Tahun 2003 tentang Mahkamah Konstitusi*).
8 Theoretically, the Constitutional Court can declare this provision as too restrictive and hence unconstitutional. In 2004, the Constitutional Court reviewed a challenge to Article 50 of the Constitutional Court Law, which stated that the Court could only review statutes that were enacted after October 19, 1999. The Court moved swiftly in declaring Article 50 to be unconstitutional and invalidating it entirely. See Constitutional Court Decision No. 066/PUU-II/2004, reviewing Law No. 1 of 1987 on the Chamber of Commerce.
9 Horowitz (2006) 132.
10 Butt and Lindsey (2012) 138.
11 Tushnet and Dixon (2014).

12 Ibid. 105.
13 Ibid. 105.
14 Ibid. 107.
15 Ibid. 107.
16 Ibid. 109.
17 In 2011, the parliament adopted Law No. 8 of 2011 on the Amendment of the Constitutional Court Law. Some of the key features of the law such as Articles 45A and 57(2a) were directly crafted to waken the Court's judicial review authority. Article 45A prohibited the Court from issuing decisions beyond what was sought by applicants. Article 57(2a) prohibited the Court from making decisions that prescribe some directives to the lawmakers or a new legal norm that override the statutory provisions that were deemed contrary to the Constitution. The Court struck down these two articles in the Constitutional Court Decision No. 48/PUU-IX/2011. Although the Court decision seemed radical, the decision did not signal a strong-form of review for two reasons: first, the Court merely struck down some provisions of an unpopular law, as the Amendment was not wholly supported by the general public. Second, long before the Mahfud Court struck down the law, the Asshiddiqie Court had shown some acts of defiance by issuing decisions beyond what were sought by the claimants. Moreover, both of the Asshiddiqie and Mahfud Courts issued many directives to the lawmakers.
18 Constitution of Republic of Indonesia 1945, Article 24C(1) and 24C(2).
19 Constitution of Republic of Indonesia 1945, Transitional Provision of the Fourth Amendment.
20 Constitution of Republic of Indonesia 1945, Article 24C(3).
21 Ibid.
22 The *Communist Party* case (n. 3).
23 Law No. 12 of 2003 on the House of Representative Election, Article 60(g).
24 For the detail of the impact of the anti-communist witch-hunts, see Heryanto (2006).
25 The *Communist Party* case (n. 3) at [36]–[37].
26 Jimly Asshiddiqie, 'Mahkamah Konstitusi: Bekas PKI Boleh Memilih dan Dipilih' (Constitutional Court: Former PKI May Cast a Vote and Elect) *Tempointeraktif* (Jakarta, February 24, 2004).
27 Ibid.
28 Law No. 23 of 2003 on the Constitutional Court, Article 47.
29 The *Communist Party* case (n. 3).
30 Tushnet (2004).
31 Ibid. 1910.
32 Ibid. 1910.
33 Dongwook Cha, 'The Role of the Korean Constitutional Court in the Democratization of South Korea' (PhD dissertation, University of Southern California 2005) 67; see also the Constitutional Court of Korea (2001) 86–93.
34 Dongwook Cha (n. 33) 68.
35 Ibid.
36 Ibid. 69.
37 Constitutional Court Decision No. 14–17/PUU-V/2007 (hereinafter the *Political Crime I* case).
38 Constitutional Court Decision No. 15/PUU-VI/2008 (hereinafter the *Political Crime II* case).
39 Law No. 23 of 2003 on the Presidential Election, Article 6 (T).
40 The *Political Crime I* case (n. 37) 134.
41 Ibid. 132.
42 Law No. 10 of 2008 on Legislative Election, Article 50(1g).
43 'Syarat Belum Pernah Dipidana Kembali Dipersoalkan' (The Requirement that a Candidate be Free from Criminal Charges has been Contested Again) *Hukumonline.*

com (26 May 2008) www.hukumonline.com/berita/baca/hol19316/syarat-belum-pernah-dipidana-kembali-dipersoalkan accessed May 14, 2015.

44 Constitutional Court Decision No. 10/PUU-VI/2008 (hereinafter the *DPD Residence* case).

45 The DPD was established by the Third Amendment of the Indonesian Constitution in 2001. The role of DPD was to represent the region in the national government. Although it was kind of the Second Chamber of the national parliament, the DPD was not given lawmaking powers, as its power was limited to submitting laws to the DPR.

46 Law No. 10 of 2008 on the Election of People Representative Council, Regional Representative Council, Regional People Representative Council, Articles 12 and 67.

47 The Court made a reference to Article 22C(1) of the 1945 Constitution, which provides that the members of the DPD shall be elected from every province through a general election.

48 The *DPD Residence* case (n. 44) 215.

49 Butt (2012).

50 Ibid. 108.

51 At the end of Chief Justice Asshiddiqie's first five-year term, there was a rumour that the President wanted to replace him because the Executive was not happy with Asshiddiqie's leadership style. By the time the Court began its new calendar year in August 2008, six new associate Justices had come to the bench and some of them were suspected to be pro-government appointees. Those Justices later ousted Chief Justice Asshiddiqie in an internal election. A few months later, Chief Justice Asshiddiqie resigned from the bench as he felt a big shame after being outmanoeuvred by the Executive and his associate Justices. For a detailed analysis of the fall of Jimly Asshiddiqie, please see Hendrianto (2016).

52 See Irawan (2014).

53 The *Mohammad Sholeh* case (n. 4).

54 Law No. 10 of 2008 on the Legislative Election, Article 55(2).

55 The *Mohammad Sholeh* case (n. 4) at [7].

56 Law No. 10 of 2008 on Legislative Election, Article 214(1).

57 Ibid. Article 1(27).

58 The *Mohammad Sholeh* case (n. 4) 7.

59 Ibid. 106.

60 Ibid. 105.

61 Ibid. 107.

62 Horowitz (2013) 185.

63 Ibid. Horowitz made reference to Law No. 12 of 2003 on Legislative Election, Articles 105, 106, and 107.

64 M.D. Mahfud, 'Suara Terbanyak Itu Kehendak Legislatif' (The Largest Votes is the Will of the Legislature) *KORAN SINDO* (Jakarta, May 10, 2014).

65 Ibid.

66 Ibid.

67 'Dicoret Jadi Caleg, M Sholeh Gugat PDIP Jatim Rp 100 Miliar' (Removed from the List, M. Sholeh sues the PDIP East Java for RP 100 Billion) *Detiknews* (Jakarta, June 1, 2009) http://news.detik.com/read/2009/01/06/113006/1063702/466/dicoret-jadi-caleg-m-sholeh-gugat-pdip-jatim-rp-100-miliar accessed May 14, 2015.

68 Constitutional Court Decision No. 102/PUU-VII/2009 (hereinafter the *ID Card* case).

69 Andra Wisnu, 'Bring KPU Members to Court, Analysts Say' *Jakarta Post* (Jakarta, July 7, 2009) www.thejakartapost.com/news/2009/07/07/bring-kpu-members-court-analysts-say.html accessed May 14, 2015.

70 Law No. 42 of 2008 on the Presidential Election, Articles 28 and 111(1).

71 The *ID Card* case (n. 68).

72 Ibid. 19.
73 Ibid. 17.
74 Constitutional Court Decision No. 110–111–112–113/PUU-VII/2009 (hereinafter the *Left over Votes* case).
75 Law No. 10 of 2008 on the Legislative Election, Article 205(4).
76 General Election Commission Regulation No. 15 of 2009, Article 23(3).
77 The Constitution provides the Supreme Court with the authority to review ordinances and regulations made under any statutes. This provision means that the right of judicial review is not uniformly given to a single court; instead, the Supreme Court and the Constitutional Court share a different judicial review authority. See Constitution Republic of Indonesia 1945, Article 24A(1).
78 Supreme Court Decision No. 15 P/HUM/2009, 8.
79 J. Kristiadi, '*Mahkamah Agung* v. *KPU*' (*The Supreme Court* v. *the General Election Commission*) (Jakarta, August 4, 2009) www.lexregis.com/?menu=news&idn=275 accessed May 14, 2015.
80 For a detailed background of the struggle over the left over votes, please see Butt (2012).
81 Law No. 10 of 2008 on the Legislative Election, Article 205(4).
82 The *Left over Votes* case (n. 74) 102.
83 Ibid. 102.
84 Ibid. 103.
85 Ibid. 104.
86 Ibid. 108.
87 Ibid. 108.
88 Ibid. 108.
89 Ibid. 108.
90 Budiarti (2010) 92.
91 'Komisioner KPU Bisa Terancam Dipidana' (The Commissioner of the General Election Commission might Face Criminal Charges) *Hukumonline* (Jakarta, February 18, 2009) www.hukumonline.com/berita/baca/hol21234/komisioner-kpu-bisa-terancam-dipidana accessed May 14, 2015; see also Rahmat Sahid, 'Kalau KPU Ngotot Akan Terjadi Bencana Besar' (There will be a Disaster if the Election Commission Refuse to Comply) *SEPUTAR INDONESIA* (Jakarta, February 21, 2009).
92 See Stefanus Hendrianto, 'Leadership Shakeup at Indonesia's Constitutional Court, April 7, 2013' www.iconnectblog.com/2013/04/leadership-shake-up-at-the-indonesian-constitutional-court accessed September 1, 2015.
93 'Mahfud Says He has No Posture for Presidency' *ANTARA News* (Jakarta, August 22, 2011) www.antaranews.com/en/news/75010/mahfud-says-he-has-no-posture-for-presidency accessed May 14, 2015.
94 Stefanus Hendrianto, 'The Indonesian Constitutional Court at a Tipping Point' International Journal of Constitutional Law and ConstitutionMaking.org Blog (October 3, 2013) www.iconnectblog.com/2013/10/the-indonesian-constitutional-court-at-a-tipping-point accessed September 1, 2015.
95 'MK Chief Justice, Golkar Lawmaker Arrested for Bribery Charges' *Jakarta Post* (Jakarta, October 3, 2013) www.thejakartapost.com/news/2013/10/03/mk-chief-justice-golkar-lawmaker-arrested-bribery-charges.html accessed September 1, 2015.
96 Indonesian Constitutional Court Decision No. 108/PUU-XI/2013 (hereinafter the *Presidential Threshold* case).
97 Law No. 42 of 2008 on the Election of President and Vice President, Article 9.
98 'Yusril and Crescent Star Party Throw Hat in 2014 Presidential Race' *Jakarta Globe* (Jakarta, December 9, 2013) http://thejakartaglobe.beritasatu.com/news/yusril-and-crescent-star-party-throw-hat-in-2014-presidential-race/ accessed September 1, 2015.
99 Constitution of the Republic of Indonesia 1945, Article 6 (2).
100 The *Presidential Threshold* case (n. 96) 12.

101 Ibid. 21.

102 In 2007, the Asshiddiqie Court ruled that the prohibition for an independent candidate to run in a regional election ran counter to the principle of equality as stipulated in the Constitution. Therefore, the Court ruled that an independent candidate can run in a regional election. See Constitutional Court Decision No. 5/PUU-V/2007. In 2012, some non-governmental organisations asked the Mahfud Court to interpret the role of the Deputy Minister within the Indonesian constitutional structure. The Court held that deputy ministers are not members of the cabinet. See Constitutional Court Decision No. 79/PUU-IX/2011.

103 Constitutional Court Decision No. 14/PUU-XI/2013 (hereinafter the *General Election Schedule* case).

104 Law No. 42 of 2008 on the Presidential Election, Article 112.

105 The *General Election Schedule* case (n. 103) 6–7.

106 Ibid. 15–16.

107 Ibid. 80–81.

108 Constitutional Court Decision No. 22/PUU-XII/2014 (the *Armed Forces Voting Right* case).

109 Law No. 42 of 2008 on the Presidential Election, Article 206.

110 Constitutional Court Decision No. 50/PUU-XII/2014 (hereinafter the *Presidential Candidate* case).

111 Law No. 42 of 2008 on the Election of President and Vice President, Article 159(1).

112 The *Presidential Candidate* case (n. 110) 40.

113 Ibid. 39.

114 There was some speculation that President Jokowi did not re-appoint Chief Justice Zoelva because the Court did not rule in favour of Jokowi's political party, the PDI-P, in some cases before the Court. For instance, the PDI-P challenged the law on the election of the Speaker of the House (commonly known as the MD3 Law). The Court held that the PDI-P had no standing to challenge the law. In addition, Zoelva's political affiliation was to the Star and Crescent Party, which opposed Jokowi in the last presidential election.

115 When Chief Justice Zoelva was approaching the end of his first five-year term, the Jokowi administration hinted that Chief Justice Zoelva would not be re-appointed for his second term. Chief Justice Zoelva could be re-appointed but he must first undergo a public competition to be a Chief Justice. Zoelva put aside his ego and applied for the position. Nonetheless, Zoelva refused to be interviewed by the selection committee. The Jokowi administration maintained that Chief Justice Zoelva would not receive any special treatment and he could not take any shortcut. As Chief Justice Zoelva refused to undergo a fit and proper test interview, the Selection Committee finally decided to drop his name. See Stefanus Hendrianto 'The Indonesian Constitutional Court in Crisis over the Chief Justice's Term Limit' International Journal of Constitutional Law and ConstitutionMaking.org Blog (February 5, 2015) www.iconnectblog.com/2015/02/the-indonesian-constitutional-court-in-crisis-over-the-chief-justices-term-limit/ accessed September 1, 2015.

References

Budiarti R.T., *On the Record: Mahfud MD Di Balik Putusan Mahkamah Konstitusi* (On the Record: Mahfud MD behind the Constitutional Court Decisions) (Konstitusi Press 2010).

Butt S., 'Indonesia's Constitutional Court: Conservative Activist or Strategic Operator?' in B. Dressel (ed.) *The Judicialization of Politics in Asia* (Routledge 2012).

Butt S. and Lindsey T., *The Constitution of Indonesia: A Contextual Analysis* (Hart Publishing 2012).

Constitutional Court of Korea, *The First Ten Years of the Korean Constitutional Court, 1988–1998* (Constitutional Court of Korea 2001).

Hendrianto S., 'The Rise and Fall of Heroic Chief Justice: Constitutional Politics and Judicial Leadership in Indonesia' (2016) *Washington International Law Journal* (forthcoming).

Heryanto A., *State Terrorism and Political Identity in Indonesia: Fatally Belonging* (Routledge 2006).

Horowitz D., 'Constitutional Court Premier for Decision Makers' (2006) 17(4) *Journal of Democracy* 125.

Horowitz D., *Constitutional Change and Democracy in Indonesia* (Cambridge University Press 2013).

Irawan A., *Biografi Mahfud: Cahayamu Tak Bisa Kutawar* (Mahfud's Biography: I Cannot Deny your Light) (Ar-ruzz Media 2014).

Mietzner M., 'Political Conflict Resolution and Democratic Consolidation in Indonesia: The Role of the Constitutional Court' (2010) 10(3) *Journal of East Asian Studies* 397.

Tushnet M., 'Social Welfare Rights and the Forms of Judicial Review' (2004) 82 *Texas Law Review* 1895.

Tushnet M. and Dixon R., 'Weak-Form Review and its Constitutional Relatives: An Asian Perspective' in R. Dixon and T. Ginsburg (eds) *Comparative Constitutional Law in Asia* (Edward Elgar 2014).

8 Election campaign regulation and the Supreme Court of Japan

Shigenori Matsui

Introduction

Election speech is an essential part of political speech and needs to be vigorously protected. It is for this reason that the United States Supreme Court, in upholding "a profound national commitment to the principle that debate on public issues should be uninhibited, robust, and wide-open,"[1] struck down a state statute that had made it a crime for the editor of a daily newspaper to write and publish an editorial on election day urging people to vote a certain way.[2] It is firmly settled in the United States that any election speech regulation is subject to very strict scrutiny and is likely to be struck down as a violation of the First Amendment.

On the other hand, in Japan, the Japanese Public Office Election Act[3] places the most restrictive regulations on election campaigning in the world, and the Supreme Court of Japan has upheld all of these regulations. As a result, all these regulations have seriously impacted elections and politics in Japan.

In this chapter, we will examine how election campaigning is regulated in Japan and how such regulations have been upheld by the Supreme Court of Japan. Then, we will critically examine whether these regulations are justified.

The legislature and elections in Japan

The Diet, Japan's national legislature,[4] is composed of the House of Representatives and the House of Councillors.[5] Members of both Houses are "elected members, representative of all the people."[6] This means that the Japanese people have a right to choose members of both the House of Representatives and the House of Councillors. Moreover, the Constitution of Japan explicitly guarantees the right to vote to all adult citizens[7] and also protects the freedom of expression.[8] The Constitution of Japan then provides in article 47 that "[e]lectoral districts, method of voting and other matters pertaining to the method of election of members of both Houses shall be fixed by law."[9]

Under the current electoral system, out of 475 members of the House of Representatives, 295 members are elected in single-member election districts, while 180 members are elected based on proportional representation.[10] Thus each voter casts two votes at the ballot box: one for a particular candidate in the election district and one for a political party.[11] The candidate who gains the most votes in the election district will win that election and each political party is allocated the number of seats that corresponds to the number of votes it received.[12] Each political party needs to publish a list of candidates for the proportional representation election. The list must indicate the candidates' names and their priority ranking on the list as the candidates will be chosen in order of that ranking to fill those seats assigned to their political party.

On the other hand, out of 242 members in the House of Councillors, 146 members are elected in election districts and 96 members are elected based on proportional representation.[13] The election district is marked by prefectural boundary.[14] Candidates who received more votes in the election districts will be elected. For the proportional representation election, each political party will publish the list of candidates in advance without indicating the priority of the candidates. In this proportional representation election, the voter may cast a vote for a political party or for a candidate listed for this proportional representation election.[15] Political parties will be allocated seats that correspond to the number of votes they or the candidates on their list gain nation-wide and the candidate who gets the most votes will be elected first.

Therefore, the election campaign is significantly different depending on whether it is a district election or a proportional representation election, and also on the number of candidates that will be elected in one election district. Here, we will focus on elections in the single-member districts of the House of Representatives.[16]

Electoral campaigning is a political activity geared to win an election. The Ministry of Internal Affairs and Communication, which is charged with the regulation of elections in Japan, defines "election campaign" as any "activity necessary directly or indirectly and useful to obtain a vote or let the candidate obtain a vote for the purpose of electing a particular candidate with respect to a particular election."[17] Such election campaigns are distinguished from other types of political speech and are subject to special regulation.

An election in Japan is triggered when the term of office for members of the House of Representatives and the House of Councillors ends: four years for the members of the House of Representatives and six years for the members of the House of Councillors. For members of the House of Representatives, the election can also be triggered when the House of Representatives is dissolved. The election for all the members of the House of Representatives is called a "general election."[18] Moreover, half of the members of the House of Councillors would be elected every three years. This election for the half of the members of the House of Councillors is called a "regular election."[19]

The election for the members of the House of Representatives whose term of office will expire must be conducted within 30 days before the expiration date.[20] The election of members of the House of Representatives must be conducted within 40 days if the House of Representatives is dissolved.[21] The general election needs to be officially announced at least 12 days prior to the election date.[22]

The regular election for the members of the House of Councillors must be conducted within 30 days before their term of office expires[23] and must be officially announced at least 17 days prior to the election date.[24] The Prime Minister of Japan will decide the election date or voting day.

The basic structure of election campaigns in Japan is that, under article 129, the candidates can engage in election campaigning after registering their candidacies upon the announcement of the election, and only during the designated election campaign period until the day before the voting day.[25] The election campaign period is different depending upon the type of election held. As we have already seen, in the case of the House of Representatives, it is generally 12 days, and, in the case of the House of Councillors, it is generally 17 days.[26]

Election campaign regulations

Election campaigning is allowed only during the election campaign period

Candidates as well as supporters are not allowed to start campaigning before the official election campaign period.[27] This means that no candidate is allowed to indicate that he/she will be running for the coming election or ask supporters to vote for him/her in the coming election before the official election campaign period.

The candidates and supporters are allowed to engage in campaigning until the day before the voting day. This means that the candidates or supporters are not allowed to engage in campaigning on the voting day.[28] As a result, election campaigning is allowed only for a very short period of time.

Restrictions on who can participate in election campaigns

Candidates and their supporters can engage in election campaigning. However, there are significant exceptions and also strict regulations on how to organise electoral campaigns.

First, it is illegal for those citizens who have been denied the right to vote or the right to run for office because of their election law violation to participate in election campaigning.[29] Second, minors are explicitly prohibited from participating in election campaigning.[30] And no one can use minors for election campaigns (except for simple assistance).[31] It must be noted that in Japan the voting age used to be 20 years old, and anyone under that age could not vote and was prohibited from participating in election campaigns. In most Western countries, minors, especially high school students, are free to participate in election campaigns. This used to be illegal in Japan. But the recent amendment has lowered the voting age to 18.[32] It would be permissible for 18 year olds to participate in election campaigns after this law takes effect.

Third, there is a restriction on participation in election campaigns for public officials involved in elections[33] and certain public workers, such as judges, prosecutors, police officers, or tax officers.[34] There is also a ban on public workers engaging in election campaigns by taking advantage of their positions as public officials.[35] There is further a ban on educators, public or private, from engaging in election campaigns by taking advantage of their positions as educators.[36]

It is of course legal for supporters to participate in election campaigns for a candidate as volunteers. But the candidate cannot pay any money or provide any benefits to them (except to election campaign car announcers and sign language interpreters). Moreover, in order to secure the fairness of election campaigning, there is a restriction on providing foods or drinks (except for serving tea) to persons engaging in an election campaign.[37] Candidates can hire administrative assistants to manage their election campaign office and pay them a fixed amount. However, each candidate needs to appoint one person responsible for campaign finance[38] and there are some restrictions on campaign spending,[39] as well as a limit on total expenditure.[40] Furthermore, the candidates need to notify the local election commission about these workers; any payments to persons not notified or extra payments to those who were hired could be regarded as election fixing and offenders could be criminally punished.[41]

Election campaign Japanese-style

In order to conduct election campaigns, each candidate is allowed to establish basically only one election campaign office in an election district.[42] The election campaign office needs to display at the front door a certificate issued from the local election commission.[43]

The candidate can also designate one vehicle as an "election campaign car" and one sound amplifier system.[44] The designated car needs to show the display designated by the election commission.[45] No more than four passengers in addition to candidate and driver can ride in that car,[46] and all those on board must wear official armbands provided by the election commission.[47]

There are many bans on what candidates and supporters can do during the election campaign period. In addition to a ban on the distribution and display of election campaign documents and door-to-door canvassing as explained below, it is illegal to collect signatures from voters in support of a candidate or in opposition to a candidate,[48] to publish the result of a popularity poll of the candidates,[49] to drive cars in tandem to demonstrate their cause,[50] or to repeat the name of a candidate for the election campaign (except when conducted at a rally, in a public speech, or from the election campaign car between 8 a.m. and 8 p.m.).[51] The candidate cannot campaign in the election campaign car except to repeat the name of the candidate and make election speeches in a parked election campaign car.[52] Repeating the names of the candidate is especially important in Japan, because the voters need to write down the full name of the candidate at the polling station when choosing their preferred candidate.[53]

Ban on distribution and display of election campaign documents

There are two methods by which the government allows dissemination of information on candidates to the voters. The first is an election bulletin board and the other is official election flyers.

When the election is officially announced, each local election commission will erect public election bulletin boards all over the district to allow candidates to post their posters.[54] Each candidate is allowed to post a poster in a designated space on the bulletin board assigned by the election commission.[55]

During the election campaign, the election commission will also prepare an election flyer to be distributed to each house.[56] This election flyer lists all the candidates and provides each candidate an opportunity to provide necessary information to the voters. There is a space limitation for each candidate. This official election flyer is intended to provide detailed information on the candidate, such as career history of the candidate, the political manifesto, or election promises.

Other than these two methods, there are very strict limitations on the printing, displaying, and distribution of election campaign documents.

First, there is a limit on the number of posters, placards, and banners that can be used in election campaigns.[57] Basically, posters can only be posted on election bulletin boards. Therefore, the number of posters which could be printed and used is strictly limited. Moreover, there is a size limitation as well.[58] Basically, this is the only document which can be posted or displayed during the election campaign period. No other election campaign document is allowed to be posted or displayed under article 143.[59]

Moreover, each candidate for the House of Representatives in the election district is allowed to print and distribute only 35,000 postcards and 70,000 flyers (limited to two styles) registered at the election commission.[60] The size of these flyers is limited[61] and they must display the name of the person who is responsible for printing and distribution as well as his address.[62] Official stamps issued by the local election commission need to be attached to these flyers.[63] These flyers need to be inserted into daily newspapers and be delivered or otherwise distributed in accordance with the cabinet order.[64] No other election campaign documents can be distributed during the election campaign period under article 142.[65]

Furthermore, no one is allowed to distribute or display any document showing the name of a candidate, his symbol mark, the name of a political party, or the name of the person who endorses or opposes a candidate in order to circumvent these bans under article 146.[66] These documents are prohibited even when the documents are not soliciting a vote or support for the election. Similarly, it is illegal to send postcards, letters, or telegrams that show the name of the candidate who plans to run for office after the dissolution of the House of Representatives,[67] distribute holiday greetings using the names of candidates or political parties in the election districts,[68] or to send postcards or letters of holiday greetings to any voter in the election districts.[69] All of these documents are prohibited in order to prevent circumvention on the ban on the distribution of documents for election campaigns.

Ban on door-to-door canvassing

The candidates or supporters are also prohibited, under article 138, paragraph 1, from conducting door-to-door canvassing for the purpose of getting votes.[70] This means that one is not allowed to visit other households in order to solicit a vote for a particular candidate during the election campaign period.

In order to prevent the circumvention of this ban, candidates and supporters are similarly prohibited from conducting door-to-door canvassing in order to announce the public rally of a particular candidate or to state the name of the candidate or political party.[71] This means that even if one is not soliciting a vote for a particular candidate, one is not allowed to visit one's friends and others to tell them that a particular candidate will have a rally on a particular day in a particular place or mention the name of a particular candidate or political party.

This ban on door-to-door canvassing is very unique and has been controversial. In most Western countries, such door-to-door canvassing is not prohibited at all.

Public rally or public gathering

Candidates can have individual public rallies and the political party can have public party rallies at public schools, civil halls, other public facilities[72] or in other facilities.[73] Candidates may only display a limited number of banners or placards in front of the venue.[74] During such political rallies, candidates can make speeches and others can make endorsement speeches.[75] In order to hold such a rally, candidates or political parties must notify the local election commission[76] and any other rallies for election campaigning are prohibited.[77] It is also illegal for a person other than a candidate to organise a joint rally of two or more candidates.[78] As a result of all these prohibitions, there is some question whether anyone can hold public debates among candidates during the election period.

Candidates can also make public speeches as well, either standing on the streets or in parked election campaign cars.[79] Candidates need to carry a flag granted from the local election commission[80] and all persons engaging in the election campaign during such public speech (limited to 15 persons) need to wear the designated armbands.[81] Public speech during the evening and night is prohibited[82] and candidates are warned not to remain in the same place for long hours.[83] Public speech at facilities owned or managed by the government, trains or railroad stations, and hospitals is prohibited.[84]

Newspapers and broadcasting

All these bans on distribution or display of election campaign documents do not prevent newspapers or magazines from carrying out news reports or comments on elections.[85] Newspapers or magazine publishers can distribute their newspapers or magazines as usual.[86] But, in order to do so, newspapers need to be regularly published at least three times every month (magazines need to be regularly published at least once a month) with charge, granted approval for special postal rate, and continuously published for one year prior to the date of the announcement of the election (for daily newspapers which publish news stories, the period is six months).[87] These limitations are meant to preclude the publication of newspapers or magazines only for election campaign purposes. Moreover, the newspapers are prohibited from abusing the freedom of expression and violating the fairness of the election by publishing false information or distorting the facts.[88]

In order to prevent undue influence on newspapers, no one is allowed to provide or promise any money, property or any other kind of benefits to the editors or owners of the newspapers to make them carry out reports or comments on election for the purpose of facilitating an electoral victory.[89] Editors or owners are also prohibited from receiving such benefits.[90] Moreover, no editor or owner of the newspaper is allowed to carry out reports or comments on elections by taking advantage of his positions for the purpose of facilitating an electoral win.[91] As a result, although there is no explicit ban on newspapers carrying editorials urging the readers to vote for a particular candidate or political party, there is an open question on the extent to which newspapers can publish such editorials.[92]

Candidates can run election campaigning ads in newspapers, but they are only allowed to carry ads in one paper for five times during the election campaign period, and the size of the ad must accord with the provisions of the government order.[93] This is not a mandatory provision for the newspaper and it is up to the newspaper to decide whether to accept the ads. In order to enforce this limitation on election ads, no candidates are allowed to carry greeting ads in newspapers.[94]

Broadcasters can broadcast any programme subject to the Broadcasting Act.[95] The Broadcasting Act mandates every terrestrial television station to observe the fairness doctrine: each station must maintain political neutrality towards controversial issues.[96] Therefore, if the broadcast station broadcasts a programme in favour of a particular candidate or a political party, then the station can be accused of being in violation of this obligation. Moreover, a broadcasting station is prohibited from abusing its freedom of expression and violating the fairness of the election by broadcasting false information or distorting the facts.[97] In addition, no one is allowed to broadcast a programme for the purpose of an election campaign using its broadcasting facilities except as provided under the Public Office Election Act.[98] These restrictions also apply to commercials. As a result, there are no television commercials endorsing candidates as well as negative television commercials against competitors in Japan, as commonly found in the United States.[99] Furthermore, candidates are prohibited from running greeting ads in the broadcast as well.[100]

On the other hand, the political party that endorses candidates can request the Nihon Hoso Kyoukai (NHK), a public broadcaster, and private broadcasters, to broadcast a programme explaining their candidates and their basic policies ("political view broadcast") for free.[101] This is a mandatory provision for the broadcasters and these broadcasters are mandated to carry out a programme as created by the political party.[102] Notice, however, that it is the political party and not individual candidates that can request this political view broadcast. Furthermore, NHK is mandated to carry a programme telling audience the names, ages, political party affiliations, and major personal histories of the candidates ("personal history broadcast") in the district.[103]

Ban on publication of false information

There is a criminal ban on the publication of false information during the election campaign. Anyone who publishes false information on candidates or those who plan to become candidate with respect to their statuses, occupations, personal histories, affiliations with political parties or other organisations, or endorsement or support by political party, in order to facilitate an electoral win can be punished with prison confinement for not more than two years or fined up to 300,000 JPY.[104] On the other hand, anyone who publishes false information or distorted facts on candidates or those who plan to become candidates in order to prevent their electoral win can be punished with prison confinement for not more than four years or fined up to one million JPY.[105]

Moreover, anyone who publishes defamatory information on candidates or those who plan to run for election could be punished for criminal defamation.[106] Furthermore, as we have already seen, if a newspaper or magazine publishes false stories or distorts the facts and infringes the fairness of the election by abusing the freedom of expression, its editor or owner can be criminally punished.[107] Broadcasters are subject to the same restriction.[108]

There is also a ban on the publication of popularity polls for candidates[109] and this ban is applicable to newspapers as well as magazines and broadcasters.[110] The ban on publication of popularity polls carries with it criminal punishment as well.[111] Moreover, if newspapers or magazines that do not satisfy the requirement for immunity carry reports or comments on the election, their editor or owner can face criminal punishment.[112] If an editor or owner, for the purpose of supporting a particular candidate and by taking advantage of his/her position, runs a story or comment in newspapers or magazines[113] or if the broadcaster runs a programme for an election campaign,[114] he/she can also face criminal sanctions.

After the elections

Even after the election is over, there are several restrictions on political speech. Basically, no one is allowed to conduct door-to-door canvassing, distribute or display any document, publish in newspapers or magazines, broadcast a programme using broadcasting facilities, or hold a celebration party, for the purpose of showing appreciation for the support with respect to the election.[115]

Applicability to the Internet

All of these regulations had been interpreted as applicable to the Internet. Activities such as creating a webpage, modifying a webpage, uploading documents, or sending messages are regarded as distribution of documents and are prohibited by the Public Office Election Act. As a result, when the election is officially announced, a candidate or his supporters are not allowed to modify their webpages.

However, a growing dissatisfaction with the regulations' applicability to the Internet ultimately led the Diet to amend the Public Office Election Act partially to liberalise these bans on the Internet. As a result, using webpages for an election campaign is now liberalised[116] and the candidates are allowed to send e-mails to voters who have consented to receive such e-mails in advance.[117] Still, voters are not free to send e-mails soliciting votes or opposing particular candidates. The use of the Internet for the election campaign is still significantly limited.

Supreme Court of Japan and election campaigning

Supreme Court of Japan on election campaign speech restrictions

These restrictions are so comprehensive and restrictive that they leave practically no room for free election campaigning. Each violation carries stiff criminal punishments.[118] Moreover, if one violates one of these restrictions, one cannot only face criminal punishments but also be denied the right to vote, as well as the right to run for office.[119]

Many of these regulations were originally introduced well before the enactment of the Constitution of Japan and pursuant to the Meiji Constitution, which declared the sovereignty of the Emperor and viewed all Japanese people as subjects to the Emperor, and denied any constitutional right to vote.[120] The ban on door-to-door canvassing was introduced when the universal male suffrage was first allowed in Japan in 1925. Apparently, the government then was afraid of the active participation of the public when the voters' franchise was significantly expanded and introduced all the restrictions in order to contain public participation in politics. Despite the radical change brought by the enactment of the Constitution of Japan, however, most of these regulations survived the constitutional change. Although the people are now regarded as sovereign and the right to vote is constitutionally granted to all adult citizens, regardless of sex, and the freedom of expression is constitutionally protected, the same old restrictions on election campaigns have been maintained.

Nevertheless, the Supreme Court of Japan, echoing its overall passive and conservative constitutional jurisprudence,[121] has consistently upheld all of these restrictions when these restrictions were challenged before it and has sustained the constitutionality of all these convictions.[122]

Supreme Court of Japan on ban on election campaigning before registration

For instance, the Supreme Court of Japan in 1969 quickly upheld the limitation of election campaigning to such a short period of time and ban on election campaigning before the official announcement and registration.[123] It is clear from previous judgments of the Supreme Court of Japan, that the freedom of expression was subject to necessary and reasonable restriction. If one allows election campaigning anytime, undue and unnecessary competition would be invited, harm to the fairness of election may be brought because of the difficulty of detection, and unnecessary cost and labour is also necessitated, bringing about unfairness due to disparity of economic power, and eventually risking corruption in elections. In order to prevent these harms and to secure the fairness of elections, it was necessary to limit the election campaign period to a reasonable length, and the imposition of the same starting date for all campaigns makes it possible for each candidate to compete in election campaigns under the same conditions. The reason why article 129 of the Public Office Election Act limits election campaigning to the period starting from the date of registration till one day before the voting day is exactly to accomplish these objectives. Securing the fairness of elections is to maintain public welfare and the limitation on the election campaign period and a ban on election campaigning prior to this period is a reasonable and necessary restriction on freedom of expression. Therefore, article 129 of the Public Office Election Act does not violate article 21 of the Constitution.

The Supreme Court of Japan has followed this precedent and has rejected all constitutional challenges against the ban on election campaigning prior to the official announcement of elections.[124]

Supreme Court of Japan on ban on door-to-door canvassing

The Supreme Court of Japan has also upheld the ban on door-to-door canvassing. The first judgment of the Supreme Court of Japan pertained to the ban proscribed in statutes before the passage of the Public Office Election Act.[125] These holdings were quite brief and simply concluded that the ban was constitutional without providing any justifications. Although some of the lower courts were reluctant to accept the Supreme Court's precedent and gave it a limited construction or struck the law down,[126] the Supreme Court of Japan was not persuaded.[127]

The Supreme Court of Japan explicitly confirmed these holdings in 1969, denying any necessity of overruling its precedent.[128] Some of the lower courts still ignored these precedents and struck down a ban, acquitting the defendants.[129] Nevertheless, the Supreme Court of Japan overturned all of these lower court judgments and affirmed the constitutionality of the ban in 1981.[130]

According to the 1981 judgment of the Supreme Court of Japan, the ban on door-to-door canvassing is not meant to restrict the expression of opinion itself but is meant to prevent harm brought by the method of expression of opinion, namely the possibility of inviting election fixing by providing benefits, the possible invasion of privacy of voters, the possibility of necessitating intolerable inconvenience and cost of competition, and the possibility of inducement of votes based on emotional influence, and to secure the fairness of elections. These objectives are legitimate and there is a rational connection between the blanket ban on door-to-door canvassing and these objectives. The cost lost by the ban on door-to-door canvassing, namely the restriction on freedom of expression by the method of door-to-door canvassing, is merely an indirect and incidental restriction resulting from a ban on a particular method. The benefits to be achieved, namely, prevention of harm arising from door-to-door canvassing and securing fair elections, far outweigh the lost interest. The blanket ban on door-to-door canvassing by article 138, paragraph 1 of the Public Office Election Act therefore does not violate article 21 of the Constitution. The Supreme Court of Japan thus concluded that the 1969 grand bench precedent should be confirmed.

The Supreme Court of Japan has confirmed this holding in another judgment in 1981[131] and has followed these judgments ever since.[132]

Supreme Court of Japan on ban on distribution and display of election documents

The Supreme Court of Japan similarly upheld the ban on distribution of election documents in article 142, the ban on display of election documents in article 143, and the ban on circumvention in article 146 in 1955.[133] The Supreme Court of Japan confirmed the constitutionality of article 142 in 1964[134] by holding that if one allows unlimited freedom of distributing documents with respect to election campaigning for public office, one might invite unnecessary competition in election campaigning, thereby creating the possibility of undermining the fairness of elections. The ban on the distribution of such documents, which is recognised as necessary and reasonable in order to prevent such harm, is an unavoidable measure to secure public welfare in order to ensure proper fairness of elections. Article 142 of the Public Office Election Act, which adopted such a measure, therefore did not violate article 21 of the Constitution.

The Supreme Court of Japan confirmed these holdings ever since.[135,136]

Reflection on the judgments of the Supreme Court of Japan

Impact on election and politics

These comprehensive election campaign regulations affirmed by the Supreme Court of Japan have significantly impacted Japanese elections and politics.

Because of all of these restrictions, it is impossible to engage in a free election campaign. Most of the time, the candidate is simply allowed to ride in the election campaign car, waving a hand covered with white globes, repeating his name and begging for a vote from morning till evening.

Moreover, the restrictions have practically made election campaigning a matter for professional experts rather than for average citizens. The practical message is clear: laymen should steer clear away from election campaigns. There are so many things that cannot be done and it is thus very dangerous for average citizens to participate in election campaigns, especially since any violations trigger stiff criminal punishments.

As a consequence, it is far better if the candidates have access to solid electoral machinery with experienced election campaign experts. This is one of the reasons why so many politicians in Japan are those who succeed in the election district as well as whole support organisations from his/her family members; when politicians die or retire, their spouses or children (sometimes grandchildren) inherit the support organisation (*koenkai*) and run for the next election in the same election districts.[137] Such politicians definitely have a significant advantage over newcomers who do not have expert support.

Furthermore, since the election campaign period is too short and there are so many election campaign restrictions, it is questionable whether candidates can provide sufficient information on their political views to the voters and whether voters would have sufficient information on the candidates, their political views, or the political issues at stake in the election. It is likely that the election result is influenced not by informed decision but by general impression such as the image of a candidate's face or familiarity with the candidate's name.

Furthermore, since the election campaign period is too short, it is all the more important for the supporter's group (*koenkai*) to provide service and assistance to voters in the election district before the election campaign. The voters will then likely reward their services and assistance by voting for the politicians during the election, even if the candidates or supporters have never expressly asked for their vote. This is another reason why the politicians who inherited the election district (as well as the supporters) from their family members perform better at elections.

Are these restrictions merely restrictions on method?

In light of the restrictions' significant impact on election and politics, it can be questioned whether the justification accepted by the Supreme Court of Japan in their judgments is indeed convincing.

First of all, the Supreme Court of Japan believes that all these restrictions are content-neutral restrictions on the method of expression and any restriction of freedom of expression is an indirect and incidental effect of the regulation. It is questionable, however, whether they can be viewed as content-neutral restrictions only on method of expression: they are regulating the speech precisely because the content of the expression is on election campaigns. They are hardly content-neutral restrictions.

Even if they are simply a regulation of the method of expression, that should not automatically justify all such regulations. Regulations on time, place, and manner of expression need to be justified as the least restrictive method to achieve important objectives. When the method regulated is vital to election campaigning, such as door-to-door canvassing or distribution of documents, regulation should not be allowed just because other methods are still available. It is questionable whether such regulations can be justified since the goal can be achieved by less restrictive means.

It is indeed very troubling that the Supreme Court of Japan reviewed all these restrictions on election campaigns under a very lenient standard of review, deferred legislative judgment, and concluded that they are reasonable and necessary restrictions to secure the fairness of elections. It had never inquired into whether it was necessary to introduce a blanket ban on these election campaign methods or whether there are less restrictive alternatives available. Although election campaigning is a vital process in a democracy, it looks as though the Supreme Court of Japan does not believe it is the role for the courts to remove impermissible restrictions on the people's political freedom.

Danger of unnecessary competition?

The Supreme Court of Japan invoked the danger that unfettered election campaigning might bring about unnecessary competition, which might lead to violations of the fairness of the election, in order to support the ban on distribution and display of election documents. But since the citizens have a freedom of expression, there is nothing wrong per se with free competition. If we allow free election campaigning, some candidates might engage in conduct such as publishing false defamatory statements against other candidates. Therefore, such conduct, which violates the fairness of the elections, would need to be sanctioned. But there is no reason to believe that all election campaign methods, which might be used by some to violate the fairness of elections, need to be banned. The mere possibility of abuse should not be a legitimate reason to prohibit all legitimate activities.

The inequality stemming from the disparate financial situations of candidates could be a serious concern. This concern was also invoked to justify the ban on door-to-door canvassing as well. However, if the candidate has a sufficient number of volunteers who are willing to work for free, there is no need to worry about the spending. Door-to-door canvassing is probably the most inexpensive way of promoting the view of candidates. As a result, this justification may be simply an excuse to help those candidates who do not have a sufficient number of volunteers.

Moreover, if the cost of election campaigns is a serious concern, then the government might be allowed to impose the limit on total amount of spending allowed in election campaigns,[138] as the Public Election Act has already imposed.[139] The government could also provide each candidate with some public funding, as it has already done.[140] It is questionable whether it is necessary to require every candidate to spend the same amount of money for election campaigning and ban any activity which might require more financial resources.

Danger of impairing the fairness of the elections?

The ban on door-to-door canvassing is justified by the courts on the basis that door-to-door canvassing can be used as a method of fixing elections and there is difficulty in detecting such illegal conduct. It is surely illegal to buy votes or to intimidate or harass voters to vote for a particular candidate. Such conduct would surely impair the fairness of elections and need to be prevented.

However, it can be questioned whether door-to-door canvassing actually has a real and imminent danger of causing such harm. The government simply insisted on the possibility of such electoral fixing and the Supreme Court of Japan simply accepted this possibility as a justification for banning door-to-door canvassing.[141] But it is questionable whether the mere possibility of election fixing could be a persuasive justification to impose such a blanket ban.[142]

Furthermore, in order to prevent election fixing, it is sufficient to impose criminal punishment to those who engage in such illegal conduct. It is indeed a crime to provide benefit to buy votes.[143] Therefore, the goal could be achieved by less restrictive means. It is questionable whether it is necessary to ban all door-to-door canvassing, even considering the difficulty of such detection.

Necessary to protect privacy of voters?

The ban on door-to-door canvassing is also justified as a measure to protect the privacy of the residents. When the candidate or supporter knocks on the door, surely some of the residents will be dismayed. The protection of privacy appears to be a very important interest to protect against unwanted intrusion.

But not all residents would want to be left alone. Some may welcome a chat with the candidate or the supporter. Even if some do not want to be disturbed, they could simply refuse to open their doors. Given the importance of door-to-door canvassing as a method of election campaigning, it is questionable whether the residents need to be protected even against a knock on the door.

Moreover, the residents could simply post a sign indicating their wishes not to be disturbed ("no solicitation, please"). In order to protect their privacy, it would suffice to prohibit any visit that ignores such signs posted in front of the residents' gates or doors. Furthermore, the legislature might be allowed to restrict the hours when door-to-door canvassing can be conducted, thus prohibiting door-to-door canvassing during the night or in the early morning.[144] It is questionable whether a total ban is necessary to protect the privacy of the residents.

Finally, door-to-door canvassing for the purpose of election campaigning is prohibited, but all other door-to-door canvassing is not. One is free to knock on the door to sell or advertise products. It is questionable whether there is a special reason to protect residents from door-to-door canvassing only for election campaigns.

Is election campaigning special?

Some of the Justices have suggested that election campaigning is somewhat different from regular political freedom and needs to be treated specially.

Justice Masami Itoh thus frankly admitted in his concurring opinion in the 1981 judgment[145] that traditional justification for the ban on door-to-door canvassing is not totally persuasive. Rather, he insisted that the ban could be justified on the premise that with respect to election campaigns, each candidate must compete under the same rules designed to secure the fairness of election and the legislature is granted discretion to decide what kinds of rules should be imposed. He relied on article 47 of the Constitution, which delegates the power to decide matters related to election to the Diet, and opined that the ban on door-to-door canvassing is justified because it is a rule set by the legislature.[146,147]

Justice Masao Ohno also implied that door-to-door canvassing is an election campaign method and needs to be treated differently from the regular exercise of freedom of expression.[148] In order to secure the fairness of elections, he pointed out, the government must provide public funding to allow for appropriate and equal opportunities for candidates to express their opinions, while prohibiting unnecessary spending and labour. He insisted that the legislature should be granted discretion on how far it could allow free election campaigns in addition to publicly funded election campaigns.

It is questionable whether such a view could be accepted in a democracy. Election is a vital process in a democracy. Election speech is the most vital part of political expression. Even the Supreme Court of Japan has admitted that the core of the protection of freedom of expression lies in the protection of political speech on matters of public importance.[149] According to Justice Itoh's view or Justice Ohno's view, however, election campaigns could be subjected to special regulations and the legislature is granted broad powers to regulate election campaigning. If we accept this view, any kinds of restriction could be justified so long as it is imposed equally to all the candidates. Such a view is utterly irreconcilable with the constitutional guarantee of freedom of expression. It is ironic that the legislature is strictly prohibited from interfering with political speech but it could easily regulate election speech, despite the fact electoral speech is indeed a vital part of political speech.

Is the applicability of political campaign regulations to the Internet justified?

Furthermore, it is utterly questionable whether these regulations, such as the ban on the distribution of election documents, should be applicable to the Internet.[150] It is doubtful as a matter of statutory interpretation whether creating or updating a webpage could be viewed as distribution of such documents. Moreover, it is also doubtful whether any kind of rationales which might be invoked to justify the ban on the distribution of these documents could be applicable to creating and updating a website. Creating and updating a website is quite inexpensive and leaving this to individual freedom raises no possibility of inequality among the candidates due to financial differences. It is totally unimaginable how allowing election campaigning on the Internet could lead to injustice or unfairness of elections. Sending e-mails for election campaigns is in itself also harmless. Sending fake e-mails could be prohibited but there is no reason to prohibit all e-mails to individual voters.

Conclusion

> Speech is an essential mechanism of democracy, for it is the means to hold officials accountable to the people.... The right of citizens to inquire, to hear, to speak, and to use information to reach consensus is a precondition to enlightened self-government and a necessary means to protect it. The First Amendment "has its fullest and most urgent application" to speech uttered during a campaign for political office.[151]

This is the reason why the United States Supreme Court has held that "political speech must prevail against laws that would suppress it, whether by design or inadvertence. Laws that burden political speech are 'subject to strict scrutiny'," which requires the Government to prove that the restriction "furthers a compelling interest and is narrowly tailored to achieve that interest."[152] However, it is this election speech that is subject to the most comprehensive and strictest regulations in Japan and these draconian regulations are constantly upheld by the Supreme Court of Japan. These regulations have a significant adverse impact on Japanese elections and politics and, in order to promote the country's democracy, it is surely an appropriate time to reconsider all these regulations.

Notes

1 *New York Times* v. *Sullivan* 376 US 254, 270 (1964).
2 *Mills* v. *Alabama* 384 US 214 (1966).
3 Koushoku senkyohō [Public Office Election Act], Law No. 100 of 1950.
4 Nihonkoku kenpō [Constitution of Japan] of 1946, art. 41.
5 Ibid. art. 42.
6 Ibid. art. 43.
7 Ibid. art. 15, paras 1 and 3.
8 Ibid. art. 21.
9 Ibid. art. 47.
10 Koushoku senkyohō [Public Office Election Act], Law No. 100 of 1950, art. 4, para. 1.
11 Ibid. art. 36.
12 For the purpose of proportional representation election, Japan is divided into 11 blocs and, in each bloc, a political party will be assigned the number of seats that corresponds to the number of votes it collected.
13 Ibid. art. 4, para. 2.
14 There are 47 prefectures and as a result there are 47 election districts. Tokyo, the most populous prefecture, has ten Councillors, while less populous prefectures such as Shimane have only two Councillors. Since half of the members need to be

elected every three years, one to five Councillor(s) need to be elected in each prefecture every three years. In 2015, the number of seats to be allocated to Tokyo was increased by two and Tottori and Shimane prefectures and Tokushima and Kochi prefectures were combined to elect two from the 2016 summer election. Koushoku senkyohō no ichibuwo kaiseisuru hōrtsu [Act to Amend Parts of the Public Office Election Act], Law No. 60 of 2015. It must be noted that the voter can cast only one vote regardless of the number of members to be elected in one prefecture.

15 Koushoku senkyohō [Public Office Election Act], Law No. 100 of 1950, art. 95-3.

16 In addition to members of the Diet, local residents have a right to choose the head of the local government as well as local legislative members. Nihonkoku kenpō [Constitution of Japan] of 1946, art. 93, para. 2.

17 Ministry of Internal Affairs and Communication, Genko no senkyo undou no kisei [Current Election Campaigning Regulation] www.soumu.go.jp/senkyo/senkyo_s/naruhodo/naruhodo10_1.html.

18 Koushoku senkyohō [Public Office Election Act], Law No. 100 of 1950, art. 31.

19 Ibid. art. 32. When there is a need to fill the vacancy in the election district after the election, a by-election will be held. Ibid. art. 33-2.

20 Ibid. art. 31, para. 1.

21 Ibid. art. 31, para. 3.

22 Ibid. art. 31, para. 4.

23 Ibid. art. 32, para. 1.

24 Ibid. art. 32, para. 3.

25 Ibid. art. 129.

26 See nn. 23, 24.

27 See n. 25.

28 However, candidates are allowed to keep the posters and/or the election campaign office intact even on the voting day.

29 Ibid. art. 137-3. See n. 119.

30 Koushoku senkyohō [Public Office Election Act], Law No. 100 of 1950, art. 137-2, para. 1.

31 Ibid. art. 137-2, para. 2.

32 Koushoku senkyohō no ichibuwo kaiseisuru hōritsu [Act to Amend Parts of the Public Office Election Act], Law No. 43 of 2015, art. 1.

33 Koushoku senkyohō [Public Office Election Act], Law No 100 of 1950, art. 135.

34 Ibid. art. 136. Moreover, all public workers are prohibited from engaging in any political activities. Kokka koumuinhō [Public Workers Act], Law No. 120 of 1947, art. 102. Supporting or opposing a particular candidate during the elections is a prohibited political activity.

35 Koushoku senkyohō [Public Office Election Act], Law No. 100 of 1950, art. 136-2.

36 Ibid. art. 137.

37 Ibid. art. 139.

38 Ibid. art. 180.

39 Ibid. art. 184. There is also a record keeping obligation and report requirement. Ibid. 185.

40 Ibid. art. 194.

41 Ibid. art. 221, para. 1, nos 1 and 3. Those who received such money or benefit will be also punished, see art. 221, para. 1, no. 4. It must be added that the administrative assistance workers are staff members who provide administrative support and need to be notified in advance. In addition to these workers, simple helpers who, for instance, attach stamps to flyers or prepare for the political rally, can be hired and paid without notification. However, anyone who actually engages in election campaigning (except for the election campaign car announcer and the sign language interpreters) cannot be paid.

42 Ibid. art. 131, para. 1. In addition, the endorsing political party can also establish one election campaign office in each election district. In order to prevent circumvention of the limitation, no one is allowed to have additional places for taking breaks or similar places, see ibid. art. 133.
43 Ibid. art. 131, para. 3.
44 Ibid. art. 141, para. 1. The use of other cars or a sound amplifier system for election campaigning is thereby prohibited, except when a candidate uses additional sound amplifiers for making speeches during the candidate's election rallies or public gatherings. Moreover, the political party that endorses candidates can use additional election campaign cars and sound amplifier systems depending upon the number of the candidates running in one prefecture, see ibid. art. 141, para. 2.
45 Ibid. art. 141, para. 5.
46 Ibid. art. 141-2, para. 1.
47 Ibid. art. 141-2, para. 2.
48 Ibid. art. 138-2.
49 Ibid. art. 138-3.
50 Ibid. art. 140.
51 Ibid. art. 140-2.
52 Ibid. art. 141-3.
53 There is no ban on making telephone calls for election campaign purposes. The use of false names when making such phone calls is, however, prohibited, see ibid. art. 235-5.
54 Ibid. art. 144-2, para. 1.
55 Ibid. art. 144-2, para. 5.
56 Ibid. art. 167.
57 Ibid. art. 143, paras 1 and 3.
58 Ibid. art. 143, para. 9.
59 Ibid. art. 143, para. 1. Any kind of documents showing the name of the candidates or any item which allows voters to guess the name of the candidate is banned, see ibid. art. 143, para. 16. It must be noted that the endorsing political parties can display an additional 10,000 posters, see ibid. art. 144, para. 1.
60 Ibid. art. 142, para. 1. In addition, the political party that endorses the candidates can print and distribute a certain number of postcards (20,000 postcards multiplied by the number of the candidates) and a certain number of flyers (40,000 multiplied by the number of candidates) in each prefecture, see ibid. art. 142, para. 2.
61 Ibid. art. 142, para. 8.
62 Ibid. art. 142, para. 9.
63 Ibid. art. 142, para. 7.
64 Ibid. art. 142, para. 6.
65 Ibid. art. 142, para. 1. The political party who endorses candidate can, however, distribute a "manifesto," a pamphlet, or document describing its important policies and basic measures to implement them, see ibid. art. 142-2.
66 Ibid. art. 146, para. 1.
67 Ibid. art. 142, para. 13.
68 Ibid. art. 146, para. 2.
69 Ibid. art. 147-2.
70 Ibid. art. 138, para. 1.
71 Ibid. art. 138, para. 2.
72 Ibid. art. 161.
73 Ibid. art. 161-2.
74 Ibid. art. 164-2.
75 Ibid. art. 162.
76 Ibid. art. 163.
77 Ibid. art. 164-3, para. 1.

78 Ibid. art. 164-3, para. 2.
79 Ibid. art. 164-5, para. 1.
80 Ibid. art. 164-5, paras 2 and 4.
81 Ibid. art. 164-7, paras 1 and 2.
82 Ibid. art. 164-6, para. 1. It is between 8 a.m. and 8 p.m. that public speeches are permitted.
83 Ibid. art. 164-6, para. 3.
84 Ibid. art. 166.
85 Ibid. art. 148, para. 1. The ban on the publication of popularity polls for candidates is applicable to newspapers.
86 Ibid. art. 148, para. 2.
87 Ibid. art. 148, para. 3.
88 Ibid. art. 148, para. 1.
89 Ibid. art. 148-2, para. 1.
90 Ibid. art. 148-2, para. 2.
91 Ibid. art. 148-2, para. 3.
92 Besides, all major newspapers in Japan are supposed to report news objectively and no major newspaper is willing to carry such partisan editorials.
93 Ibid. art. 149. The political party can also carry ads for a limited number of times depending upon the number of candidates.
94 Ibid. art. 152.
95 Ibid. art. 151-3.
96 Hosouhō [Broadcasting Act], Law No. 132 of 1950, art. 4, para. 1.
97 Koushoku senkyohō [Public Office Election Act], Law No. 100 of 1950, art. 151-3.
98 Ibid. art. 151-5.
99 However, there is no ban on television commercials run by the political party for political purposes.
100 Ibid. art. 152.
101 Ibid. art. 150.
102 Ibid. Candidates as well as political parties are required to maintain decency and are not allowed to defame others or violate public order or good morality, see ibid. art. 150-2.
103 Ibid. art 151, para. 1. The NHK is required to carry such programmes at least once on television and roughly ten times on radio but it is encouraged to carry it more often, see ibid. art. 151, para. 2.
104 Ibid. art. 235, para. 1.
105 Ibid. art. 235, para. 2.
106 Keihō [Criminal Code], art. 230, para. 1.
107 Koushoku senkyohō [Public Office Election Act], Law No. 100 of 1950, art. 148, para. 1, and art. 235-2, no. 1.
108 Ibid. art. 151-3; art. 235-4, no. 1.
109 Ibid. art. 138-3.
110 Ibid. art. 148, para. 1 and art. 151-3.
111 Ibid. art. 242-2. However, newspapers or magazines can publish their election predictions based on their own research.
112 Ibid. art. 235-2, no. 2.
113 Ibid. art. 148-2, para, 3, and art. 235-2, no. 3.
114 Ibid. art. 151-5, and art 235-4, no. 2.
115 Ibid. art. 178.
116 Ibid. art. 142-3.
117 Ibid. art. 142-4.
118 Ibid. art. 243 (punishable by confinement for not more than two years or by fine for not more than 500,000 JPY), and art. 244 (punishable by confinement for not more than one year or by fine for not more than 300,000 JPY).

119 Ibid. art. 252 deprives the defendant who is convicted and sentenced to a fine of his/her right to vote and run for office for five years after the sentence is finalised and deprives the defendant who is convicted and sentenced to prison confinement of his/her right to vote and run for office for five years after finishing the sentence.
120 Dainihonteikoku kenpō [Meiji Constitution], 1889.
121 Matsui (2010, 2011).
122 Usaki (1990) 141.
123 Saikō Saibansho [Sup. Ct], April 23, 1969, grand bench, 23 Saikō Saibansho Hanreishu Keiji [Keishu] 235.
124 Saikō Saibansho [Sup. Ct], July 21, 1981, 3rd petty bench, 35 Saikō Saibansho Hanreishu Keiji [Keishu] 568; Saikō Saibansho [Sup. Ct], February 23, 1988, 3rd petty bench, 248 Saikō Saibansho Saibanshu Keiji [Shukei] 313; Saikō Saibansho [Sup. Ct], September 10, 2002, 3rd petty bench, 282 Saikō Saibansho Saibanshu Keiji [Shukei] 251; Saikō Saibansho [Sup. Ct], January 28, 2008, 2nd petty bench, 293 Saikō Saibansho Saibanshu Keiji [Shukei] 11.
125 Saikō Saibansho [Sup. Ct], September 27, 1950, grand bench, 4 Saikō Saibansho hanreishu Keiji [Keishu] 1799.
126 Tokyo Chihō Saibansho [Tokyo Dist. Ct], March 27, 1967, 493 Hanrei jihō 72; Matsue Chihō Saibansho [Matsue Dist. Ct], March 27, 1969, 234 Hanrei Times 30; Matsue Chihō Saibansho [Matsue Dist. Ct], March 27, 1969, 234 Hanrei Times 32.
127 Saikō Saibansho [Sup. Ct], November 21, 1967, 3rd petty bench, 21 Saikō Saibansho Hanreishu Keiji [Keishu] 1245.
128 Saikō Saibansho [Sup. Ct], April 23, 1969, grand bench, 23 Saikō Saibansho Hanreishu keiji [Keishu] 235.
129 Matsuyama Chihō Saibansho Saijō Shibu [Matsuyamaya Dist. Ct, Saijō Branch], March 30, 1978, 915 Hanrei jihō 135; Matse Chihō Saibansho Izumo Shibu [Matsue Dist. Ct, Izumo Branch], January 24, 1979, 923 Hanrei Jihō 141; Fukuoka Chihō Saibansho Yanagawa Shibu [Fukuoka Dist. Ct, Yanagawa Branch], September 7, 1979, 944 Hanrei jihō 133; Morioka Chihō Saibansho Toono Shibu [Morioka Dist. Ct, Toono Branch], March 25, 1980, 962 Hanrei jihō 130. The Hiroshima High Court, Matsue Branch was the first High Court judgment that struck down a ban on door-to-door canvassing. Hiroshima Kōtō Saibansho, Matsue Shibu [Hiroshima High Ct, Matsue Branch], April 28, 1980, 964 Hanrei jihō 134.
130 Saikō Saibansho [Sup. Ct], June 15, 1981, 2nd petty bench, 35 Saikō Saibansho Hanreishu Keiji [Keishu] 205.
131 Saikō Saibansho [Sup. Ct], July 21, 1981, 3rd petty bench, 35 Saikō Saibansho Hanreishu Keiji [Keishu] 568.
132 Saikō Saibansho [Sup. Ct], October 11, 1994, 3rd petty bench, 264 Saikō Saibansho Saibanshu Keiji [Shukei] 109; Saikō Saibansho [Sup. Ct], September 9, 2002, 1st petty bench, 282 Saikō Saibansho Saibanshu Keiji [Shukei] 5; Saikō Saibanso [Sup. Ct], September 10, 2002, 3rd petty bench, 282 Saikō Saibansho Saibanshu Keiji [Shukei] 251; Saikō Saibansho [Sup. Ct], January 28, 2008, 2nd petty bench, 293 Saikō Saibansho Saibanshu Keiji [Shukei] 11.
133 Saikō Saibansho [Sup. Ct], April 6, 1955, grand bench, 9 Saikō Saibansho Hanreishu Keiji [Keishu] 819.
134 Saikō Saibansho [Sup. Ct], November 18, 1964, grand bench, 18 Saikō Saibansho Hanreishu Keiji [Keishu] 561.
135 Saikō Saibansho [Sup. Ct], April 23, 1969, grand bench, 23 Saikō Saibansho Hanreishu Keiji [Keishu] 235; Saikō Saibansho [Sup. Ct], March 23, 1982, 3rd petty bench, 36 Saikō Saibansho Hanreishu Keiji [Keishu] 339; Saikō Saibansho [Sup. Ct], February 23, 1988, 3rd petty bench, 248 Saikō Saibansho Saibanshu Keiji [Shukei] 313; Saikō Saibansho [Sup. Ct], September 9, 2002, 1st petty bench, 282 Saikō Saibansho Saibanshu Keiji [Shukei] 5; Saikō Saibansho [Sup. Ct], January 28, 2008, 2nd petty bench, 293 Saikō Saibansho Saibanshu Keiji [Shukei] 11.

136 The Supreme Court of Japan also confirmed its position on the constitutionality of art. 146. Saikō Saibansho [Sup. Ct], September 9, 2002, 1st petty bench, 282 Saikō Saibansho Saibanshu Keiji [Shukei] 5.

137 "Seshu seiji ni mirai wa arunoka" [Is There a Future for Politicians Who Succeeded the Seat for the Diet?] *J-cast News* (12 December 2014) www.j-cast.com/2014/12/12223016.html (noting that half of the Prime Ministers have fathers who are Diet members and one-quarter of all the Diet members succeeded their seats from their fathers or grandfathers).

138 Saikō Saibansho [Sup. Ct], July 21, 1981, 3rd petty bench, 35 Saikō Saibansho Hanreishu Keiji [Keishu] 568 (Itoh, J, concurring).

139 See n. 40.

140 Thus, printing postcards, flyers, and posters designated by the Public Office Election Act is a publicly funded activity. Koushoku senkyohō [Public Office Election Act], Law No. 100 of 1950, art. 142, para. 10, and art. 143, para. 14.

141 Justice Itsuo Sonobe frankly remarked that he could not rule out the possibility that such illegal conduct could take place during door-to-door canvassing under the current situation, while he was open to reconsidering the matter in the future. Saikō Saibansho [Sup. Ct], October 11, 1994, 3rd petty bench, 264 Saikō Saibansho Saibanshu Keiji [Shukei] 109 (Sonobe, J, concurring).

142 Saikō Saibansho [Sup. Ct], July 21, 1981, 3rd petty bench, 35 Saikō Saibansho Hanreishu Keiji [Keishu] 568 (Itoh, J, concurring). While some voters might be influenced by personal relationships if one allows door-to-door canvassing, this mere possibility might not be sufficient to justify a total ban on door-to-door canvassing.

143 Koushoku senkyohō [Public Office Election Act], Law No. 100 of 1950, art. 221, para. 1. Violence or intimidation against a voter taking advantage of its special relationship is also a crime, see ibid. art. 225.

144 Saikō Saibansho [Sup. Ct], July 21, 1981, 3rd petty bench, 35 Saikō Saibansho Hanreishu Keiji [Keishu] 568 (Itoh, J, concurring).

145 Ibid.

146 He also expressed the same view with respect to the ban on the distribution of election documents. Saikō Saibansho [Sup. Ct], March 23, 1982, 3rd petty bench, 36 Saikō Saibansho Hanreishu Keiji [Keishu] 339 (Itoh, J, concurring).

147 Justice Itoh confirmed his view in subsequent judgments. Saikō Saibansho [Sup. Ct], February 23, 1988, 3rd petty bench, 248 Saikō Saibansho Saibanshu Keiji [Shukei] 313 (Itoh, J, concurring).

148 Saikō Saibansho [Sup. Ct], October 11, 1994, 3rd petty bench, 264 Saikō Saibansho Saibanshu Keiji [Shukei] 109 (Ohno, J, concurring).

149 Saikō Saibansho [Sup. Ct], June 11, 1986, grand bench, 40 Saikō Saibansho Hanreishu Minji [Minshu] 872 (Hoppou Journal Case).

150 Wilson (2011).

151 *Citizens United* v. *FEC*, 558 US 310, 339 (2010).

152 Ibid. 340.

References

Matsui S., *The Constitution of Japan: A Contextual Analysis* (Hart Publishing 2010).

Matsui S., 'Why is the Japanese Supreme Court So Conservative?' (2011) 88 *Washington University Law Review* 1375.

Usaki M., 'Restrictions on Political Campaigns in Japan' (1990) 53:2 *Law and Contemporary Problems* 133.

Wilson M.J., 'E-Elections: Time for Japan to Embrace Online Campaigning' (2011) *Stanford Technology Law Review* 4.

9 The electoral process and the judicial review of elections in the Republic of Korea

Woo-Young Rhee

Introduction

In recent years, the constitutional democracy in the Republic of Korea has stabilised. Many of the structural issues in South Korean society, such as the under-representation of women and other minorities in the political process, are now addressed and resolved through legislative and judicial mechanisms. At the same time, South Korean society is rapidly becoming more pluralised politically, socially, and culturally; the nation now confronts the challenge of incorporating these changes while sustaining its commitment to the core values of constitutional democracy and fundamental rights protection for minorities. South Korea has been committed to establishing democracy and the rule of law particularly since the adoption of the current Constitution in 1988; yet, it is not spared from political tension as seen most recently in the case of dissolution of a political party as petitioned by the government in 2013 and resolved by the Constitutional Court in December 2014.[1]

The Constitution of the Republic of Korea provides that the Republic of Korea is a democratic republic.[2] The Constitution of the Republic of Korea was established and came into effect in July 1948. The nation's Constitution thereafter went through nine revisions, with the most recent constitutional revision in 1987 that established the current Constitution of the Republic of Korea, which came into effect in February of 1988. The revision to the current Constitution of 1988 was epitomised by the 'June 1987 Civilian Movement' representing the democratisation movements in the 1980s through which South Korean citizenry demanded the direct election of the nation's president and the substantive guarantee of fundamental rights. Six of the nation's presidents have been directly elected by the voters and served their presidential terms in full since the current Constitution of the Republic of Korea came into effect in February 1988. The Constitutional Court of the Republic of Korea, which was established under the current Constitution in September 1988, has proactively exercised its constitutionally vested function of constitutional adjudication for over twenty-five years with more than 500 decisions holding the statute at issue to be unconstitutional, thereby contributing to the realisation of the constitutional values of fundamental rights protection.

In the public election context, the Constitutional Court of the Republic of Korea since its establishment in 1988 has proactively reviewed the constitutionality of the various aspects of Korea's public election law, through the mechanisms of constitutional adjudication. Whereas the Constitutional Court has taken activist positions in the areas such as electoral district reapportionment and the proportional representation system, the Court has taken relatively passive positions in reviewing the constitutionality of statutory provisions regulating election campaign activities.[3] This chapter will seek to explore the law and the decisions pertaining thereto in the Korean context.

Overview of the public election law of the Republic of Korea

The Public Election Act[4] is the general and integrated public election law in the Republic of Korea. It primarily seeks to secure the fair administration of public elections by preventing corruption (Article 1 of the Public Election Act). The Public Election Act applies to the election of the president, the members of the National Assembly, the chief executive officers of local governments, and the members of the local legislatures (Article 2 of the Public Election Act). This statute was first enacted in March 1994 under the current Constitution as a major part of political reform, along with the statute regulating political funds and donations,[5] and has been revised practically every year.

The general election to constitute the National Assembly consists of two different types of elections: one is to elect representatives from the electoral districts, with election of a single representative from each electoral district by simple relative majority (246 out of 300 seats at the National Assembly); and the other is to elect proportional representatives (fifty-four out of 300) from a single nation-wide electoral district through party lists.[6] In the general election held in 2000 to constitute the sixteenth National Assembly (2000–2004 term), each voter cast one vote for both elections. However, in 2001, the Constitutional Court held this 'one person one vote' system to be unconstitutional.[7] From the general election held in 2004 to constitute the seventeenth National Assembly (2004–2008 term) onwards, each voter casts two votes, one for his or her preferred electoral district representative and the other for his or her preferred political party to elect the proportional representative from the party list. At the presidential election, the simple relative majority rule also applies, with the exception of applying the minimum percentage standard when there is only one candidate.[8] The simple relative majority rule applies to the elections of the chief executive officers of the local governments and of members of the local legislatures as well.

Analysis of major decisions of the Supreme Court and the Constitutional Court

Statutory regulations to ensure electoral fairness and transparency

The Public Election Act[9] mandates fair competition among political parties and candidates (Article 7), requires the public media to engage in fair reporting (Articles 8 through 8-7), requires the neutrality of public officials (Article 9), and prohibits unfair election practices by the national and local election commissions (Articles 10-2 and 10-3). The Act also requires mandatory verification by Internet service providers of the real name and identity of the users posting opinions on Internet media's online bulletin boards during the election campaign period (Article 82-6).

With respect to the real name verification obligation on the part of the Internet service providers on online bulletin boards, the Constitutional Court has held that the relevant statutory provisions do not violate the Constitution as they are indispensable to securing the fairness of the public elections during the election campaign period.[10] However, the Constitutional Court held the real name verification provision to be unconstitutional if it obliged the Internet service providers to verify the identity of all users of the Internet media's online bulletin boards outside the designated election campaign period.[11]

Statutory provisions on the eligibility to vote and run for public office

The Constitution of the Republic of Korea provides that all citizens have the right to vote (Article 24 of the Constitution) and the right to run for public office (Article 25 of the Constitution). The Public Election Act[12] further contains more specific statutory provisions on the right to vote and the right to run for public office. The right to vote is vested in all Korean nationals of or over nineteen years of age on the day of the public election, and listed in the voter register (Articles 3, 15(1), and 17 of the Act). Furthermore, all Korean nationals who are otherwise not ineligible to serve in public office and are of or over forty years of age for presidency (and twenty-five years of age for the membership at National Assembly) are eligible to run for the respective offices (Article 16 of the Act).

At issue in the election law context has been the restriction on the right to vote vis-à-vis individuals of Korean nationalities but who reside overseas. This has been particularly at issue in Korea because of individuals residing in North Korea or Japan with certain legal links to North Korea. The Constitutional Court held in 1999 that the then relevant statutory provision denying the right to vote to Korean nationals residing overseas was constitutional as there were technical and administrative difficulties in implementing the law should the right to vote be vested to such individuals. It was also justified on the basis of the individuals' failure to satisfy their tax obligations and military duties.[13] However, the Constitutional Court changed its position in 2007, and held that the statutory provisions restricting the right to vote of nationals residing overseas to be unconstitutional in light of the principle of universal suffrage and the right to equality.[14]

With respect to the deprivation of the right to vote of convicts (Article 18(1)(ii) of the Act), the Constitutional Court held in its 2014 decision that the restriction of the right to vote of the individuals under probation to be unconstitutional while such restriction on the convicts serving prison terms was held not to be in compliance with the Constitution, and the National Assembly was asked to choose the appropriate means in revising such part of the provision so that the relevant part would be in compliance with the Constitution.[15]

As to the restrictions on the right to vote and the right to run for office, the Constitutional Court of the Republic of Korea held that the right to vote and the right to run for public office are core fundamental rights, any limits or restrictions thereon should be minimal, and the extent and severity of the restrictions should be proportional to the nature of the crime or other grounds for the restriction.[16]

Apportionment of electoral districts

Under Korean law, the electoral districts for the general election are apportioned by the Electoral District Apportionment Commission. For the upcoming twentieth general election to be held in April 2016, the Commission will be established within the National Election Commission as an independent institution for the first time in Korea's history of public elections.[17] The Commission consists of up to eleven commissioners, as recommended and appointed by the Speaker of the National Assembly with the advice and the consent of the representatives of respective negotiation groups within the National Assembly.[18] The apportionment of the electoral districts has constitutional significance, and the authority of the Commissioners to redistrict, and the method they use, and the standard applicable to the apportionment, are also critical to the public election process as a whole and its legitimacy.

Most importantly, at issue have been the permissible difference in population among different electoral districts and the geographic standards for apportionment to prevent gerrymandering. The relevant provision in Korea provides that the administrative districts, population, geography, transportation, and other relevant conditions should be taken into account in apportionment and redistricting (Article 25(1) of the Public Election Act).[19] The Constitutional Court has held that the apportionment conducted by the Electoral District Apportionment Commission is an act of legislative nature and that, as such, the apportionment and redistricting should be conducted in the legislative form to legitimately bind the voter-public, and not as an internal administrative matter to be conducted by an ad hoc committee established within the National Assembly.[20]

In apportioning the electoral districts for the election of the electoral district representatives, the Constitutional Court held in 1995 that the disparity between the most populous and the least populous districts should be no more than four-to-one.[21] Subsequently, in 2001, the Constitutional Court held that the three-to-one ratio should be the standard for constitutionality.[22] In 2014, the

Constitutional Court held that the two-to-one ratio of population difference should be the standard for constitutionality in the apportionment of electoral districts.[23] Accordingly, the electoral districts will be reapportioned or redistricted by the end of 2015, with approximately sixty currently existing electoral districts affected. The upcoming general election to be held in April 2016 to constitute the twentieth National Assembly (to be in session 2016–2020) of the Republic of Korea will be held under the new standard of two-to-one population ratio.

The 2014 Constitutional Court decision that altered the population difference standard from three-to-one to toe-to-one has brought the applicable standard in Korea to comparable standards adopted by most of the OECD member states and other mature and stable democracies.[24] The Constitutional Court took into account certain elements that might justify a lower standard in the unique Korean context and reality, such as its unicameral legislature mandating individual members of the National Assembly to serve the role as the representatives of the voters as a whole yet simultaneously as the regional representatives, and the reality of greater concentration of population in urban areas. However, the Constitutional Court held that such justifications did not justify further appeasement of the standard beyond the two-to-one population ratio among different electoral districts, and thereby limited the legislative discretion on this issue.[25]

Proportional representation system

The proportional representation system with a single nation-wide electoral district was initially adopted by the Constitution of the Third Republic (1969–1972) with the intention to benefit the political party with the most number of seats at the National Assembly, which was the ruling party. Under the Constitution of the Fifth Republic (1980–1988), the number of proportional representatives was set at one-half of the number of the representatives elected from the electoral districts, with the allocation of two-thirds of the proportional representation seats to the political party that obtained the most number of seats at the electoral district election, which was also the ruling party, while the rest or one-third of the proportional representation seats were allocated in proportion to the number of votes obtained by each party with five or more seats at the electoral district election (Article 130 of the now repealed National Assemblyperson Election Act).[26] The benefit given to the political party with the most number of seats at the electoral district election was abolished in 1991 through the revision of the election law under the current Constitution (1988 to present). Under the current law, the proportional representation seats are allocated in proportion to the votes obtained by each of the political parties at the electoral district election.

Under the current proportional representation system in South Korea, fifty-four out of 300 members of National Assembly are proportional representatives, while the remaining 246 members are elected through the electoral district election. The proportional representatives are elected from the lists that respective political parties timely prepare with fixed orders (Article 49(2) of the Public Election Act).[27] The National Election Commission allocates the proportional representation seats to the political parties that have obtained either five or more seats at the electoral district election or 3 per cent of valid votes at the proportional representation ballot, in proportion to the votes such parties have obtained at the proportional representation ballot.[28]

Through the general election held in 2000 to constitute the sixteenth National Assembly (2000–2004 term), the electoral district representatives and the proportional representatives were both elected by a single vote cast by each of the voters under the then-current election laws. The Constitutional Court held in 2001 that the 'one person one vote' rule was not in compliance with the Constitution to the extent that it did not allow a separate vote to be directly cast for his or her preferred political party.[29] The relevant election law provisions were thereby revised pursuant to the holding of the above Constitutional Court decision, and the one person two votes system has been part of the Korean election law for the election of the National Assembly and local legislature members and, so that each voter casts one vote for his or her preferred individual candidate for the election of the electoral district representatives and the other for his or her preferred political party for the election of proportional representatives. This has occurred since the 2004 general election that constituted the seventeenth National Assembly (2004–2008 term). The Constitutional Court decided the above case primarily on the ground that the presumption of the will and the intent of the voters indicated at the electoral district election for determining the voter preference over the political party for the proportional representation purposes, was in violation of the principles of direct voting and equality in voting.[30]

Recently, in February 2015, the National Election Commission of the Republic of Korea submitted its legislative opinion to the National Assembly concerning directions for election law revisions facing the upcoming general election to be held in April 2016 to constitute the twentieth National Assembly (to be in session in 2016–2020). It has suggested, *inter alia*, to increase the proportional representation seats, to sever the current nation-wide single district for proportional representation into six regional districts, and to allow the concurrent candidacy for electoral district election and the proportional representation election.

Expenses of public election and the trust money deposit system

Korean election law requires the deposit of trust money in order for a candidate to be properly registered at any public election, along with the submission of various information and documents concerning, for example, payment of property tax, military service or the exemption thereof, and criminal record (Article 49(4) of the Public Election Act).[31] The requirement of trust money deposits has been challenged on several occasions. In 1996, the Constitutional Court held that the election law's requirement of trust money deposit as one of the preconditions for registration as a candidate in public elections did not violate the Constitution, as such a deposit would serve as an advance payment to cover expenses for the official campaign bulletin and potential fines for violating election laws and regulations. As to the justifiable amount of trust money to be deposited, the Constitutional Court held that it should be determined by taking into account the characteristics of each type of public election and that it might be set at a fixed amount for each type of public election.[32] Relatedly, the Constitutional Court has held that requiring different amounts for party-nominated candidates and independent candidates with no party nomination would be unconstitutional.[33]

Under the current Korean election law, a candidate should deposit KW300 million for presidential election, and KW15 million for National Assembly election. The National Election Commission or its local offices should return the amount, pursuant to the schedule under the Public Election Act, within thirty days of the public election. The amount not refundable reverts to the government (Article 57(1) of the Public Election Act).[34] For national elections to elect the president and general election to elect members of the National Assembly, the amount in full is to be returned in cases where the candidate is elected, dies, or obtains 15 per cent or more of the valid votes; and one-half of the amount deposited is to be returned where the candidate obtains 10 per cent or more but less than 15 per cent of the valid votes.[35] For proportional representation elections, the amount in full is to be returned should anyone on the party list be elected as a proportional representative.[36]

Election campaign regulations

The election law of Korea takes the position that, in principle, anyone may freely conduct election campaign activities (Article 58(2) of the Public Election Act).[37] However, many statutory provisions specifically set forth detailed regulations and standards applicable to those who may conduct election campaign activities, and when and in which manner an individual may conduct election campaign activities (Articles 58, 59, 60, and subsequent provisions of the Act). Such a stance of the Korean election law may be traced back to Korea's unique experience under authoritarian rule prior to the adoption of the current Constitution.[38]

The Korean election law designates and regulates the election campaign period, or the time period during which the election campaign activities may be conducted (Articles 59 and 60-3 of the Public Election Act).[39] This connotes that election campaign activities are not permitted and thus are unlawful if conducted outside the designated election campaign period. The time period is currently set at twenty-three days for the presidential election and fourteen days for the general election and the local elections (Articles 33, 34, 59, and 60-3 of the Act). The Constitutional Court has held that the designation of an election campaign period is constitutional.[40] It has also held that the restriction of the time period for campaign activities under Korean election law is not unconstitutional as such restriction is necessary and reasonable in light of the legislative purpose, the degree and content of the restriction, and the actual practice of campaign activities conducted in Korea.[41]

As to the methods of election campaign activities, current election law contains regulations in considerable detail applicable to specific elements of election campaigning, including the specific format and contents of the election bulletin (Article 65 of the Public Election Act),[42] the posters (Article 64 of the Act), the banners (Article 67 of the Act), and the arm and chest bands (Article 68 of the Act); the specific format, size, and length of the newspaper advertisements (Article 69 of the Act), broadcast advertisements (Article 70 of the Act), candidates' speech through broadcast media (Articles 71 and 72 of the Act), broadcast of candidates' careers (Articles 73 and 74 of the Act), speeches and debates in public forum (Articles 79, 81, 82, 82-2, and 82-3 of the Act), advertisements via the Internet (Article 82-7 of the Act), election campaigns through information communication network (Article 82-4 of the Act), the Internet media's online bulletin users' real name verification (Article 82-6 of the Act), and the specific regulations and limits applicable to the use of the amplifiers (Article 91 of the Act). Most peculiarly, Article 109 of the Public Election Act[43] provides that nobody may conduct election campaign activities by way of transmitting letters, telegrams, facsimiles, or other means of electronic communication, unless permitted by the Act. As such, the expression of opinions and ideas in the public election context through various means of social network services might violate this provision, which has raised considerable concern from the freedom of expression perspective.

One statutory provision provides that a candidate may only transmit text messages as part of election campaign activity up to five times by using the number previously reported to and registered with the election commission; the candidate is exempted from the above restriction if he or she had posted a statement or transmitted an electronic mail via an Internet homepage or its bulletin board. The Constitutional Court has upheld this provision to be constitutional.[44] It has also held that, while excessive restrictions on who may conduct campaign activities are unconstitutional,[45] the ban preventing non-governmental organisations and other organisations with social causes from conducting election campaign activities is not unconstitutional.[46]

Conclusion

The Constitutional Court of the Republic of Korea since its establishment under the current Constitution of the Republic of Korea in 1988 has proactively reviewed the constitutionality of various aspects of public election law and the electoral process of Korea. Its decisions have far-reaching ramifications insofar as the body of the election law has moved in a more democratic direction and reinforced representative democracy in Korea. Such examples include the reforms ushered in by the decisions of the Constitutional Court on the electoral district apportionment and the proportional representation system, contributing to addressing and implementing in Korea such values, issues, and concerns as equality in public election and minority representation in the lawmaking institution and process.

On the other hand, while the election law of Korea has idiosyncratic grounds for regulating and restricting in detail various aspects of election campaign activities with stiff penalty and punishment, the Constitutional Court has been passive in reviewing the constitutionality of such statutory provisions. Such stance has been analysed to be part of the remaining vestiges of authoritarian regimes in the past, when the incumbent regimes intended to curb regime change through public election by ostensible campaign activities influenced by the government. This passive stance might chill and hinder the citizenry's active participation in the electoral process and the exercise of freedom of expression in the election context by voters. The Constitutional Court of Korea is thus urged to take a more proactive stance in reviewing the constitutionality of such provisions pertaining to election campaign activities in Korean public election law.

Notes

1 Constitutional Court Decision Issued December 19, 2014, 2013 Hun-Da 1 (Dissolution of a Political Party).
2 Article 1(1) of the Constitution of the Republic of Korea.
3 Constitutional Court Decision Issued April 20, 1995, 93 Hun-Ma 4 (*re* time period and method of public election campaign); Constitutional Court Decision Issued May 25, 1995, 95 Hun-Ma 105 (*re* election campaign by groups and legal persons); Constitutional Court Decision Issued July 21, 1995, 92 Hun-Ma 177 (*re* limiting publication or release of the result of election poll for a certain period preceding the election date). For analysis on such decisions, see Sung (2012) 6–36; Sung (2015) 156–260.
4 Law No. 13497, with the most recent revision effective August 13, 2015.
5 Political Fund Act, Law No. 11376, with the most recent revision effective February 29, 2012.
6 For a general understanding on Korea's proportional representation system in the Korean context and a comparative perspective, see Ka (2009); Yoon (2009); Yoon (2007); Ka *et al.* (2007); Kim and Shim (2002); Cho (2001); Farrell (2001); Park (2000); Ahn (2000); Ahn (1998); Ahn (1995); Chung and Shin (1994); Shin (1994).
7 Constitutional Court Decision Issued July 19, 2001, 2000 Hun-Ma 91 (Constitutional Complaint on the Constitutionality of Articles 56, 146(2), and 189 of the Public Election Act).
8 Article 67(3) of the Constitution of the Republic of Korea ('If and when there is only one presidential candidate, such candidate shall not be elected President unless he or she receives at least one-third of the total valid votes.').
9 Public Election Act (n. 4).
10 Constitutional Court Decision Issued February 25, 2010, 2008 Hun-Ma 324 (Constitutional Complaint on Constitutionality of Article 82-6(1) of the Public Election Act).
11 Constitutional Court Decision Issued August 23, 2012, 2010 Hun-Ma 47 (Constitutional Complaint on Constitutionality of Article 44-5(1) of the Act for Promotion of Information Communication Network and for Protection of Information, and of Articles 29 and 30(1) of the executive order thereof).
12 Public Election Act (n. 4).
13 Constitutional Court Decision Issued January 28, 1999, 97 Hun-Ma 253; Constitutional Court Decision Issued March 25, 1999, 97 Hun-Ma 99 (Constitutional Complaint on Constitutionality of Article 38(1) of the Public Election Act).
14 Constitutional Court Decision Issued June 28, 2007, 2004 Hun-Ma 644 (Constitutional Complaint on Constitutionality of Article 15(2) of the Public Election Act); Constitutional Court Decision Issued June 28, 2007, 2005 Hun-Ma 772 (Constitutional Complaint on Constitutionality of Article 38 of the Public Election Act).

15 Constitutional Court Decision Issued January 28, 2014, 2012 Hun-Ma 409 (Constitutional Complaint on Constitutionality of Article 18(1)(ii) of the Public Election Act). The Constitutional Court held that the provision remains applicable until December 31, 2015, with the mandate that the National Assembly should revise such provision in pursuance of the Constitutional Court decision by the above date. The National Assembly revised the provision at issue accordingly, which took effect on August 13, 2015.
16 Constitutional Court Decision Issued December 24, 1997, 97 Hun-Ma 16 (Constitutional Complaint on Constitutionality of Article 18(3) of the Public Election Act).
17 Article 24 of the Public Election Act (n. 4). For a historical account of applicable laws and debates for changes of electoral district apportionment for Korea's National Assembly, see Hwang (2002).
18 Ibid.
19 Public Election Act (n. 4).
20 Constitutional Court Decision Issued February 26, 2004, 2003 Hun-Ma 285.
21 Constitutional Court Decision Issued December 27, 1995, 95 Hun-Ma 224 (Constitutional Complaint on Constitutionality of Table 1 incorporated in the Public Election Act).
22 Constitutional Court Decision Issued October 25, 2001, 2000 Hun-Ma 92 (Constitutional Complaint on Constitutionality of Table 1 incorporated in the Public Election Act).
23 Constitutional Court Decision Issued October 30, 2014, 2012 Hun-Ma 190, 192, 211, 262, 325; 2013 Hun-Ma 781; 2014 Hun-Ma 53 (Consolidated) (Constitutional Complaint on Constitutionality of Electoral District Apportionment per Table 1 Attached to Article 25(2) of Public Election Act), published in the Constitutional Court Official Gazette No. 217, 1725 *et seq.*
24 Ibid.
25 Ibid.
26 Law No. 4739, March 16, 1994 (Repealed).
27 Public Election Act (n. 4).
28 Article 189 of the Public Election Act (n. 4).
29 Constitutional Court Decision Issued July 19, 2001, 2000 Hun-Ma 91 (Constitutional Complaint on the Constitutionality of Articles 56, 146(2), and 189 of the Public Election Act).
30 Ibid.
31 Public Election Act (n. 4).
32 Constitutional Court Decision Issued August 29, 1996, 95 Hun-Ma 108 (Constitutional Complaint on Constitutionality of Article 56 of the Public Election Act).
33 Constitutional Court Decision Issued September 8, 1989, 88 Hun-Ga 6 (Constitutionality Review on Article 33 of the (now repealed) National Assemblyperson Election Act); Constitutional Court Decision Issued November 27, 2008, 2007 Hun-Ma 1024 (Constitutional Complaint on Constitutionality of Article 56(1)(i) of the Public Election Act); Constitutional Court Decision Issued July 19, 2001, 2000 Hun-Ma 91.
34 Public Election Act (n. 4).
35 Ibid., Article 122-2(1)(i).
36 Ibid., Article 122-2(1)(ii).
37 Ibid.
38 Rhee (2012).
39 Public Election Act (n. 4).
40 Constitutional Court Decision Issued September 29, 2005, 2004 Hun-Ba 52 (Constitutional Complaint on Constitutionality of Article 59(1) of the Public Election Act).
41 Constitutional Court Decision Issued October 30, 2008, 2005 Hun-Ba 32; Constitutional Court Decision Issued August 30, 2001, 99 Hun-Ba 92.
42 Public Election Act (n. 4).

43 Ibid.
44 Constitutional Court Decision Issued June 24, 2010, 2008 Hun-Ba 169 (Constitutional Complaint on Constitutionality of Article 59(iii) of the Public Election Act).
45 Constitutional Court Decision Issued July 29, 1994, 94 Hun-Ga 4.
46 Constitutional Court Decision Issued May 25, 1995, 2005 Hun-Ma 105; Constitutional Court Decision Issued August 30, 2001, 2000 Hun-Ma 121.

References

Ahn K.W., 'Rule of Law and Minority Protection' (1995) 12 *Law and Society* 6.

Ahn S.C., *A Comparison of Electoral Systems: Institutional Impact and Political Influence* (Bobmun Sa Publishing Co. 2000).

Ahn W.K., 'Relationship between Electoral System and Political Party Structure in Korea' (1998) 7 *Korea North East Association Journal* 23.

Cho J.K., 'To Improve the Quality of Korean Democracy' (2001) 7(1) *Korean Journal of Legislative Studies* 6.

Chung Y.K. and Shin M.S., 'National District Proportional Representation System and National Assembly' (1994) Korean Legislative Studies Institute 1992–1993 Research Project Paper.

Farrell D.M., *Electoral Systems: A Comparative Introduction* (Palgrave Macmillan 2001).

Hwang A.R., 'Introduction of One Person Two Votes System in the 17th General Election' (2006) 12(2) *National Strategies* 61.

Hwang A.R., 'Suggestions for the National Assembly Electoral District Reform' in Youngjae Jin (ed.), *Election in Korea* (IV) (Korean Social Science Data Center 2002).

Ka S.J., 'A Comparative Study of Ideological Differences between Proportional Representatives and District Representatives' (2009) 14(1) *Legislative Studies* 109.

Ka S.J., Son B.K., Yoon J.B., and Choi J.Y., 'A Comparison of Characteristics and Outcome of Legislative Activities between Electoral District Representatives and Proportional Representatives in National Assembly' (2007) Korean Legislative Studies Institute Research Paper.

Kim M.G. and Shim J.Y., 'Strategic Intentions in Changes in Electoral System in Korea' (2002) 36(1) *Korean Political Science Association Journal* 139.

Park C.W., *Proportional Representation System* (Pakyoung Publishing Co. 2000).

Rhee W.Y., 'Constitutionalism and the Discussions for Constitutional Revision in the Republic of Korea, in the First Decade of the 21st Century', (2012) 42(1) *Hong Kong Law Journal* 43.

Shin M.S., 'A Critical Analysis of the National District Electoral System in Korea' (1994) 28(2) *Korean Political Science Association Journal* 239.

Sung N.I., 'Election System and Election Campaign' (2012) 130 *Justice (Korean Legal Center)* 6.

Sung N.I., *Constitutional Law* (15th edn, Bobmun Sa Publishing Co. 2015).

Yoon E., 'Analysis of the Gender Quota for Proportional Representation System in Korea' (2009) 11(2) *Korean Autonomous Local Government Society Journal* 69.

Yoon J.B., *Election and Democracy in Korea* (Jipmoondang 2007).

10 Judicial strategies to resolving presidential election disputes

The case of Taiwan

Wen-Chen Chang and Yi-Li Lee

Introduction

Direct presidential elections were adopted in Taiwan in the course of its democratic transition and constitutional reform in the 1990s. The first direct presidential election was held in 1996, and since then five presidential elections have taken place. In all of these five presidential elections, numerous legal and political charges were made between presidential candidates and challenges against election results took place as well. So far, since the first presidential election, there have been dozens of lawsuits brought to the courts for judicial resolution. These litigations include lawsuits against the validity of elections and the elected office, politically-charged civil and criminal suits, and litigation concerning the legality of presidential election regulations.

Most well-known was the gunshot incident that occurred one day before the presidential election in 2004 and the subsequent months-long protests staged by the losing candidate in the front of the presidential office. In addition, several civil and criminal defamation lawsuits were lodged before the courts while charges were made between presidential candidates and their campaigns during or after presidential elections. For example, the former President Chen Shui-bian as the 2000 presidential candidate launched criminal litigation against the spokesperson of James Soong's presidential campaign for defamation. Another example is James Soong, a vice presidential candidate of the *Pan-Blue* alliance[1] in the 2004 presidential election. He filed a civil defamation lawsuit against the former President Lee Teng-hui. Soong alleged that public statements of President Lee damaged his reputation. In addition to these civil or criminal lawsuits, public prosecutors – before or during the election – were often called upon to investigate and decide whether to prosecute the candidates who were alleged to have received inappropriate and even illegal donations.

This chapter is aimed at systematically examining these presidential election litigations and analysing the ways and the extent to which the courts have strategically dealt with these disputes. Apart from this Introduction and the Conclusion, this chapter is divided into three main sections. The next section explores the institutional dynamics of presidential elections since 1996. The third section examines presidential election lawsuits concerning the validity of the presidential elections and the elected offices, the decisions of election commissions in electoral regulations, civil and criminal defamation, and prosecutorial decisions. The fourth section analyses the judicial strategies that the courts have used to address the presidential disputes.

Against the backdrop of a highly politicised society, this chapter argues that judicial deference to the decisions of the Election Commission as well as the results of presidential elections is critical to the development of democratic politics and the maintenance of judicial integrity. To prevent political revenge, the courts may try to detach themselves from contentious politics and often do not intervene in criminal defamation disputes. Yet, it is interesting to note that the courts may become more actively involved in civil defamation litigation so as to safeguard the right of the individual's reputation.

Direct presidential election and democratic transition

When democratic transitions in Taiwan began in the late 1980s, several bold transitional measures towards political transformation were taken by the government. Not only were certain restrictions on demonstrations, free associations and media finally lifted, access to political offices was also opened to fair competition through elections.[2] The election for the presidency was no exception, and the first presidential election was held in 1996. In addition, the presidential powers were transformed through constitutional revisions during the periods of democratic transition. The presidency became the most powerful government institution that directed the development of the state. It was not difficult to predict that the confrontation among political parties in the presidential election had increasingly intensified as a result of this 'winner-takes-all' system.[3]

The adoption of a direct presidential election and presidential powers

After forty years of authoritarian rule by the Nationalist Party, Kuomintang (KMT), large-scale constitutional reforms were undertaken one after another in the early 1990s to open up legislative and presidential elections.[4] In the process of constitutional reforms, the establishment of a presidential system and the conduct of direct presidential elections were placed high on the constitutional reform agenda. Through numerous political negotiations among political parties, it finally took two rounds of constitutional revisions in 1992 and 1994 to provide for fully-fledged direct elections for the presidency.[5] The 1994 constitutional revision decided that the President and the Vice President shall be directly elected by the entire electorate in the free area of the Republic of China (ROC).[6] Later, the Legislative Yuan[7] passed the Presidential and Vice Presidential Election and Recall Act in August 1995.[8] The first direct presidential election was held in 1996, and since then five presidential elections have been held.

The powers and status of President have long been an issue of debate. Some argue that the President is placed under the 1947 ROC Constitution as the head of state under the parliamentary system[9] and only owns ceremonial powers.

These ceremonial powers include the power to issue and promulgate laws and regulations with the counter-signature of the President of the Executive Yuan[10] or to confer honours and decorations.[11] However, others assert that the ROC Constitution also provides the President with some substantial powers, such as serving as the Commander in Chief to command the armed forces,[12] declaring martial law with the approval of the Legislative Yuan,[13] appointing and removing civil and military officials,[14] and issuing emergency decrees subject to resolutions of the Executive Yuan.[15]

The debate over presidential powers became complicated during the era of the authoritarian regime. The powers of the President were expanded through the enactment and revisions of the 'Temporary Provisions Effective during the Period of National Mobilisation for Suppression of the Communist Rebellion' (Temporary Provisions) at the expense of the Executive Yuan, beyond the original design of the ROC Constitution.[16] As a result, two former Chiang presidents, Chiang Kai-shek and Chiang Ching-kuo, wielded unlimited powers in real politics without any checks.[17]

In the beginning of democratic transition in the early 1990s, the removal of the expanded presidential powers became the subject of debate. However, those powers not only went unrevoked, but were even codified and consolidated by the subsequent constitutional revisions.[18] For example, the 1994 constitutional revision not only provided that the President and Vice President should be directly elected by the people in Taiwan, but also removed the requirement of the Premier's counter-signature in the appointment of officials by the President and decisions to dissolve the Legislative Yuan.[19] In addition, the 1997 constitutional revision expanded the presidential powers again by removing the requirement of obtaining the Legislative Yuan's consent to the appointment of the Premier by the President.[20] Through those constitutional revisions, the presidency has become the most powerful government institution and the Premier has functionally become the Chief Executive Officer of the President.

Such expansion of presidential powers has also been confirmed by the Constitutional Court. For instance, the Court in *JY Interpretation No. 627* indicated that 'subject to the scope of his executive powers granted by the Constitution and the Amendments to the Constitution, the President is the highest executive officer and has a duty to preserve national security and national interests'.[21] It is evident that the President has become the Chief Executive through the incremental constitutional change.

Confrontational presidential elections

To date, there have been five presidential elections since 1996. These elections were held in different political contexts. The first and second presidential elections in 1996 and 2000 were held over the course of Taiwan's democratic transition. The other three elections after 2000 were held during a period of divided politics in which intensive political competition between two major political alliances led to serious confrontations.

Presidential elections in the context of democratic transition

The first presidential election was held over the course of the political transition and political fragmentation within the ruling party, KMT. After severe political struggles between *Mainstream Factions* and *Non-Mainstream Factions* within the KMT,[22] President Lee Teng-Hui as the leader of *Mainstream Factions* successfully consolidated his power and secured control over the party. With the support of the KMT, President Lee won the nomination of the KMT for the presidency. He chose Premier Lien Chan as his running mate. In addition, there were three other tickets in this presidential race. Due to the split within the KMT, a few political figures from the *Non-Mainstream Factions* left and established the New Party. With the endorsement of the New Party, Lin Yang-kang and Hau Pei-tsun, who were Vice Presidents of the KMT and had a close relationship with *Non-Mainstream Factions*, decided to run for election independently. In addition, Chen Li-an, who was the former President of the Control Yuan,[23] also left the KMT to be an independent presidential candidate. Wang Ching-feng, a former member of the Control Yuan, served as his running mate.

To compete with the KMT for the presidency, the opposition party Democratic Progressive Party (DPP) nominated former Professor of National Taiwan University Department of Political Science Peng Ming-min, a long-time political dissident in exile and the pioneer of the Taiwanese Independent Movement, as the presidential candidate after two rounds of primary elections within the party.[24] The DPP member of the Legislative Yuan, Frank Hsieh, was his running mate.

The political temperature became increasingly intense during the 1996 presidential campaign. To nip the growth of Taiwan nationalism, the People's Republic of China in the mainland attempted to use intimidation tactics to interfere with the election.[25] The US government dispatched one fleet to respond to this threat across the Taiwan Strait. Amidst these tensions, the first direct presidential election was held on March 23, 1996, wherein President Lee Teng-hui and Premier Lien Chan defeated other political campaigns and won by a landslide victory.[26]

The second direct presidential election was held on March 18, 2000. There were five teams in this election. Similar to the first presidential election, the KMT faced an internal split over the choice of its presidential candidate. In the presidential election year, the incumbent governor James Soong of Taiwan Province attempted to win the KMT's nomination to run the presidential election.[27] However, the KMT led by President Lee Teng-hui did not support James Soong but instead supported Vice President Lien Chan. Lien was finally nominated as the presidential candidate of the KMT, with Premier Vincent Siew as his running mate. Soong eventually left the KMT and ran the presidential election as an independent. He picked a physician, Chang Chao-hsiung, as his running mate.[28]

Similar to the KMT, the opposition party DPP also faced a split in the process of nomination. The former DPP chairperson Hsu Hsin-liang and the former mayor of Taipei City Chen Shui-bian competed with each other for the nomination. The DPP finally nominated Chen Shui-bian as its presidential candidate, and Chen chose the former magistrate of Taoyuan County and long-time advocate for women rights, Annette Lu, as his vice presidential running mate. Disappointed with the DPP, Hsu Hsin-liang announced his decision to leave the party and run for the presidency independently. He finally selected the female legislator of the New Party, Chu Hui-liang, as his running mate. In addition, the New Party nominated Li Ao as its presidential candidate and selected Fung Hu-hsiang as the vice presidential candidate.[29]

As a result of these political splits, Chen defeated other political opponents and won the presidency in the 2000 election with only 39.30 per cent of the popular vote.[30] This election marked the first peaceful transfer of government power from the KMT that had ruled Taiwan for more than half a century, to the long-time opposition party.[31] As a consequence of losing the election, President Lee Teng-hui resigned as chairperson of the KMT under pressure. After leaving the KMT, he formed a new party, the Taiwan Solidarity Union. After losing the presidential election, James Soong formed a new political party, the People First Party (PFP), and collaborated with the KMT against the new ruling party, DPP.[32]

Presidential elections in the context of divided politics

Although the KMT lost the presidency in 2000, it still retained a strong majority in the legislature. Since the political branches of government were controlled by two different political campaigns, the *Pan-Green* (the DPP and its alliance party, Taiwan Solidarity Union) and the *Pan-Blue* (the KMT and the PFP), partisan confrontations became increasingly intensified. The phenomenon of divided-government politics emerged and continued even after the presidential and parliamentary elections in 2004.

In order to win the 2004 presidential election, the *Pan-Blue* campaign decided to cooperate for one unified ticket. In late March 2003, the Chairman of the KMT, Lien Chan, and the Chairman of the PFP, James Soong, were nominated as the presidential candidate and vice presidential candidate to run the election.[33] The third direct presidential election was held on March 20, 2004. It was the first election in Taiwan with only two teams in the presidential race.

After two days of the passage of Referendum Act in December 2003, President Chen Shui-bian launched the first two referendum proposals. The first proposal advocated for the acquisition of anti-missile weaponry to strengthen Taiwan's self-defence capabilities. The second proposal advocated for negotiations with the People's Republic of China on the basis of parity with the aim of establishing a peace and stability framework for cross-strait interactions.[34] One day before the election, an unexpected gunshot incident concerning President Chen and Vice President Lu occurred. Chen and Lu won against the challengers Lien and Soong, who rejected the election result. Neither referendum proposal mentioned above was passed since the turnout of the referendum did not meet the required threshold.[35] The supporters of the *Pan-Blue* campaign staged months-long protests in front of the presidential office, and two lawsuits challenging the result and validity of the election were launched. Amidst the political and legal turmoil, the Central Election Commission announced that DPP President Chen Shui-bian won the election by a slim victory.[36] Both the result and validity of this contentious election were eventually upheld and confirmed by the two decisions of the Supreme Court, discussed below.

Following this controversial election, the political division between the *Pan-Blue* and the *Pan-Green* widened. Massive demonstrations and protests against Chen were fuelled by the allegations arising from the gunshot incident. Since early 2006, allegations of corruption against Chen and his family also emerged one after another, which triggered even more political confrontations and constitutional disputes.[37]

Amidst such political turmoil, the next presidential election drew close. Two groups of candidates ran in this election. After a relatively competitive nomination process, the former Premier Frank Hsieh and Premier Su Tseng-chang won the DPP presidential primary in early 2007. In the meantime, the former Mayor of Taipei, Ma Ying-jeou, was nominated to be the presidential candidate by the KMT in 2007. The fourth presidential election was held in January 2008. Along with the presidential election, two referendum proposals were initiated by the ruling party, the DPP, and the opposition party, the KMT. The proposal submitted by the DPP concerned whether the government should seek United Nations membership under the name 'Taiwan'. The counter-proposal of the KMT was for Taiwan to rejoin the United Nations and participate in other international organisations under the name 'Republic of China', 'Taiwan' or any other name that upholds successful and national dignity.[38] Eventually, the DPP's presidential ticket lost the election. Ma Ying-jeou won a landslide victory in the 2008 election. However, both referendum proposals failed because of low voter turnout rate.[39]

The fifth direct presidential election was held on January 14, 2012. Three teams of candidates participated in this election. In 2011, President Ma Ying-jeou was seeking re-election for his second term and won the KMT nomination. Premier Wu Den-yih was selected as President Ma's running mate. The same year, DPP Chairwoman Tsai Ing-wen was nominated as the presidential candidate after winning the selection process. She chose the Secretary of the DPP, Su Jia-chyuan, as her running mate. The chairperson of the PFP, James Soong, decided to run for the presidency again and picked Professor Lin Ruey-shiung to be his vice presidential candidate. After a highly competitive campaign, President Ma Ying-jeou was re-elected[40] (Table 10.1 illustrates the candidates and the turnout of five presidential elections since 1996.)

Presidential election disputes since 1996

Taiwan held its first direct presidential election in 1996, and since then there have been five presidential elections. As illustrated above, these presidential elections were held against the backdrop of transitional and divided politics, leading to political contentions and even lawsuits. So far, since the first presidential election, there have been dozens of lawsuits relating to these presidential

Table 10.1 Candidates and turnout of five presidential elections since 1996

Year	*Presidential and vice presidential candidates/party*	*Votes*	*Percentage*
1996	Lee Teng-Hui Lien Chan/KMT (elected)	5,813,699	54.00
	Peng Ming-min, Frank Hsieh/DPP	2,274,586	21.12
	Lin Yang-kang, Hau Pei-tsun/Independents	1,603,790	14.90
	Chen Li-an, Wang Ching-feng/Independents	1,074,044	9.98
2000	Chen Shui-bian, Annette Lu/DPP (elected)	4,977,697	39.30
	James Soong, Chang Chao-hsiung/Independents	4,664,972	36.84
	Lien Chan, Vincent Siew/KMT	2,925,513	23.10
	Hsu Hsin-liang, Chu Hui-liang/Independents	79,429	0.63
	Li Ao, Fung Hu-hsiang/New Party	16,782	0.13
2004	Chen Shui-bian, Annette Lu/DPP (elected)	6,471,970	50.11
	Lien Chan, James Soong/KMT	6,442,452	49.89
2008	Ma Ying-jeou, Vincent Siew/KMT (elected)	7,659,014	58.45
	Frank Hsieh, Su Tseng-chang/DPP	5,444,949	41.55
2012	Ma Ying-jeou, Wu Den-yih/KMT (elected)	6,891,139	51.60
	Tsai Ing-wen, Su Jia-chyuan/DPP	6,093,578	45.63
	James Soong, Lin Ruey-shiung/PFP	369,588	2.77

Sources: authors.

elections. These litigations include lawsuits against the validity of elections and elected offices, politically charged civil and criminal suits, and litigation concerning the legality of presidential election regulations.

Litigation against the validity of elections and elected offices

According to the Presidential and Vice Presidential Election and Recall Act, there are two types of electoral litigation: litigation against the validity of elections and litigation against the elected office.

With regard to litigation against the validity of a presidential election, wherein the conduct of the Election Commission illegally affects the election result in question, the candidate or the prosecutor may file a lawsuit against the Election Commission within fifteen days after the official announcement of the election results. With regard to the lawsuit against the elected office, if an electee has been involved in any violent or illegal action during the election, or the number of votes that the electee allegedly gained is false, the other candidate, the prosecutor and the Election Commission can initiate a lawsuit against the elected office within thirty days after the public release of the impugned results.

Article 110 of the Presidential and Vice Presidential Election and Recall Act provides that the jurisdiction over presidential elections and recall lawsuits is exclusively vested with the High Court, which is located in the same city as the central government. There are only two tiers of review provided – one with the High Court and the other with the Supreme Court – each of which must be concluded within six months.

To date, two lawsuits against the validity of elections and two lawsuits against the elected offices have been instituted. Among these lawsuits, the two commenced by the *Pan-Blue* campaign after the 2004 presidential election are most well known.

2004 election disputes and litigations

BACKGROUND

As mentioned above, several controversies surrounded the 2004 presidential election. One dispute was concerned with the legality of holding the referendum along with the presidential election. Upon the passage of the Referendum Act in December 2003, President Chen Shui-bian launched two referendum proposals, and the Executive Yuan decided to hold the referendum along with the upcoming presidential election in 2004.[41] The method to take and cast ballots was also decided: when entering the polling station, the voters would first cast their vote in the referendum ballot and then cast their vote in the presidential election ballot. The *Plan-Blue* campaign condemned the holding of referendum along with the presidential election as a manipulative decision by President Chen to boost the votes to his election advantage.[42] They also questioned the sequence of casting the referendum ballot first and then the presidential ballot, because they believed that President Chen's supporters were more likely to vote for the referendum, and this voting arrangement would violate the principle of secret ballot, since it might reveal who had voted for President Chen and who had not.

In addition to the dispute on the referendum, an unexpected gun shooting incident gave rise to other controversies. Before the election day, President Chen Shui-bian and Vice President Annette Lu were shot during their last campaign rally. Because of the gun shooting, President Chen launched a national security protocol, and ordered 200,000 military and police personnel to uphold national security and be on emergency alert.[43] After the polls closed, President Chen won the re-election by a very narrow margin. Yet, the referendum proposals failed due to the low voter turnout rate.

However, after the results were announced, the *Pan-Blue* campaign refused to accept the election result and challenged the election. The campaign requested a vote recount of all ballots cast. In the end, the Central Election Commission conducted a recount and confirmed President Chen's narrow victory. However, the *Pan-Blue* campaign rejected this result and decided to launch two lawsuits in the High Court. One lawsuit challenged the validity of the presidential election and the other challenged the validity of elected office.[44] During the litigation, both parties agreed to recount the election ballots once again. In order to preserve the evidence, the High Court ordered all ballot boxes to be sealed.[45]

LITIGATION TO INVALIDATE THE PRESIDENTIAL ELECTION

The first lawsuit filed by the *Pan-Blue* campaign to the High Court was to challenge the validity of the presidential election. The defendant was the electoral commission in charge of election administration. Four issues were raised before the Court. They included: (1) whether the holding of a referendum alongside the 2004 presidential election was in violation of Article 17 of the Referendum Act, (2) whether the requirement of casting the referendum ballot first followed by the presidential election ballot exposed voters' preferences and thus violated the principle of a secret ballot, (3) whether the decision of the Central Election Commission not to revoke the election after the March 19 gunshot incident was illegal and (4) whether the Election Commission was grossly negligent in administrating the election.[46] On January 25, 2005, the High Court rendered the decision, dismissing all of the claims alleged by the *Pan-Blue* campaign.[47]

With regard to the above issues, the Court held that the power to decide whether a referendum should be held belonged to the Executive Yuan. The Central Election Commission only had the power to implement this decision under the supervision of the Executive Yuan. In addition, Article 17 of the Referendum Act allows the President to initiate the so-called 'defensive referendum' with a resolution from the Executive Yuan. The Election Commission had no power to review this decision. Holding the so-called 'defensive referendum' together with the presidential election was an appropriate means to save time and resources, which was consistent with Article 19 of the Referendum Act.[48]

Although the *Pan-Blue* plaintiff claimed that the initiation of the referendum was a manipulative strategy to boost the votes for the Chen campaign, it was hard to prove that the procedure to cast the referendum ballot had any tangible impact on the voters' will to cast the presidential ballot. Furthermore, since the two campaigns had never requested to postpone the election or change the date to vote after the gunshot incident, the Central Election Commission had no discretionary power to decide whether to suspend the election.[49] The decision to launch the national security protocol did not prevent the military soldiers from casting their vote, and there was no evidence that the national security mechanism increased the number of military and police personnel on duty and had any impact on the result of the election in favour of Chen's campaign.[50] In addition, the polling stations' design of a U-shaped queue that directed the voters to take the referendum ballot first and then the presidential election ballot did not actually reveal whether or not the voters would vote for President Chen and thus did not violate the principle of secret ballot. The final result of recount found 3,000 invalid ballots, but the number of disputed ballots did not change the election result.[51]

The High Court thus rejected the suit of Lien and Soong, who immediately appealed to the Supreme Court. The Supreme Court confirmed the ruling of the High Court. In its judgment, the Supreme Court not only validated the total recount of the national vote ordered by the High Court, but also held that the holding of the referendum along with the election did not violate the principle of secret ballot and that the implementation of the national security mechanism had no influence on the election.[52]

LAWSUIT TO INVALIDATE ELECTED OFFICE

As mentioned above, the *Pan-Blue* campaign also filed a lawsuit challenging the validity of elected office, namely, the elected status of the candidates who won the election. Four issues were raised before the Court. The key issues were whether the ballots in favour of Chen's ticket were miscounted and whether the number of invalid ballots was unusually high. Other issues were quite similar to those that arose in the lawsuit against the validity of the election: whether the alleged assassination attempt on President Chen was credible, and whether holding the referendum in tandem with the presidential election was illegal. The *Pan-Blue* campaign alleged that the gunshot incident was an instance of electoral fraud, and was designed to boost the votes for the Chen campaign, and thus illegally influenced the voters' choice. The national emergency declaration which President Chen subsequently issued was also alleged to have impacted the voter turnout in favour of the Chen campaign.[53] The High Court rendered its judgment on November 4, 2004, and rejected all claims made by the *Pan-Blue* campaign.

With regard to the first issue, the *Pan-Blue* campaign asserted that the Election Commission miscounted the ballots and requested that the Court apply its criteria to recount the ballots and exclude those disputed ballots in favour of President Chen. However, the Court rejected such assertion as the Presidential and Vice Presidential Election and Recall Act did not sanction the suggested criteria to recount the ballots as raised by the *Pan-Blue* campaign. After the recount, the campaign of Chen and Lu won with only a 25,563 vote margin. The original margin was reported as 29,518. The Court reasoned that the result of the recount did not have any impact on the election.[54] In response to the second issue, the Court indicated that even though the presidential decision to hold the defensive referendum with the election did not meet the requirements of Article 17 of the Referendum, it did not constitute a threat, violence or any other illegal means that forced the voters to vote against their free will.[55]

In addition, the conclusion of the forensic analysis report by Henry Lee, a well-known forensic expert hired by the government at the request of the defendant, indicated that the gunshot incident was impossible to be staged in advance. It was insufficient to prove that the gunshot illegally interfered with the election since no voters were forced to cast their ballots against their free will. There was no evidence that proved that the campaign of Chen and Lu improperly manipulated this incident to influence the election.[56] Finally, several military personnel and heads of police departments also testified that the national security mechanism implemented following the gunshot incident did not hinder military soldiers' or the police forces' ability to vote.[57] The High Court overruled the suit of Lien and Soong, who appealed to the Supreme Court. But the Supreme Court also confirmed the original ruling of the High Court.[58]

Other election lawsuits

After the 2000 presidential election, a lawsuit was launched to challenge the status of the winning candidates, Chen and Lu, on the ground that both Chen and Lu had been sentenced for libel and sedition during the authoritarian era. However, the High Court ruled that the challenger lacked the standing to sue as the Act regulating Presidential and Vice Presidential Election permitted only the prosecutor or the candidates themselves to launch the litigation against the status of the winning candidates.[59] After the 2012 presidential election, a lawsuit that questioned the validity of the presidential election was also brought before the Court. Similarly, as the challenger against the election result had to be prosecutors or the candidates themselves, this case was dismissed due to the fact that the litigant was neither the prosecutor nor a candidate.[60]

Litigation regarding presidential election regulation

In Taiwan, the Central Election Commission was created in 1980 after the passage of the Public Officials Election and Recall Act. The powers of the Commission include: to make the plans for the elections and recalls, to examine candidates' qualifications, to supervise and inspect the elections and recalls, to establish and manage polling stations and ballot counting stations and, finally, to examine and confirm election results. In addition, the Central Election Commission was also responsible for prescribing the measures governing campaign propaganda or activities of political parties via television or other broadcast media.[61]

To avoid electoral fraud, Article 2 of the Act on Property-Declaration by Public Servants provides that the presidential and vice presidential candidates and candidates who run for county (city) election should declare their properties when they register to run. In 2000, the vice presidential candidate Feng Hu-hsiang of the New Party refused to make such a declaration. Pursuant to the aforementioned Act, the Central Election Commission fined him NT$300,000. He then filed a suit to the High Administrative Court. However, the Supreme Administrative Court dismissed his claims.[62]

During the campaign period, polling reports are allowed on television and radio stations. To secure the fairness of elections, the former Article 47 of Presidential and Vice Presidential Election and Recall Act prohibited individuals, political parties and organisations from releasing opinion polls on the election through any means, and also prohibited the reporting of such poll results in the last ten days of campaigning. In March 2000, the Chinese Television Company broadcast the result of an opinion poll on the eve before the polling day. The Central Election Commission subsequently fined the company NT$500,000. The Chinese Television Company brought a lawsuit against the Election Commission. The Supreme Administrative Court however found in favour of the Election Commission.[63]

A similar case occurred during the 2004 presidential election. On March 17, 2004, the Formosa TV Company broadcast a political advertisement of the Chen campaign on Election Day. The Central Election Commission decided to fine the company NT$500,000. The Formosa TV Company opposed this decision and filed a suit against the Election Commission. The Supreme Administrative Court also dismissed this lawsuit.[64]

Civil and criminal defamation lawsuits

In Taiwan, Article 11 of the Constitution guarantees the freedom of speech. This freedom is essential for nurturing diversity in a democratic society. At the same time, however, reputation is also regarded as a fundamental right and is an aspect of human dignity, against which the freedom of expression must be balanced.[65] In light of these two conflicting rights, the civil and criminal law of defamation has – perhaps not surprisingly – become the centre of litigation in the course of these presidential election campaigns.[66] In all of the five presidential elections discussed in this chapter, numerous defamation charges were lodged between presidential candidates and their respective campaigns. As expected, these disputes came before the courts for final resolution.

Criminal defamation lawsuits

During the 2000 presidential election, a member of the Taipei City Council from the New Party, Li Qing-yuan, who had published a book, held a press conference to accuse Chen Shui-bian, the presidential candidate of DPP, of having extra-marital affairs.[67] Chen Shui-bian and his wife filed a civil and criminal defamation lawsuit against this member of the Taipei City Council.

The court in this criminal defamation decision used the standard developed by the Constitutional Court in *JY Interpretation No. 509*. In this interpretation, the Constitutional Court stated:

> Article 310, the first sentence of Paragraph 3, of the Criminal Code … prescribes the elements of a defence; that is, a perpetrator who originated or circulated a defamatory statement may be found not guilty of criminal defamation, if the statement is true. Nevertheless, it does not imply that the accused must carry the burden of proof that the defamatory statement is in fact a truthful statement. In the case where the accused has no way of showing the truthfulness of the statement, the court must find the accused not guilty when the evidence proffered for the court's review shows that the accused has reasonable grounds to believe that the statement was true at the moment of dissemination.[68]

The Constitutional Court narrowly construed criminal defamation to exclude those who failed to demonstrate the truth of a defamatory statement but nevertheless had reasonable grounds to believe that the statement was true with evidence to support their belief. It also emphasised that prosecutors should carry the burden of proof to demonstrate that there was any intention on the part of the accused.[69] In other words, if the accused had offered evidence to support the veracity of the distributed speech, even though he neglected to check the facts, the accused still lacked intention to disseminate defamatory speech.

Based upon such a constitutional standard, the court in Chen's defamation case ruled that the rumours about extra-marital affairs were already known to the media and thus were not fabricated by the member of the Taipei City Council himself. Hence, the act to publish such facts by the member of the Taipei City Council lacked the requisite intent and did not constitute defamation.[70]

In addition, during the 2000 election, the presidential candidate of DPP, Chen Shui-bian, also filed another criminal defamation lawsuit against Qiu Yi, the spokesman of the independent candidate James Soong. During the campaign period, Qiu Yi held a press conference accusing Chen of being improperly involved in the transaction of stocks, alleging that the accumulation of Chen's property was illegal. Chen Shui-bian filed a lawsuit against Qiu Yi. He claimed that Qiu Yi wilfully spread false and unverifiable information, which had produced negative effects to his campaign, and argued that this act constituted defamation.[71]

The court again referred to the constitutional standard developed in *JY Interpretation No. 509*. It reasoned that if the speech of the accused related to matters of public interest, and, based on the evidence available to him, there was a reasonable ground for the accused to believe that the statements were true, such acts would not constitute defamation. Since the defendant had difficulty verifying the transaction of stocks and the amount of funds held by the plaintiff, Chen Shui-bian, the Court held that the defendant had no intent to spread false facts and his actions did not amount to defamation. Furthermore, the integrity of the presidential candidate was a matter of public interest. While the defendant had reasonable grounds to believe that the facts he reported were true, he did not have the requisite intent and no defamation was established.[72]

Civil defamation lawsuits

The contentious nature of Taiwan's presidential election has led to numerous legal and political charges made between competing presidential candidates, their relatives, the members of the presidential campaigns and other public figures. Dozens of civil defamation lawsuits have been filed before the courts. These civil defamations lawsuits can be categorised into five types according to the identity of the plaintiffs and defendants. These five types include: (1) lawsuits by a candidate against others, (2) lawsuits by relatives of the candidates against members of other presidential campaigns, (3) lawsuits by relatives of the candidates against others, (4) lawsuits by the members of a presidential campaign against others, (5) lawsuits by other public figures.

LAWSUITS BY A CANDIDATE AGAINST OTHERS

As mentioned above, in the 2000 presidential election, a member of the Taipei City Council, Li Qing-yuan, accused Chen Shui-bian of having extra-marital affairs. Chen filed both civil and criminal defamation lawsuits against Li. Although Li was cleared of any criminal wrongdoing, he was nevertheless found liable by the civil court for damaging Chen's reputation. The civil court ruled that Li was negligent in verifying the facts and thus damaged Chen's reputation, and even ordered Li to publish an apology in the main newspapers for one day.[73]

After the 2004 presidential election, the vice presidential candidate of the joint ticket from KMT and PFP, James Soong, filed a civil defamation suit against former President Lee Teng-hui, who had alleged that Soong was playing mahjong while his supporters were protesting in front of the presidential office in November 2005. The civil court ruled that former President Lee could not prove that the facts he stated were true and had not verified the facts. Since his statement was beyond the protection of fair comment, former President Lee had to bear tortious liability.[74]

LAWSUITS BY RELATIVES OF THE CANDIDATES AGAINST MEMBERS OF OTHER PRESIDENTIAL CAMPAIGNS

During the period of the 2003 election year, the DPP lawmaker Tuan Yi-kang held a press conference to accuse Lien Chan, the KMT Chairman, of illegally helping his daughter to evade NT$400 million in taxes, and the tax authorities launched a probe into the alleged tax evasion by Lien's daughter. Lien Hui-hsin, the daughter of Lien Chan, brought a civil lawsuit against the allegations made by DPP lawmaker Tuan Yi-kang. The court found that the investigation of the tax authority had nothing to do with the alleged tax evasion. The court confirmed

Table 10.2 Information about lawsuits by a candidate against others

Election year	*Plaintiff*	*Defendant*	*Time to sue*	*The final judicial decision*	*Result of lawsuit*
2000	Chen Shui-bian	Li QingYuan	2005	April 18, 2012	Chen Shui-bian won the lawsuit
2004	James Soong	Lee Teng-hui	2005	April 19, 2007	James Soong won the lawsuit

Sources: authors.

Table 10.3 Information about lawsuits by relatives of the candidates against the members of another presidential campaign

Election year	*Plaintiff*	*Defendant*	*Time to sue*	*The final judicial decision*	*Result of lawsuit*
2004	Lien Hui-hsin	Tuan Yi-kang	March 2004	August 16, 2007	Lien Hui-hsin won the lawsuit

Sources: authors.

that the statement made by DPP lawmaker Tuan Yi-kang improperly attacked the reputation of Ms Lien and ordered DPP lawmaker Tuan Yi-kang to publish an apology in the main newspapers for one day.[75]

LAWSUITS BY RELATIVES OF THE CANDIDATES AGAINST OTHERS

In the 2008 presidential election, the vice director of the Taiwan Society North, Chang Chi-tien, publicly mentioned during the DPP presidential campaign that the then first lady Mei-ching Chow stole newspapers at the Harvard-Yenching University Library when she stayed at Harvard. Chow Mei-ching then filed a civil defamation suit against Chang, claiming that her reputation was damaged. The civil court ordered Chang to publish an apology in the main newspapers for one day and to compensate NT$600,000 to the first lady.[76]

LAWSUITS BY THE MEMBERS OF A PRESIDENTIAL CAMPAIGN AGAINST OTHERS

During the 2012 presidential election, the Executive Director of President Ma's campaign, King Pu-tsun, alleged that the statement of a spokeswoman Kang Yu-cheng of the DPP at a public conference implied that he was a male chauvinist, and that he had lied that President Ma had ever met the Cabinet Secretariat of Japan Shinzō Abe during his visit to Japan. Arguing that such a statement damaged his reputation, King filed a defamation lawsuit against Kang in 2011. The Supreme Court, however, did not rule in favour of King since the statement made by the defendant Kang was an appropriate comment, and that there was no evidence to show that the defendant had the intention or was negligent in attacking the reputation of King.[77]

Table 10.4 Information about lawsuits by relatives of the candidates against others

Election year	*Plaintiff*	*Defendant*	*Time to sue*	*The final judicial decision*	*Result of lawsuit*
2004	Chow Mei-ching	Chang Chi-tien	2009	July 30, 2010	Chow Mei-ching won the lawsuit

Sources: authors.

Table 10.5 Information about lawsuits by the members of a presidential campaign against others

Election year	*Plaintiff*	*Defendant*	*Time to sue*	*The final judicial decision*	*Result of lawsuit*
2004	King Pu-tsun	Kang Yu-cheng	2011	April 30, 2015	King Pu-tsun lost the lawsuit

Sources: authors.

LAWSUITS BY OTHER PUBLIC FIGURES

Sometimes, civil defamation lawsuits were not brought by presidential candidates, their relatives or members directly involved in the campaign, but by other public figures who were active in the political arena. For example, after the 2000 presidential election, the former New Party lawmaker, Hsieh Chi-ta, held a press conference to claim that Tseng Wen-hui, the wife of former President Lee Teng-hui, had attempted to flee to New York and accused Tseng of bringing dozens of suitcases stuffed with money to the United States. Tseng Wen-hui filed a civil lawsuit against Hsieh Chi-ta. The civil court held that there was no evidence for Hsieh to believe that the facts were true, and thus Hsieh's statement constituted an attack on the reputation of Tseng. The court also ordered Hsieh to publish an apology statement in the main newspapers for one day, and declare that his accusation made against Tseng after the 2000 presidential election was not true and that she had apologised to Tseng.[78]

The sexual orientation of DPP chairwoman Tsai Ing-wen became an issue during the 2012 election. The former chairperson Su Tseng-chang launched a lawsuit against a political commentator, Jerry Fan, demanding a public apology and compensation for his damaged reputation. This commentator stated on a talk show that Su questioned Tsai's sexual orientation, but Su rejected that he had ever made such a statement and argued that such a fabrication made by Fan seriously damaged his reputation. The High Court, however, did not rule in favour of Su as it reasoned that Fang's view represented one perspective among many, and was not defamatory.[79]

In the same presidential election year, the former Prime Minister Frank Hsieh in the DPP presidential campaign criticised the poor performance of President Ma. A political commentator, Qiu Yi, argued on a talk show that the statement of Frank Hsieh was peppered with the use of indecent words. Hsieh denied such a statement, arguing that the commentator had distorted his statement and attacked his reputation. Hsieh filed a civil lawsuit against this commentator. The High Court ruled that the commentator should pay NT$300,000 to Hsieh as compensation.[80]

Table 10.6 Information about lawsuits by others against others

Election year	*Plaintiff*	*Defendant*	*Time to sue*	*The final judicial decision*	*Result of lawsuit*
2000	Tseng Wen-hui	Hsieh Chi-ta	2001	May 6, 2010	Tseng Wen-hui won the lawsuit
2012	Su Tseng-chang	Jerry Fan	2011	January 22, 2015	Su Tseng-chang lost the lawsuit
2012	Frank Hsieh	Qiu Yi	2011	August 13, 2013 (High Court)	Frank Hsieh lost the lawsuit

Sources: authors.

Prosecutorial decisions

In highly competitive elections, the candidates and their campaigns are often alleged to have received inappropriate donations or even to have been involved in illegal investments. In such a case, public prosecutors may be required to initiate investigations into the allegation and to decide whether or not to prosecute the candidates. Until now, in Taiwan, three well-known cases of such nature have occurred before or during presidential elections.

In the 2000 presidential election, a KMT legislator accused the independent candidate, James Soong, of being involved in irregular money transactions. The legislator alleged that Soong transferred over NT$100 million to an account under the name of his son at the Chung Hsing Bills Finance Corporation and questioned the sources of the funds. In addition, the legislator also alleged that another questionable sum of NT$116 million was deposited in the account of Soong's son. Soong explained that these funds were transferred under the instruction of President Lee to provide financial aid for ex-President Chiang Ching-kuo's family and for other tasks. However, President Lee denied that he gave such instructions. The KMT also alleged that Soong embezzled party assets while he served as the party secretary. In response, the prosecutor launched an investigation into Soong's campaign in December 1999. It became known as the 'Chung Hsing Bills Finance Corporation scandal'. After a year of investigation, the prosecutor dropped embezzlement charges against Soong in January 2001 due to the absence of substantial evidence.[81]

The second example is the case of Fubon Bank's acquisition of Taipei Bank. When Ma Ying-jeou was the Mayor of Taipei City, the relationship between Ma and big corporations was questioned by the *Pan-Green* opposition party. While the proposal to merge Taipei Bank with Fubon Bank was discussed, a *Pan-Green* Taipei City councillor alleged that Ma attended five luxurious banquets held by Fubon Group in its guesthouse. Since this acquisition was at a suspiciously low price, Ma was accused of illegally favouring the Fubon Bank. When Ma was nominated as the KMT presidential candidate in 2007, this case re-emerged as a hot topic during the election. After several rounds of investigation, the prosecutor eventually dropped all charges against Ma in 2009.[82]

The third well-known example is the case of Yu Chang Biologics. In 2007, Tsai Ing-wen was invited to be the chairperson of the Yu Chang Company by several scientists who persuaded Tsai that her expertise in negotiation and fund-raising would help the company. In 2011, when Tsai Ing-wen was nominated as the DPP candidate for the presidential election, she was accused of improper involvement in the Yu Chang Biologics Company. It was alleged that Tsai's family received improper benefits from the company, and that she violated the law regulating conflict of interests upon leaving her cabinet office as Deputy Premier. After several months of investigation, the prosecutor dropped all charges against Tsai in August 2012.[83]

Judicial strategies to resolve presidential election litigations

Globally, national courts may strategically respond to electoral disputes against the backdrop of partisan politics and serious political confrontations. The most prominent example is *Bush* v. *Gore*, in which the US Supreme Court was called upon to adjudicate the vote-counting controversy between the Bush and Gore campaigns in the 2000 presidential election.[84] Strategic judicial responses to electoral disputes have also occurred in Taiwan. A close scrutiny of courts' decisions within the context of divided politics reveals four main strategies adopted by the judges in dealing with the above-mentioned election disputes.

Upholding election results

Partisan politics can occasionally provide courts with the opportunity to decide on the results of an election. Highly charged political controversies challenge and test the strength of state institutions, including the courts. But such judicial decisions are difficult and can easily lead to backlash.[85] As shown above, Taiwanese courts were required to address the validity of election results and elected offices in the context of divided politics where the branches of government were controlled by different political parties.

Political confrontations between the two major political parties surfaced in Taiwan when the long-time opposition party DPP won the 2000 presidential elections. Although the KMT lost the presidency that it dominated for an extended period, it still retained a strong majority in the legislature. President Chen faced a hostile *Pan-Blue*-dominated legislature from the outset of his presidency in 2000. Partisan hostility intensified, and the phenomenon of divided government continued even after the presidential and parliamentary elections in 2004. One main reason for political confrontation between the two campaigns was that the *Pan-Blue* camp refused to accept the 2004 presidential election results because of the gunshot incident that occurred one day before the election. The *Pan-Blue* campaign believed this incident was designed to manipulate public sentiment in favour of Chen. Lawsuits against the validity of the election and the elected office were filed before the courts by the *Pan-Blue* campaign. The courts eventually dismissed these suits and upheld the election results. In these two lawsuits, the courts carefully examined the procedure of the election that was critical to the fairness and impartiality of the election. After reviewing the number of invalid ballots, the legality of the referendum that was held alongside the election, and the national security emergency order, the courts confirmed the validity of the election and the elected office.

Taiwan has experienced five direct presidential elections over the course of its democratic transition and divided politics. Major political parties have won and lost elections, and they sometimes split or unite after winning or losing elections.[86] The rules of the game – democratic elections – have been accepted by all political parties and reflect the will of the people. Within the context of highly competitive presidential politics, the institutional role of courts is to preserve, until the next election, a presidential leadership democratically chosen in accordance with the existing rules.[87] The decisions of the courts demonstrate that they would defer to the result of an election if it is held in a fair and impartial manner.[88] To the courts, one main function in contemporary constitutionalism is to uphold democracy. A fair and impartial election is indeed one of the basic requirements in a democracy. Hence, if the election is held fairly and consistently with the rules of democracy, the court would without any doubt uphold the election and endorse the election result. The courts in a constitutional democracy must recognise their roles in solemnly respecting, not changing, the result of elections undertaken in accordance with democratic rules. Hence, judicial deference to the results of elections is the best strategy that the courts have adopted, as it is ultimately beneficial both for addressing contentious politics and upholding judicial integrity.

Respecting the Election Commission's authority

Before democratisation, Taiwan's elections were manipulated by the authoritarian government. By the mid-1980s, a new law concerning the election protocol for all offices at the national and local levels was enacted. The new election protocol not only institutionalised a set of rules for campaigns and elections, but also established an independent Central Election Commission under the Executive Yuan to hold and supervise all levels of elections.[89] However, the independence and neutrality of the Central Election Commission have often been threatened and questioned, and its members have been alleged to be influenced by partisan politics. Even after Taiwan's democratisation, it continues to face the challenging issue as to how the independence and authority of the Election Commission should be preserved.[90]

As illustrated above, the Central Election Commission has – since Taiwan's democratisation – exercised effectively its regulatory powers. For example, the Commission punished presidential candidates who refused to declare their property, or media companies that illegally broadcast the results of polling or advertisements of political campaigns. Although the decisions of the Central Election Commission were challenged, the courts always upheld the decisions of the Commission. Judicial endorsement of the Election Commission not only upholds the integrity of elections, but also secures the authority of the Election Commission. In Taiwan, the courts, particularly administrative courts, have not always deferred to the authority of administrative agencies. On the contrary, recent studies have demonstrated that its courts are more likely to reverse the decisions made by administrative agencies in a few regulatory areas, such as the environment.[91] Facing contested elections, it is clear that Taiwanese courts have adopted the judicial strategy of respecting the regulatory authority of the Election Commission in the interest of democracy.

Preventing political retaliation

In the context of serious political confrontations, the courts and prosecutors may strategically detach themselves from contentious politics. As demonstrated above, such a strategy can be observed in judicial decisions concerning criminal defamations and prosecutorial decisions on corruption allegations. Such judicial non-intervention into highly politically charged cases is to uphold judicial integrity and to avoid political retaliation against political contestants or even against the courts.

Decisions of non-prosecution

In the context of divided politics, it is inevitable that numerous political charges before or during the election are made between presidential candidates and campaigns, alleging corruption or improper financial relationships with big corporations. Public prosecutors are often demanded to initiate an investigation into electoral disputes and to decide whether or not to prosecute the candidates. Thus far, no presidential candidate in Taiwan has been prosecuted after these investigations. All non-prosecution decisions were made after presidential elections. The timing in the issuance of these non-prosecution decisions also demonstrates that the public prosecutor strategically avoids intervening in such electoral disputes. This strategy upholds the impartiality of public prosecutors in contentious elections.

Judicial attitude towards criminal defamation lawsuits

Like other countries, Taiwan has enacted the rules of defamation in the Criminal Code that seek to protect personal reputation from false speech attacks, and to restore and vindicate the person maligned through damages.[92] Observing the defamation cases discussed above, the timing of the Court's decisions and the standard applied by the Court demonstrate that the courts have strategically detached themselves from the defamation cases within the context of highly competitive electoral politics.

As competitive elections may involve strong criticism or even defamatory statements made against candidates or other political figures in the election, these defamatory statements with political motivations to influence voters may eventually be litigated in court. The timing of the courts in dealing with these cases becomes critical. As shown above, in Taiwan, the courts would not usually hand down any decision until the end of the election. This shows that the courts intentionally avoided being directly involved in such cases while the election was still proceeding. One main reason for such a strategy is to uphold judicial integrity and its institutional authority especially within the context of contentious politics.

In addition, the courts in criminal defamation cases provided greater protection for free speech than for the right to reputation. As shown above, in criminal settings, even if a statement was not true, so long as the speaker had a reasonable ground to believe his or her speech actually was true, the speaker bore no responsibility. Decisions concerning defamation that arose from election campaigns were more likely to emphasise the democratic function of speech in triggering dialogue among different opinions and facilitating democracy. For the courts, since speech made during elections may influence votes and the election outcome, the protection of free speech supersedes the reputation of the candidates. Interestingly, however, the courts may develop quite different strategies in balancing free speech and right to reputation in the civil liability context.

Protecting right to reputation in civil defamation lawsuits

In civil defamation decisions discussed above, it can be observed that the strategies employed by civil courts to strike a balance between free speech and right to reputation have not been consistent with the criminal courts, which have provided greater protection for free speech. Three key features are noticeable.

First, civil courts have recognised that both free speech and right to reputation are basic human rights, and that the damage to reputation in civil settings should be resolved differently from penal defamations. To the civil courts, reputation is a part of an individual's personality; whether or not the reputation has been damaged shall be based on public perception. If the act or statement is made with the requisite intent or negligence and has diminished the public perception of the victim, it constitutes a tort of defamation.[93]

Second, civil courts pay special attention to the distinction between facts and comments, which are more subjective. A democratic and diverse society must tolerate different comments. Yet, facts based upon truth are often intertwined with commentary and are thus difficult to distinguish. When striking a balance between free speech and the right to reputation, the veracity of facts should be taken into consideration. For civil courts, when the reporting of facts has destroyed the reputation of others and the reporter cannot prove that such facts are true, even if such facts are from the speech made by others, such an act may still constitute an act that intentionally or negligently damages the reputation of others and thus the speaker must bear civil liability.[94] In other words, unlike criminal courts, civil courts may find intentional misrepresentation or reports without any investigation liable for reputation damage, even though the reporters may have reasonable grounds to believe the truthfulness of such statement.

Third, for the civil courts, the reputation of a public figure who has voluntarily entered the public domain is usually given less protection than free speech. If a comment is made about a public figure or about a public affair by an honest person without malice, the burden of proof on the truthfulness of facts would be usually discharged.[95] However, if a comment is intermingled arbitrarily with other untrue facts which have damaged one's reputation, such act of the accused is still subject to liability.[96]

The difference between the requirements of civil and criminal defamation as well as their respective severity of punishment has led the civil and criminal courts to render different defamation decisions. Such differences drawn from civil and criminal defamation judgments are not surprising and can in fact be beneficial to the development of competitive politics. Criminal courts emphasise the importance of political speech and exercise restraint in imposing criminal responsibility on those involved in politics and competitive elections. At the same time, however, civil courts warn those involved in politics that civil liability must still be borne when individuals damage the reputation of others.

Conclusion

In Taiwan, direct presidential election was adopted amidst its transition to democracy. In all of the five presidential elections since 1996, numerous legal and political charges were made between presidential candidates, and challenges against election results were lodged. These disputes inevitably require judicial resolution.

Having systematically examined election disputes and litigations since the first direct presidential election, this chapter reveals that judicial deference has been commonplace in the resolution of electoral disputes against the backdrop of a highly politicised society. This chapter argues that judicial deference to the decisions of the Election Commission as well as the presidential election results has been critical to the development of democratic politics and the maintenance of judicial integrity. To prevent political retaliation or backlash, courts have also tried to detach themselves from contentious politics and often do not impose liability in criminal defamation. Yet, it is interesting to note that courts may be more actively involved in civil defamation litigation in order to protect an individual's right to reputation.

Notes

1 After the 2000 presidential election, the political branches of government were separately controlled by two different political campaigns, the *Pan-Green* (the Democratic Progressive Party and its alliance party, Taiwan Solidarity Union) and the *Pan-Blue* (the Nationalist Party, Kuomintang and the People First Party). The development of presidential politics will be discussed in the second section of the chapter.
2 Yeh (2010) 913.
3 Linz (1990) 51–69.
4 Yeh (2002) 47–77.
5 Hwang *et al.* (2003).
6 ROC Constitutional Revision 1994, s. 2.
7 'Yuan' means branch. The legislative Yuan is the legislature, while the Executive Yuan is the executive and the Judicial Yuan is the judiciary.
8 The full text of the Presidential and Vice Presidential Election and Recall Act, available at http://law.moj.gov.tw/Eng/LawClass/LawContent.aspx?PCODE=D0020053.
9 ROC Constitution 1947, s. 35.
10 Ibid. s. 37.
11 Ibid. s. 42.
12 Ibid. s. 36.
13 Ibid. s. 39.
14 Ibid. s. 41.

15 Ibid. s. 43.
16 Yeh (2002) 49–51.
17 Ibid.
18 Hwang *et al.* (2003).
19 ROC Constitutional Revision 1994, s. 2.
20 ROC Constitutional Revision 1997, s. 2.
21 *JY. Interpretation No. 627* [2007] Constitutional Court [2007] reasoning para. 2 (Taiwan).
22 After the death of the former President Chiang Ching-Kuo on January 13, 1988, Vice President Lee Teng-Hui succeeded to the presidency. Owing to the disagreements over political reforms, the KMT suffered internal strife. It was divided into two factions, the *Mainstream Faction* which supported President Lee Teng-Hui in launching the political and constitutional reforms, and *Non-Mainstream Faction* that resisted Lee from undertaking democratic reforms. See Chu (1992) 38–44; Tien and Chu (1994) 14.
23 The 1947 ROC Constitution adopted a central government composed of five Yuans, proposed by the revolutionary leader Sun Yat-sen in 1906. The five Yuans are the Executive Yuan, the Legislative Yuan, the Judicial Yuan, the Examination Yuan and the Control Yuan. According to Article 90 of the ROC Constitution, the Control Yuan is the highest control body which vests power to impeach, censure, correct and audit government officials and their executions of public duties.
24 Cheng (1997) 43.
25 Ibid. 44.
26 Ibid. 43–44; Rawnsley (1997) 47–61.
27 Copper (2000) 12–14.
28 Wu (2001) 41–43.
29 Copper (2000) 22–32.
30 Niou and Paolino (2003) 721–740.
31 Diamond (2001) 48–49.
32 Wu (2001) 43.
33 Copper (2004) 3–12; Chan (2005) 54–55.
34 The detailed information of referendum proposals can be found in the official website of the Central Election Commission, available at http://web.cec.gov.tw/files/11-1000-2243-1.php.
35 Article 30 of Taiwan's Referendum Act provides that the passage of the referendum proposal shall meet two thresholds. The first threshold is that more than half of the eligible voters shall cast in a referendum. The second is that the 'yes' votes shall exceed more than half of the ballots. For further discussion on this referendum, see Huang (2008) 122.
36 Ibid.
37 Chang (2010) 887–888.
38 Central Election Commission (n. 34).
39 Copper (2008) 52–60.
40 Copper (2012) 40–52.
41 Mattlin (2011) 165.
42 Bedford and Hwang (2006) 61–81.
43 Ibid.; Copper (2004) 3–12.
44 Bedford and Hwang (2006) 167–171.
45 *Lien & Soong* v. *Central Election Commission* [2004] Gaodeng Fayuan [High Ct.], Civil Division, [2004] 93 Hsuan 4 (Taiwan).
46 Ibid.
47 Ibid.
48 Ibid.
49 Ibid.

50 Ibid.
51 Ibid.
52 *Lien & Soong* v. *Central Election Commission* [2005] Zuigao Fayuan [Sup. Ct], Civil Division, [2005] 94 Tai-Shang 1720 (Taiwan).
53 *Lien & Soong* v. *Chen & Lu* [2004] Gaodeng Fayuan [High Ct], Civil Division, [2004] 93 Hsuan 2 (Taiwan).
54 Ibid.
55 Ibid.
56 Ibid.
57 Ibid.
58 *Lien & Soong* v. *Chen & Lu* [2005] Zuigao Fayuan [Sup. Ct], Civil Division, [2005] 94 Tai-Shang No. 1117 (Taiwan).
59 Article 104 of the Presidential and Vice Presidential Election and Recall Act only allows the prosecutor or the candidate of President and Vice President to bring a lawsuit against the status of the winning candidates. Since the challenger was a layperson, his lawsuit was dismissed by the Court. *Luan* v. *Chen & Lu* [2000] Gaodeng Fayuan [High Ct], Civil Division, [2000] 89 Hsuan Su 3 (Taiwan).
60 Article 102 of the Presidential and Vice Presidential Election and Recall Act only allows the prosecutor or the candidate of President and Vice President to bring a lawsuit challenging the result of a presidential election. As a layperson, the plaintiff cannot be allowed to file the suit to the Court. *Huang* v. *Central Election Commission* [2012] Gaodeng Fayuan [High Ct], Civil Division, [2012] 101 Hsuan Su 1 (Taiwan).
61 Public Officials Election and Recall Act 1980 ss 6–13.
62 *Feng* v. *Central Election Commission* [2004] Zuigao HsingCheng Fayuan [Sup. Admin. Ct], [2004] 93 Pan 353 (Taiwan).
63 *Chinese Television Company* v. *Central Election Commission* [2003] Zuigao HsingCheng Fayuan [Sup. Admin. Ct], [2003] 92 Pan 466 (Taiwan).
64 *Formosa TV* v. *Central Election Commission* [2008] Zuigao HsingCheng Fayuan [Sup. Admin. Ct], [2008] 97 Pan 200 (Taiwan).
65 Chang *et al.* (2014) 704–705.
66 *JY. Interpretation No. 509* [2000] Constitutional Court [2000] reasoning para. 1 (Taiwan).
67 *Prosecutor* v. *Li* [2008] Zuigao Fayuan [Sup. Ct], Criminal Division, [2008] 97 Tai-Shang No. 4613 (Taiwan).
68 Ibid.
69 *JY. Interpretation* (n. 66) reasoning para. 3 (Taiwan).
70 Ibid.
71 *Prosecutor* v. *Qiu* [2007] Gaodeng Fayuan [High Ct], Criminal Division, [2007] 95 Shang-Su 3769 (Taiwan).
72 Ibid.
73 *Chen* v. *Li* [2012] Zuigao Fayuan [Sup. Ct], Civil Division, [2012] 101 Tai-Shang 526 (Taiwan).
74 *Soong* v. *Lee* [2007] Zuigao Fayuan [Sup. Ct], Civil Division, [2007] 96 Tai-Shang 793 (Taiwan).
75 *Lien* v. *Tuan* [2007] Zuigao Fayuan [Sup. Ct.], Civil Division, [2007] 96 Tai-Shang 1810 (Taiwan).
76 *Chow* v. *Chang* [2010] Gaodeng Fayuan [High Ct], Civil Division, [2010] 98 Shang 1243 (Taiwan).
77 *King* v. *Kang* [2015] Zuigao Fayuan [Sup. Ct], Civil Division, [2015] 104 Tai-Shang 774 (Taiwan).
78 *Tseng* v. *Hsieh* [2010] Zuigao Fayuan [Sup. Ct], Civil Division, [2010] 99 Tai-Shang 791 (Taiwan).
79 The Supreme Court reasoned that the statement of Fang on the talk show represented one perspective among the many, and although his statement came from the speech

made by others, this statement did not express any extreme views. *Su* v. *Fan* [2015] Zuigao Fayuan [Sup. Ct], Civil Division, [2015] 104 Tai-Shang 106 (Taiwan).

80 *Hsieh* v. *Qiu* [2013] Gaodeng Fayuan [High Ct], Civil Division, [2013] 102 Shang 14 (Taiwan).

81 Copper (2000) 19–20.

82 Ibid.

83 Ibid.

84 *Bush* v. *Gore* 531 US 98 (2000).

85 Chang (2010) 887–888.

86 Chang (2010) 907–908.

87 Ibid.

88 Ginsburg (2013) 57–58.

89 Chang (2001) 326–328.

90 In 2009, a bold step of reform was finally undertaken with the passage of the Organic Law of the Central Election Commission. Soon, an independent Election Commission was formally established.

91 Yeh (2012) 97.

92 Chang *et al.* (2014) 704–705.

93 *Soong* v. *Lee* (n. 74); *Su* v. *Fan* [2014] Gaodeng Fayuan [High Ct], Civil Division, [2014] 102 Chung-Shang 812 (Taiwan).

94 *Chen* v. *Li* (n. 73).

95 *King* v. *Kang* [2014] Gaodeng Fayuan [High Ct], Civil Division, [2014] 101 Shang 1405 (Taiwan); *Tseng* v. *Hsieh* (n. 78).

96 *Tseng* v. *Hsieh* (n. 78).

References

Bedford O. and Hwang K.K., *Taiwanese Identity and Democracy: The Social Psychology of Taiwan's 2004 Elections* (Palgrave Macmillan 2006).

Chan S., 'Taiwan in 2004: Electoral Contests and Political Stasis' (2005) *Asian Survey* 45(1) 54.

Chang W.C., 'Transition to Democracy, Constitutionalism and Judicial Activism: Taiwan in Comparative Constitutional Perspective' (SJD Dissertation, Yale Law School 2001).

Chang W.C., 'Strategic Judicial Responses in Politically Charged Cases: East Asian Experiences' (2010) *International Journal of Constitutional Law* 8(4) 885.

Chang W.C., Thio L.A., Tan Kevin Y.L. and Yeh J.Y., *Constitutionalism in Asia: Cases and Materials* (Hart Publishing 2014).

Cheng T.J., 'Taiwan in 1996: From Euphoria to Melodrama' (1997) *Asian Survey* 37(1) 43.

Chu Y.H., *Crafting Democracy in Taiwan* (Institute for National Policy Research 1992).

Copper F.J., 'Taiwan's 2000 Presidential and Vice Presidential Election: Consolidating Democracy and Creating a New Era of Politics' (2000) 12–14, http://digitalcommons.law.umaryland.edu/mscas/vol. 2000/iss2/1 accessed August 10, 2015.

Copper F.J., 'Taiwan's 2004 Presidential and Vice Presidential Election: Democracy's Consolidation or Devolution?' (2004) 3–12, http://digitalcommons.law.umaryland.edu/mscas/vol. 2004/iss1/1/ accessed August 10, 2015.

Copper F.J., 'Taiwan's 2008 Presidential and Vice Presidential Election: Maturing Democracy' (2008) 52–60, http://digitalcommons.law.umaryland.edu/mscas/vol. 2008/iss1/1/ accessed August 10, 2015.

Copper F.J., 'Taiwan's 2012 Presidential/Vice Presidential and Legislative Elections: Assessing Current Politics and Charting the Future' (2012) 40–52, http://digitalcommons.law.umaryland.edu/mscas/vol. 2012/iss1/1// accessed August 10, 2015.

Diamond L., 'Anatomy of an Electoral Earthquake: How the KMT Lost and the DPP Won the 2000 Presidential Election' in Alagappa M. (ed.), *Taiwan's Presidential Politics: Democratization and Cross-Strait Relations in the Twenty-First Century* (Routledge 2001).

Ginsburg T., 'The Politics of Courts in Democratization' in Kapiszewski D., Silverstein I.G. and Kagan R.A. (eds), *Consequential Courts: Judicial Roles in Global Perspective* (Cambridge University Press 2013).

Huang C., 'Referendum and Democracy: The Experience of Taiwan' in Paolino P. and Meernik J. (eds), *Democratization in Taiwan: Challenges in Transformation* (Ashgate 2008).

Hwang J.Y., Liao F.T. and Chang W.C., 'Development of Constitutional Law and Human Rights in Taiwan Facing the New Century' (2003) IDE Asian Law Series No. 24, www.ide.go.jp/English/Publish/Download/Als/24.html accessed August 10, 2015.

Linz J., 'The Perils of Presidentialism' (1990) *Journal of Democracy* 1(1) 51.

Mattlin M., *Politicized Society: The Long Shadow of Taiwan's One-Party Legacy* (NIAS Press 2011).

Niou E. and Paolino P., 'The Rise of the Opposition Party in Taiwan: Explaining Chen Shui-bian's Victory in the 2000 Presidential Election' (2003) *Electoral Studies* 22(4) 721.

Rawnsley D.G., 'The 1996 Presidential Campaign in Taiwan: Packaging Politics in a Democratizing State' (1997) *Harvard International Journal of Press/Politics* 2(2) 47–61.

Tien H.M. and Chu Y.H., 'Taiwan's Domestic Political Reforms, Institutional Change and Power Realignment' in Klintworth G. (ed.), *Taiwan in the Asia-Pacific in the 1990s* (Allen & Unwin 1994).

Wu Y.S., 'Taiwan in 2000: Managing the Aftershocks from Power Transfer' (2001) *Asian Survey* 41(1) 40.

Yeh J.R., 'Constitutional Reform and Democratization in Taiwan 1945–2000', in Chow P. (ed.), *Taiwan's Modernization in Global Perspective* (Greenwood Publishing Group 2002).

Yeh J.R., 'Presidential Politics and the Judicial Facilitation of Dialogue between Political Actors in New Asian Democracies: Comparing the South Korean and Taiwanese Experiences' (2010) *International Journal of Constitutional Law* 8(4) 911.

Yeh J.R., Transitional Environmentalism: Democratic Institutions, Courts, and Civil Society in Taiwan' in Mori A. (ed.), *Democratization, Decentralization, and Environmental Governance in Asia* (Kyoto University Press 2012) 97.

11 Thailand

An abuse of judicial review

Khemthong Tonsakulrungruang

Thailand's backsliding democracy

Vibrant democracy needs more than the holding of periodic elections. Around the world, newly democratised regimes are being toppled because the public are disappointed by election results.[1] Instead of recruiting a government responsive to the people's will, an election oftentimes acts as a gateway for corrupt politicians to form a government and enrich themselves. Thus, while elections may mark the beginning of the country's democratisation, an unfair and dishonest election could also mark its end.[2] Judicial review of an electoral process is necessary to ensure the fairness of the poll. Review by an independent and professional judiciary would improve the legitimacy of the government, and ultimately ensures the survival of the regime.

The 1997 political reform aimed to consolidate Thailand's democracy.[3] Although it has been 80 years since the official democratisation took place, Thailand still oscillates between authoritarianism and weak democracy. One key factor that contributes to an incomplete democratic consolidation is the low public confidence in the electoral process, one that has historically produced corrupt governments. As a result, a significant number of Thais do not regard democracy as the only game in town. The 1997 Constitution as applicable then established the Constitutional Court and assigned to it the duty of reviewing the constitutionality of the government's actions.[4]

However, the more the Constitutional Court has exercised its judicial review over elections, the worse Thailand's politics has become. Since 2005, a series of Constitutional Court's decisions has left Thailand with two coups d'état and a badly divided nation. The latest is the coup d'état of May 22, 2014, which paved the way for General Prayuth Chan-Ocha to assume the premiership. Despite widespread violation of basic human rights, Prayuth's regime is supported by a large portion of Thais who prefer the authoritarianism of the military to the corruption of electoral politics.

Although the Constitutional Court is not solely responsible for the backsliding of the nation's democratisation, it has played a significant role leading to it. Why has judicial review of Thailand's electoral process failed to achieve fair and honest elections that facilitate democratic consolidation? This chapter will examine all cases of judicial review of an election and their consequences. It will try to examine the judiciary's mistakes against the background of Thailand's ideological and social conflicts.

Legal framework for judicial review

This study covers a decade of the Constitutional Court's jurisprudence. The year 2005 marked the beginning of its aggressive judicial review over elections. Since then, Thailand has witnessed two constitutions and two interim charters.[5] Such changes affect the direction both of the election laws and judicial reviews. At the time of writing, the 2007 Constitution has been abolished and the replacement charter has not been finalised. Thailand is currently operating under the 2014 Interim Charter.

Since 1997, Thailand's judiciary has been divided into four independent courts: the Court of Justice, the Constitutional Court, the Administrative Court, and the Military Court. The Constitutional Court was part of the political reforms to control the political process pursuant to the 1997 Constitution. It replaced the constitutional tribunal, which had been regarded as too political.[6] This newly created court was intended to act as the core mechanism to implement and realise the political reforms enshrined in the 1997 Constitution.[7] It was established to ensure that the government was transparent and effective, as well as to resolve political confrontations in a constitutional way.[8]

The Constitutional Court is a panel of judges who are either legal or political science experts. The term is non-renewable nine years.[9] Previously, the panel was composed of 15 judges, five of whom were the Supreme Court judges, two of whom were the Supreme Administrative Court judges, five legal experts, and three political science experts.[10] The Supreme Court nominated five judges and the Supreme Administrative Court nominated two. The selection of the other eight experts was carried out by the nomination committee composed of the President of the Supreme Court, four deans of law schools, four deans of schools of political science, and four representatives of political parties that have seats in the House of Representatives.[11] The nomination would be complete if the Senate subsequently approved the list.[12] The prime minister was prohibited from being involved in the process so as to prevent any political interference in the appointment process.[13]

The 2007 Constitution downsized the Constitutional Court judges to nine: three Supreme Court judges, two Supreme Administrative Court judges, two legal experts, and two political scientists.[14] It also simplified the composition of the nomination committee by including only the President of the Supreme Court, the President of the Supreme Administrative Court, the Speaker of the House of Representatives, the Opposition Leader, and the President of the Independent Agency.[15] The constitutional change reflected the drafters' distrust of politicians, thus further reducing their participation in the selection process.

However, briefly from 2006 to 2007, the Constitutional Court judges were dismissed by the Council of National Security (CNS) and were replaced by an ad hoc panel.[16] The current panel was appointed in 2008.

Three main functions of the Constitutional Court are to review the constitutionality of statutes,[17] to determine the eligibility of political office holders,[18] and to decide the jurisdictional disputes between constitutional agencies.[19] It can declare an act unconstitutional or disqualify a politician. It can also demarcate other agencies' jurisdictional turfs. But the Constitutional Court has only a limited right to review an election.

Since 1997, the duty to arrange an election was transferred from the Ministry of Interior to the independent Election Commission (EC). The 1997 Constitution mandated the EC to discharge the duty of arranging a fair and honest election as an independent body.[20] The Commission also investigates accusations of electoral fraud in conjunction with the Court of Justice's Election Department, which decides the punishment for the accused. Its independent status limits judicial review of its depositions, rules, or orders. The Constitution forbids the Administrative Court from reviewing an independent agency's exercise of power.[21] Also, there is no clause that allows the Constitutional Court to review the independent agency's rules and orders. The only explicit channel that provides the ground for judicial review by the Constitutional Court pertains to the dissolution of a political party.[22]

Direct channel

Dissolution of a political party was not mentioned in the 1997 Constitution as it was not considered important. According to the 1998 Political Party Organic Act, dissolution could be executed only if the party is accused of carrying out one of the following four activities:[23]

1 an act to overthrow the democratic regime with the King as the Head of the State or to acquire power by unconstitutional means;
2 an act that is adverse to the democratic regime with the King as the Head of the State under the Constitution;
3 an act that endangers the national security or in violation of laws or public order and good morals; or
4 an act violating Section 23 paragraph 1, Section 52, or Section 53, which is an attempt to recruit non-Thai members or failure to comply with campaign finance regulations.

The Registrar, who is also the President of the EC, shall file a complaint to the Attorney General. If the Attorney General agrees, he shall then submit the case to the Constitutional Court.

For an ordinary member, because the 1997 Constitution required a Member of Parliament to be a member of a political party, the dissolution of the party automatically disqualified the members from office unless they could be admitted to another party within 60 days.[24] But the party's executives were not allowed to establish a new party or assume an executive position in another party for a period of five years.[25]

The 2007 Constitution took the matter more seriously. It attached more severe consequences to dissolution. If it appeared to the Constitutional Court that the leader or an executive member of that political party has acknowledged, ignored, or failed to prevent a violation of the election law, resulting in an unfair and dishonest election, that political party is assumed to have sought to gain power by undemocratic means.[26] Section 68 ordered the Constitutional Court to dissolve the party and revoke the party's executive members for five years.[27] Revocation means these executive members would not be able to vote or become a candidate in any election. The charge is almost impossible to dispute as the Constitution was drafted in very strict language. For the Constitution Drafting Assembly, dissolution became the means to establish a fair and honest election by collectively punishing all party executives for an individual's offence.[28]

The 2007 Political Party Organic Act then expanded the grounds for dissolution in accordance with the new constitutional mandate. A political party shall be dissolved if it carries out one of the following acts:[29]

1 an act overthrowing a democratic regime with the King as the Head of the State or gaining power by unconstitutional means or acting in the way that the Constitution deems an undemocratic gaining of power;
2 an act in violation of an election act or the EC's rules and regulations, resulting in an unfair election;
3 an act that is adverse to the democratic regime with the King as the Head of the State;
4 an act that endangers national security, internally and externally, or in violation of laws or public order and good morals; or
5 an act violating Section 21 paragraph 1, Section 43, Section 65, Section 66, Section 69, or Section 104 which is an attempt to recruit non-Thai members or failure to comply with campaign finance regulations.

Even a minor mistake in an election can be fatal, as a party can easily fall foul of one of these grounds.

Indirect channel

Strictly speaking, both the 1997 and 2007 Constitutions allowed judicial review only in a case of party dissolution. However, historically, the Constitutional Court claimed its jurisdiction to review an election indirectly vis-à-vis the Ombudsman.

The Ombudsman, another independent agency created by the 1997 Constitution, has the duty to investigate complaints and act accordingly. In some cases, it may notify the concerned agency but in others it might file a lawsuit. In the 1997 Constitution, if the Ombudsman believes that a provision of law, a regulation, or an act is unconstitutional, it shall petition the Constitutional Court or the Administrative Court.[30]

The language of Section 198 of the Political Party Organic Act was problematic as it did not clearly point out which case went to which court. Generally, a dispute over a provision of law refers to a dispute over a statute or an organic act, so it falls within the Constitutional Court's jurisdiction. A dispute over an administrative rule or adjudication would belong to the Administrative Court. But the Constitutional Court once claimed its jurisdiction over the royal decree for scheduling a general election.[31] Normally, because a royal decree is a cabinet's disposition, it is an administrative rule and is subject to review only by the Administrative Court.

The 2007 Constitution was aware of the above confusion so it explicitly stated that a dispute regarding constitutionality of the provision of law is under the Constitutional Court's jurisdiction while that of the rule, order, or other act of the administrative agency is under the Administrative Court's.[32] However, the Constitutional Court still maintained that a royal decree scheduling a general election is subject to its jurisdiction. The Constitutional Court, in 2014, claimed that the royal decree was not a rule, but a provision of law and thus reviewable.[33] This move was seen as a judicial manoeuvre to undermine the 2007 Constitution's attempt to clarify the Ombudsman's role.

A decade of judicial review

The past decade of judicial review can be divided into three phases. The saga of judicial review began in 2006 when the Constitutional Court invalidated the general election. It was followed by a series of dissolution of political parties from 2007 to 2008. There was a gap before the Constitutional Court invalidated another general election in February 2014.

2006

The first review of Thailand's elections took place in 2006. Thaksin Shinawatra's Thai Rak Thai party (TRT) won the 2005 general election. On one hand, this victory was a crucial benchmark in Thai politics as it made Thaksin the first elected prime minister who completed his first term and also won the second. More importantly, Thaksin won by a landslide. He won a super-majority, forming a single-party government. On the other hand, this landslide victory left the opposition, the Democrat and Chart Thai parties, with too few seats to initiate even a parliamentary debate.[34] The check and balance mechanism could no longer function.

Despite a dysfunctional opposition, the Thaksin administration was far from smooth. The public grew uneasy with what they perceived as abuses of power; populist policies, attempts to dominate independent agencies and the Senate, corruption, and suppression of dissidents. Politics eventually moved from the Parliament to the street.[35] Thaksin's opponents then formed the People's Alliance for Democracy (PAD) and staged a month-long protest. As pressure mounted, Thaksin dissolved the House of Representatives on February 24 and called for a snap election on April 2, 2006.[36]

In the event that the House is dissolved, the Constitution required a general election within 60 days.[37] The period was reduced to 45 days if the term of the House expired.[38] Thus, Thaksin's move was perfectly legal. But the opposition front, the Democrat, Chart Thai, and Mahachon parties, still denounced the election date, which was considered too rushed.[39] The period of 37 days left Thaksin's opponents little time for preparation. They asked the Supreme Administrative Court to review the royal decree scheduling an election date, which the Supreme Administrative Court refused because the choice of the election date was deemed a political question.[40] The opposition then boycotted the April general election, leaving TRT the only main party to run in several constituencies. According to the Election Organic Act, when there is only one party running for an election, a candidate must obtain no less than 20 per cent of constituent votes.[41] To circumvent the 20 per cent requirement, TRT hired several small parties to compete with it. Meanwhile, PAD campaigned for an election boycott to show the public's disapproval of Thaksin.

Despite obstacles, the EC managed to carry out the poll. There were incidents – for example, when a voter deliberately tore a ballot in front of TV cameras in order to express his opposition[42] – but TRT won more than 90 per cent of the seats regardless. There was a high number of ballots that were destroyed or had voted against all candidates. Moreover, in several districts, TRT candidates failed to win even 20 per cent of the vote. This election was chaotic, and the result was worrisome. If the public accepted the results, Thailand would have witnessed a house without opposition. If the public refused, the country might slide into civil unrest.

On April 25, 2006, His Majesty the King Bhumibol delivered speeches urging the judiciary to "do your duty" to uphold democracy and end the electoral debacle. The message was delivered twice on the same day to Administrative Court judges and Court of Justice judges. The three court presidents called for a meeting and issued a joint statement confirming that the judiciary would follow His Majesty's instruction.[43] The Supreme Administrative Court was the first to review the constitutionality of the election. It then ordered an injunction, halting re-elections in several districts, citing possible unconstitutionality.[44] The Ombudsman then took the case to the Constitutional Court.

The Ombudsman asked the Constitutional Court to review the constitutionality of the royal decree scheduling the general election and the EC's resolution on arranging the voting venue. The Ombudsman accused the government and the EC, in the royal decree, of setting the election date too early. This move reflected the unfairness of this April's poll as the EC showed preferential treatment towards Thaksin's party. Furthermore, the EC resolved to change the voting practice by re-positioning the voting booth. This new position of the voting booth allowed by-standers to see whom the voters chose, hence it was a breach of the confidentiality of the vote.

The Constitutional Court agreed that the royal decree was a kind of rule. Because of the ambiguity in the text of Section 198 of the Constitution, the Ombudsman could request the Constitutional Court's review of a rule.

In the royal decree, although the Constitutional Court rejected to review the decision to dissolve the House because it was a political question, it claimed that setting an election date was not. The EC argued that several past elections had also been scheduled shortly after the house dissolutions, without any challenge to their constitutionality. Moreover, the EC argued that it did its best to persuade the opposition to join the election, and even offered to postpone the election date. But the opposition was firm on boycotting the poll.

The Constitutional Court decided that the royal decree scheduling a general election was unconstitutional because the date was held too early. The election result showed that, if one combined the number of invalid ballots and ballots that abstained from choosing any candidate, the number exceeded the valid ballots. The Court also pointed out the irregularity of the result as TRT won most seats in the Parliament. TRT's unnatural victory meant the House lacked an opposition. This was contrary to the Constitution's objective of establishing a check-and-balance system within parliament through an election. When the election could not realise this constitutional purpose, it was unconstitutional.

The Constitutional Court then reviewed the EC's resolution to change the voting booth's position. The EC was an independent agency established by the Constitution. It was not under the cabinet's oversight. Thus, its resolution was not an administrative rule that fell within the administrative court's jurisdiction. The Constitutional Court concluded that it could then review the EC's disposition.

The EC argued that the practice of turning the booth outward was common in several countries without affecting the confidentiality of the vote. Besides, the chance of bystanders observing a voter's choice was unlikely. Any attempt to harass a voter would be detected by an EC local committee who guarded the booth on the election date. The Constitutional Court disagreed. Citing that an EC local committee was composed of the parties' representatives, this allowed representatives of political parties to observe for whom an individual voted. The EC's practice also breached the confidentiality principle of a democratic election, which was described in Section 104 of the Constitution.[45]

Because the election result did not produce a functional parliament with a check-and-balance system, and because the manner of voting exposed voters' confidential decision, the Constitutional Court invalidated the 2006 general election.[46]

The 9/2549 Decision led to an imprisonment of members of the EC for failing to duly perform its duty[47] and the Democrat's petition to dissolve TRT. It also intensified the political conflict. Thaksin set the new election date in July 2006 but the Court's decision boosted PAD's confidence and leverage. The party stepped up the pressure for Thaksin to withdraw himself from politics. With no prospect of having a new government in the foreseeable future, the Royal Thai Army seized power on September 19, 2006.

2007–2008

The CNS seized power and abolished the 1997 Constitution. It dismissed members of several independent agencies, including the Constitutional Court judges, but the CNS installed a new panel to try pending cases.[48] This move tainted the Court's impartiality.

Complication was added when the CNS issued an order commanding that, in the event of a party's dissolution, the party's executive shall be banned from political activities for a period of five years.[49] As the CNS was an actual supreme ruler, its order had the same legal effect as a statute or even a charter.[50] But the CNS did not clarify whether this ban was to be applied to pending cases or only future ones. This ambiguity led to a debate as to whether the Constitutional Court could apply the ban on TRT retroactively.

The Constitutional Court delivered its ruling a year later. In May 2007, the Constitutional Court dissolved TRT and two smaller parties.[51] TRT, the Court found, hired two smaller parties to compete with it in the 2006 general election to circumvent the 20 per cent requirement. Such behaviour constituted an act intending to acquire power by undemocratic means as well as an act that endangered the national security, public order, or good morals. The two other parties agreed to receive TRT's money so they were acting adversely to the democratic regime with the King as the Head of the State.

TRT challenged the new panel of the Constitutional Court claiming that the Constitutional Court was gone as the 1997 Constitution was abolished. Besides, it was against the rule of law to create a panel to try a specific case. The Court confirmed its competence relying on the CNS's order. This followed the long-held precedence that the judiciary shall never question the validity and legitimacy of coup makers.

Although TRT had never formally ordered its executive to hire small parties to run in the 2006 election, the Court assumed TRT's involvement by examining the surrounding circumstances. No sensible party leader would formally acknowledge or admit to the commission of the crime but the Court held that the crime clearly benefited TRT as a whole and it was almost impossible for an executive to commit such a crime without a mandate from TRT.

The evidence left no doubt that TRT did violate the law, and the law was clear that the party had to be dissolved. The debate focused on whether the Constitutional Court could ban TRT's executives from political activities for five years according to the CNS's order. The order was made after TRT's crime had been committed. Punishment should not be applied retroactively. But the Constitutional Court finally decided to apply the ban to all 111 executives of TRT. Despite its unanimity elsewhere in the case, the panel split over this issue. The majority of six reasoned that retroactive law was prohibited only in criminal law. The measure herein deprived people of their basic rights, but only temporarily to prevent executives of the dissolved party from harming the country. The other three judges insisted that any provision of law could not be applied retroactively if it had negative effects on individual rights and liberties.

The lesser known sister case concerned the petition to dissolve the Democrat party. The Democrat party is the oldest party that has survived Thailand's political turmoil. It led the opposition against the TRT government and relied on support from the elite and the middle class in Bangkok and the South, who are also PAD members. Thaksin's political base was from the North and the Northeast. Thus, it easily became Thaksin's nemesis. Abhisit Vejajiva, the Democrat leader, launched the campaign to boycott the 2006 election, which resulted in its invalidation and subsequently the military coup. The Democrat party was accused of defaming Thaksin during the 2006 election campaign and fabricating evidence that TRT hired smaller parties to fake competition. The Constitutional Court acquitted the Democrat party because the party's speech was only criticism made in good faith. Also, the Democrat party was not involved in the fabrication of evidence, which was carried out independently by third parties.[52]

The CNS order was later incorporated into Section 237 of the 2007 Constitution.[53] Should an executive acknowledge, or even ignore to prevent, a violation of election laws and regulations, it would be deemed an act acquiring power through undemocratic means. The party would be dissolved and the political rights of all executives had to be collectively revoked for five years. The 2007 Constitution Drafting Committee justified this draconian measure as necessary for producing a fair and honest election. The problem of an unfair election was so severe that a radical and harsh measure was needed.[54]

When the 2007 Constitution was enacted, democracy in Thailand resumed. The junta-appointed Constitutional Court judges stepped down and the new panel assumed the office. A general election was scheduled at the end of 2007. In reality, TRT's dissolution failed to stop Thaksin or the other 111 TRT executives from coming back to politics. Although he was in exile, Thaksin quickly founded the People's People Party (PPP) that was run by his proxy, Samak Sundaravej. Other former TRT executives also openly masterminded their puppeteer parties through their partners or relatives.[55]

PPP easily won the election and formed the coalition government. But PPP was short lived. The newly installed Constitutional Court axed Samak pursuant to a conflict of interest charge. Samak ran a cooking show on a TV channel while he was prime minister. Although the crime was minor, the Court found that he violated the ban on politicians receiving other sources of income than their salary.[56] Its deputy chairman, Yongyuth Thiyapairat, was found by the Supreme Court to have illegally provided financial support to a group of village leaders in Northern Thailand, thus tainting the election.[57] According to Section 237, PPP had to be dissolved and all executives revoked of their political rights because of Yongyuth's vote buying.

At the same time, PAD regrouped too and mobilised massive street protests not long after. But PAD became more violent. The protest continued in an anarchical manner that included occupying the government's offices, assailing anti-riot policemen, and finally seizing two international airports in Bangkok.[58] The seizure of airports highlighted the peak of PAD's desperate attempt to oust Thaksin's proxies. It paralysed transportation and caused huge chaos but the government was undeterred. Somchai Wongsawat, the then prime minister, refused to resign and declared an Emergency. Before the situation got worse, the Constitutional Court dissolved PPP and banned its 39 executives.[59] PAD immediately disbanded. Together with PPP, the Constitutional Court dissolved two of PPP's coalition parties, the Chat Thai and Matchima Thippatai parties, under the same charge.[60]

Section 237 was drafted in language so clear that even the Constitutional Court found it unambiguous. Nonetheless, the 20/2551 Decision was criticised for a procedural flaw. While leaders of both the Chat Thai and Matchima Thippatai parties were allowed to present their final oral testimonies, those belonging to PPP were not. The Constitutional Court seemed to be in such a hurry to rescue the country that it did not follow proper procedure.

The PPP's dissolution suddenly shifted Thailand's political landscape. The Democrat party, who had lost in four consecutive general elections, was then able to make a pact with PPP's former coalition to form a government under the army's brokerage.[61] Abhisit Vejajiva, the Democrat leader, became the prime minister.

Besides a change in the government, the 20/2551 Decision led to more violence. Thaksin's supporters were upset by both the TRT and PPP dissolutions. The grassroot majority believed that the judiciary had hijacked their government in order to pave the way for the unpopular Democrat government. Anger and disappointment built up before exploding in 2010, which saw a massive protest by Thaksin's supporters under the name of the United Front for Democracy against Dictatorship (UDD).[62] UDD shut down Bangkok's business area for months before Abhisit ordered a crackdown, resulting in 93 deaths including unarmed civilians, foreign correspondents, and soldiers.[63]

The Democrat party was the only party that survived Section 237. It was accused of misusing the political development fund in 2005. In 2010, in the four:two decision, the Constitutional Court acquitted the Democrat party because of a technical error.[64] Two reasons were given. For the majority judges, the dissolution case could only be filed by the Political Party Registrar. According to the Political Party Organic Act, the EC president is the Political Party Registrar, *ex officio*.[65] But, in this case, the Constitutional Court considered that Apichart Sukhagganond was acting in capacity of the EC president, not the Registrar, when he decided to file a dissolution charge. Thus, the EC had failed to follow the proper procedure. A judge in a concurring opinion accused Apichart of missing the 15-day deadline that the Registrar had to observe for filing a complaint after acknowledging the wrongdoing.[66] When the EC meeting resolved that the Democrat party should be dissolved, Apichart appointed another body to investigate the case for four more months. The 15-day period had passed and the case had expired. The acquittal raised double-standard issues since the Constitutional Court had never questioned the 15-day period, which had also been missed, in the TRT dissolution case.[67]

2014

The 2010 crackdown was considered successful from the military's point of view because it ended the attempt by Thaksin's supporters to dethrone the Democrat government. But it also ensured the Democrat party a defeat in the 2011 general election when Yingluck Shinawatra became Thailand's first female prime minister.

By the time Yingluck won the election, political parties became cautious of appointing key persons to executive positions because they would be vulnerable to a five-year political ban. When Thaksin established the Pheu Thai party (PT), his third party, it was left without functioning heads for years. He only proposed Yingluck, his youngest sister, a candidate for premiership 49 days before the 2011 election. But she was neither a party chairman nor an executive of PT.

The PT government was always at the constant risk of dissolution. When it proposed to amend the 2007 Constitution, the opposition prepared a dissolution petition to the Constitutional Court.[68] However, the Yingluck administration managed to survive the harassment until she tried to pass an amnesty bill in late 2013. The bill was a grave mistake. It was criticised as an attempt to bring her brother back from exile by providing amnesty indiscriminately to every party in the conflict. Both Thaksin's supporters and opponents objected against the bill because it pardoned their enemies. People marched and Yingluck recalled the bill. But the Democrat party saw another opportunity to oust Thaksin's men and become the government. The Democrat party, under the disguise of the People's Democratic Reform Council (PDRC), led a month-long protest, demanding that Yingluck resign and leave the country for good.[69] When the PDRC tried to occupy the government's House, Yingluck dissolved the House and called for another general election on February 2, 2014.[70] But the PDRC was not satisfied. Knowing that the Democrat party would definitely lose at the poll, it campaigned for boycotting the election until major reforms were carried out to clean up politics.[71]

The proposal for reform was hollow. The PDRC could not provide any concrete plan other than the postponement of an election indefinitely and requesting a benevolent royal appointee as the prime minister.[72] Yingluck rejected the plan as it was unconstitutional.

There were similarities and differences between situations surrounding the 2006 and the 2014 elections. Both were the result of street protests. But Yingluck was more compromising as she set the election date 56 days after the dissolution, much later than her brother did. Obviously she was trying to prevent the Democrat party from claiming that the date was too early and using it as an excuse to boycott the election, the mistake that led to the Constitutional Court's invalidation of the 2006 election. As a result, other parties, excluding the Democrat party, agreed to contest in this election. Unfortunately, the PDRC was more violent and stubborn than the PAD. It aimed to uproot Thaksin's influence. Instead of advocating that the public should abstain from voting, it urged its followers to obstruct the February election with all possible means, including the use of force. Again, the Democrat party boycotted this election. Another difference was that the 2014 EC was not under Thaksin's influence. It strongly objected to the election and only half-heartedly conducted the poll.

Signs of violence began when the PDRC blocked the registration venue. The blockade was fatal. Voters in 28 constituencies in the South, the Democrat's stronghold, could not vote because candidates could not register in time.[73] This was a new phenomenon in the history of Thai politics as the election could only be conducted in parts of the country. The EC asked the government to consider a new election date. The interim cabinet declined for fear that the new date would exceed the 60 day constitutional mandate. The EC then asked the Constitutional Court whether the election date could be moved and who was entitled to request such a change. The Constitutional Court agreed that, in times of necessity, the date may be rescheduled. It also pointed out that the power to reschedule the date was the joint power of the prime minister and the president of the EC.[74] However, despite the Constitutional Court's suggestion, the government insisted on February 2.

Violence intensified with reports of serious armed clashes.[75] On the voting day, many voting units were deserted because staff feared for their safety. PDRC surrounded the booths and assaulted voters who showed up. Some units had to end their operation abruptly.[76] PT managed to win the election but voting did not occur in every constituency. The Ombudsman then challenged the constitutionality of this election in the Constitutional Court.

This was the second time the Constitutional Court authorised itself to review the election. The Constitutional Court conceded that the Election Department in the Court of Justice could review an individual case. But it claimed that the power to review the overall electoral process was within the Constitutional Court because the royal decree scheduling the general election was a provision of law. Because of the clear language in the 2007 Constitution, the Court could not claim a royal decree to be a rule as it did in 2006.

Normally, a royal decree would be an administrative rule as it relies on statutory mandate to be promulgated. However, the power to promulgate a royal decree scheduling a general election derives directly from the Constitution, not a statute; hence, its special status as a provision of law was similar to statutes.

The government defended its decision not to postpone the election date because the constitution mandated that a general election must be held within 60 days. The date of February 2 was already 56 days, long enough for the opposition to prepare their campaigns. Moreover, it was the EC's fault for failing to operate voting booths.

The Constitutional Court dismissed the defence. According to Section 108 of the Constitution, the election date shall be set the same day across the country so that voters may vote without undue influence of knowing the election outcome from other constituencies.[77] When there were 28 constituencies left without candidates, there were no elections in those constituencies. Thus, the February 2 election was not held on the same date across the country. The government did not take into account objections and concerns from relevant parties, including the Court in the previous decision. The government proceeded with the election during the period when Thailand was seriously divided. Thus, obstruction was expected. Blaming the government's disregard of its warning, the Constitutional Court announced that the February election was voided.[78]

The EC is currently planning to ask Yingluck Shinawatra to cover all the expenses of the 2014 election.[79]

Again, the 5/2557 Decision produced a deadlock for Yingluck and increased the PDRC's leverage. The PDRC demanded that Yingluck and her interim cabinet members resign unconditionally. This political vacuum would justify the appointment of the third-party prime minister who would, according to the PDRC, reform Thailand into a transparent system. Yingluck tried to discuss with the EC about the new election date, which was likely to be in October but the Constitutional Court disqualified Yingluck from the caretaker prime minister position in another case that involved an unlawful transfer of a high-ranking civil servant.[80] Finally, the Royal Thai Army seized power from the PT administration.

Impact of judicial review on Thailand's political conflict

Since 2006, the Constitutional Court has invalidated two general elections and dissolved six parties. Also, it revoked the political rights of several hundreds of politicians. But this aggressive style of review failed to promote fair elections and strengthen Thailand's democracy. On the contrary, it undermined the importance of electoral politics by giving momentum to anti-democratic movements and catalysing two coup d'états.

The general impression of a judicial review of Thailand's election is that the judiciary is trying to uproot Thaksin's regime. The Constitutional Court's decisions resulted in major changes in the Thai political landscape. The first invalidation triggered the call for military intervention, ousting Thaksin's administration. The successive TRT dissolution theoretically suspended his key men for five years. In reality, they just continued to operate behind the scenes. The PPP dissolution also paved the way for Thaksin's enemy, the Democrat party, to become the government. The 2014 election invalidation created another deadlock and a justification for the army to oust a democratic government led by Yingluck, Thaksin's sister.

It may be premature to conclude definitively that the Constitutional Court was targeting only Thaksin's men. But evidence seems to point in that direction. The Court applied two different standards of review when reviewing the case of Thaksin and his opponents. Twice it dissolved Thaksin's parties. Twice it acquitted the Democrat party. While hearing Thaksin's cases, the Court forcefully stressed the importance of building a transparent and democratic Thailand. The Court was much more lenient with the Democrat party, which was the lone survivor of all dissolution lawsuits.

On the surface, the ongoing conflict in Thailand is between Thaksin's supporters and opponents. But deeper down it is a more complicated struggle between the grassroot majority and the elite minority.[81] The elite are the network of senior bureaucrats, bureaucrats, academics, and businessmen who long dominated governmental public policies.[82] The former had long been ignored by government until Thaksin came into power. He understood the desire of urbanised countrymen to ascend to improved standards of living and greater involvement in politics.[83] He then used his populist policies to build his political base and forever changed Thailand's politics. The elite, whose status quo was threatened, then struck back. While Thaksin's strategy is to win the election, his enemy sought help from non-elected institutions such as the judiciary and those independent agencies.[84] Although these bodies could not initiate public policies in the minority's favour, they could easily obstruct the Legislative and the Executive branches from operating smoothly.[85]

The judiciary has long been the key supporter of the elite faction. It gains legitimacy not from the ballot box, but from its high moral standing and from serving under the name of the king. But despite the claim that it is the protector of the rule of law and important public institutions, the judiciary always defers to the junta's authoritarian exercise of power. The judicial reviews of Thailand's elections could be seen as part of a network of the old establishment's aim to get rid of Thaksin's regime. The judiciary, as a whole, has produced numerous decisions that attacked Thaksin's men.

The Constitutional Court, in particular, is prone to becoming the minority's tool to harass Thaksin. Constitutional Court judges are not career officers similar to those in the Court of Justice or the Administrative Court. They are nominated from an ad hoc committee with little political interference. The 2008 panel had in fact recruited several figures who were known critics of the Thaksin regime.[86] Their personal attitudes were displayed publicly during trials and in decisions.

In addition to dissolutions and invalidations, the Constitutional Court disqualified Thaksin's proxy prime minister and stopped several public policies of his, such as his high-speed railway, water management scheme, and constitutional amendments.[87] While Thaksin's parties, TRT, PPP, and PT, suffered from hostile judicial review, the Democrat party, the political representative of the elite minority, is the only beneficiary. Its potential competitors were banned and, for once, it successfully brokered its way into power.

The Constitutional Court might argue that invalidation of elections and dissolutions were meant to uphold democratic principles such as transparency, a fair election, or genuine representation of the people. But the display of double standards makes such a claim doubtful. In reality, these decisions threaten political parties with insecurity and portray electoral politics as a filthy game of power – they have become a hindrance to Thailand's democratisation.

Aggressive exercise of judicial review is a dangerous tactic. Not only does it weaken Thailand's electoral politics, but it also causes deterioration of the judiciary's legitimacy. These decisions expose the judiciary's departure from the politically neutral stance to which it is supposed to adhere. These judges are helping the minority to entrench its domination in Thai politics. The move will further deepen the division in Thai society.

Because of its revered status and rigorous constitutional protection, the Constitutional Court enjoys almost absolute impunity. It is unlikely to be held accountable for its abuses of judicial review power. This is a difficult dilemma for Thais who have to choose between corrupt elected politicians and an arbitrary court.

Notes

1 Saxer (2014) 2–3.
2 Ibid.
3 The 1997 political reform was the consequence of the 1992 Black May incident when the emerging middle class protested against the military's attempt to dominate Thailand's politics. These middle class protesters were a result of decades of economic success under authoritarian regimes in the 1960–1970s. The clash left many dead and several people missing. The military was defeated. The deadly clash spurred the call for reform to create a more democratic constitution that would introduce transparency and stability into Thailand, and permanently secure democratisation. See Baker and Pongpaichit (2009) 246–257 and Ginsburg (2008) 89–91.
4 Imaizumi (2003) 8 and Ginsburg (2008) 94.
5 The Constitution of the Kingdom of Thailand, BE 2540 (1997) [Thai Constitution 1997]; the Interim Charter of the Kingdom of Thailand, BE 2549 (2006) [Thai Interim Charter 2006]; the Constitution of the Kingdom of Thailand, BE 2550 (2007) [Thai Constitution 2007]; the Interim Charter of the Kingdom of Thailand, BE 2557 (2014) [Thai Interim Charter 2014].
6 Imaizumi (2003) 8, 19.
7 Ibid. 23.
8 Ibid. 8 and 36.
9 Thai Constitution 2007 § 208 para. 1.
10 Thai Constitution 1997 § 255.
11 Ibid. § 257 (1).
12 Ibid. § 257 (2).
13 Ginsburg (2008) 95.
14 Thai Constitution 2007 § 204.
15 Ibid. § 206 (1).
16 The Council for Democratic Reform under Constitution Monarchy Decoration No. 3 BE 2549 (2006).
17 Thai Constitution 2007 § 211–212.
18 Ibid. § 91.
19 Ibid. § 214.
20 Ibid. § 235.
21 Ibid. § 223 para. 2. As the EC is not part of the legislative branch, its rules are not considered provisions of law, as the term "law" specifically refers to a parliamentary act passed with the consent of people's representatives. Thus, there is also no clause in the Constitution allowing the constitutional court to review the EC's actions. However, the EC is also the head of the EC secretariat office. If the EC is exercising its power in its capacity as the head of the EC secretariat office, for example, issuing an internal guideline or demoting its staff, it is acting as an administrative agency. In this case, its decision is reviewable by the Administrative Court.
22 Political Party Organic Act BE 2541 (1998) § 66; Political Party Organic Act BE 2550 (2007) § 69.
23 Political Party Organic Act 1998 § 66.
24 Thai Constitution 1997 § 116.

25 Political Party Organic Act 1998 § 69.
26 Thai Constitution 1997 § 237.
27 Thai Constitution 2007 § 68 para. 2.
28 The Constitution Drafting Assembly was a body of 100 experts from various sectors, e.g. bureaucracy, academic, business, and civil society, that undertook the drafting of the 2007 Constitution. Members were selected by the 2006 coup makers. Interim Charter 2006 § 19, 22, and 23.
29 Political Party Organic Act 2007 § 69.
30 Thai Constitution 1997 § 198.
31 Decision 9/2549 [2006] Constitutional Court of Thailand.
32 Thai Constitution 2007 § 245.
33 Decision 5/2557 [2014] Constitutional Court of Thailand.
34 Baker and Pongpaichit (2009) 268; Ginsburg (2008) 97.
35 Pongsudhirak (2008) 142.
36 Royal Decree Dissolving the House of Representatives 2006 (Thai).
37 Thai Constitution 1997 § 116.
38 Thai Constitution 1997 § 115.
39 Baker and Pongpaichit (2009) 270.
40 Decision No. 29/2549 [2007] Supreme Administrative Court of Thailand.
41 Election Organic Act BE 2542 (1999) § 69.
42 'Academic Rips up Ballot Paper' *Nation* (Bangkok, April 4, 2006) www.nationmultimedia.com/2006/04/03/politics/politics_30000798.php accessed May 1, 2015.
43 Supphasiri (2010) 174.
44 Decision No. 620/2549 [2007] Supreme Administrative Court of Thailand.
45 Thai Constitution 1997 § 104:

> In a general election, a voter shall have the right to cast ballot for only one list of candidates prepared by the political party and, in an election on a constituency basis, for one candidate in that constituency. In an election of a member of the House of Representatives to replace the member of the House of Representatives elected on a constituency basis whose office becomes vacant under section 119(2), a voter shall have the right to cast ballot for one candidate in that constituency. The election shall be by direct suffrage and secret ballot. In each constituency, the counting of votes from every polling station altogether shall be conducted and the result of the vote-counting shall be announced publicly at any single place in that constituency as designated by the Election Commission, except that in the case where necessity arises in a particular locality, the Election Commission may provide otherwise in accordance with the organic law on the election of members of the House of Representatives and senators. The provisions of paragraph four shall apply mutatis mutandis to the counting and announcement of votes received by each party-list in each constituency under section 103.

46 Decision No. 9/2549 [2007] Constitutional Court of Thailand.
47 Thomas Fuller, 'Thai Court Convicts 3 for Election Missteps' *New York Times* (Bangkok, June 26, 2006) www.nytimes.com/2006/07/25/world/asia/25iht-thai.2286019.html?_r=0 accessed May 1, 2015; Harding and Leyland (2011) 66.
48 The panel consisted of the President of the Supreme Court, the President of the Supreme Administrative Court, five Supreme Court judges, and two Supreme Administrative Court judges. See the Interim Charter 2006 § 35.
49 The Council of National Security Order No. 27 BE 2549 (2006).
50 Decision 45/2496 [1953] Supreme Court of Thailand.
51 Decision 3–5/2550 [2007] Constitutional Court of Thailand.
52 Decision 1–2/2550 [2007] Constitutional Court of Thailand.
53 Thai Constitution 2007 § 237:

A candidate in an election who commits an act or causes or supports another person to act in violation of the organic law on election of members of the House of Representatives and acquisition of senators or regulations or notifications of the Election Commission which resulting in the election not to be honest and fair, his right to vote at an election shall be suspended under the organic law on election of members of the House of Representatives and acquisition of senators. If it appears convincing evidence, through an act of the person under paragraph one, that the President or an executive board or director of a political party connives or neglects at such commission or such commission is known to him but he fails to deter or revise such commission for the maintenance of honest and fair election, it shall be deemed that such political party doing an act for the acquisition of the power to rule the country by means which is not in accordance with the provisions of this Constitution under section 68. In such case, if the Constitutional Court orders to dissolve such political party, the right to vote at an election of the President or the executive board of directors of a political party shall be suspended for the period of five years as from the date such order is made.

54 'Jarun-Chue-Rattatharmmanoon-Mart-Tra-237-Kae-Pan-Ha-Sue-Siang-Dai' [Jarun believes Section 237 could Solve Vote Buying Problem] *Manager Online* (Bangkok, June 9, 2009) www.manager.co.th/Home/ViewNews.aspx?NewsID=9520000064995 accessed May 1, 2015.

55 In 2008, some of the 111 former TRT executives sent their spouses or relatives to join the government. Chai Chidchob, the Speaker of the House of Representatives, was the father of Newin Chidchob. Anongwan Thepsutin, the Minister of Natural Resources and Environment, was Somsak Thepsutin's wife. Ranongrak Suwanchawee, the Minister of Information and Communication Technology, was the wife of Pairoj Suwanchawee.

56 Decision 12-13/2551 [2008] Constitutional Court of Thailand. See also 'Where Cookery is Crookery' *The Economist* (Jakarta, September 11, 2008) www.economist.com/node/12209856 accessed July 18, 2015.

57 Decision No. 2236–37/2550 [2007] Supreme Court of Thailand.

58 Ian MacKinnon, 'Thailand Protest Strands Thousands of Tourists at Bangkok Airport' *Guardian* (Bangkok, November 26, 2008) www.theguardian.com/world/2008/nov/26/thailand-protests-airport accessed May 1, 2015.

59 Decision 20/2551 [2008] Constitutional Court of Thailand.

60 Decision 18–19/2551 [2008] Constitutional Court of Thailand.

61 Jenny Percival, 'Thai Opposition Leader Becomes PM' *Guardian* (Bangkok, December 15, 2008) www.theguardian.com/world/2008/dec/15/thailand-prime-minister accessed July 15, 2015.

62 UDD was the group of Thaksin loyalists as well as anti-coup activists. It was formed in response to the creation of PAD. See also Nostitz (2014).

63 Ibid. 183–185.

64 Decision 15/2553 [2010] Constitutional Court of Thailand.

65 Political Parties Organic Act 2007 § 6.

66 Political Parties Organic Act 2007 § 93.

67 Harding and Leyland (2011) 183.

68 Saksith Saiyasombat, 'Thai Court Quashes Changes to Senate, Spares Pheu Thai Party' *Asian Correspondent* (Bangkok, November 20, 2013) http://asiancorrespondent.com/116112/thai-constitutional-court-rules-charter-amendments-unlawful-spares-pheu-thai-party/ accessed May 1, 2015.

69 Jeffrey Hays, '2013 Political Crisis after Yingluck Government Tries to Pass Amnesty Bill that would Allow Thaksin to Return to Thailand' *Facts And Details* (May 2014) http://factsanddetails.com/southeast-asia/Thailand/sub5_8a/entry-3201.html accessed May 1, 2015.

70 Royal Decree Dissolving the House of Representatives 2013.

71 James Hookway and Wilawan Watcharasakwet, 'Thailand Opposition Democrat Party to Boycott Election' *Wall Street Journal* (Bangkok, December 21, 2013) www.wsj.com/articles/SB10001424052702304866904579271862159417896 accessed May 1, 2015.

72 'Thailand's Political Crisis: Like Two Countries' *The Economist* (Bangkok, January 15, 2014) www.economist.com/blogs/banyan/2014/01/thailands-political-crisis accessed May 1, 2015.

73 Ibid.

74 Decision 2/2557 [2014] Constitutional Court of Thailand.

75 See n. 72.

76 Kocha Olarn, Pamela Boykoff, and Holly Yan, 'Thailand Elections Marred by Violence, Delays' *CNN* (Bangkok, February 2, 2014) http://edition.cnn.com/2014/02/02/world/asia/thailand-election/ accessed May 1, 2015.

77 Thai Constitution 2007 § 108:

> The King has the prerogative to dissolve the House of Representatives for a new election of members of the House. The dissolution of the House of Representatives shall be made in the form of a Royal Decree in which the day for a new general election must be fixed for not less than forty-five days but not more than sixty days as from the day the House of Representatives has been dissolved and such election day must be the same throughout the Kingdom. The dissolution of the House of Representatives may be made only once under the same circumstance.

78 Decision 5/2557 [2014] Constitutional Court of Thailand.

79 Manop Thip-Osod, 'EC takes Flak for Poll Fund Redress Plan' *Bangkok Post* (Bangkok, December 23, 2014) www.bangkokpost.com/news/general/451612/ec-takes-flak-for-poll-fund-redress-plan accessed May 1, 2015.

80 Yingluck removed the National Security Chief without proper justification and replaced that vacancy with her relative. This act was contrary to the Constitution's prevention of any conflict of interest. Decision 9/2557 [2014] Constitutional Court of Thailand. See also 'Out of Luck' *The Economist* (Bangkok, May 10, 2014) www.economist.com/news/asia/21601871-court-ousts-yingluck-shinawatra-pushing-country-further-towards-political-breakdown-out accessed May 1, 2015.

81 Saxer (2014) 7–13.

82 McCargo (2005) 501–510; Duncan McCargo, 'The Elite Cannot Turn Back the Tide of Thai Politics' *Financial Times* (May 8, 2014) www.ft.com/intl/cms/s/0/8a3b6ed4-d6b8-11e3-b251-00144feabdc0.html#axzz3fwtG2olJ accessed May 1, 2015.

83 McCargo (2005) 501–510 and McCargo (n. 82).

84 Laothamatas (1996).

85 Ibid.

86 Opas Boonlom, 'Outgoing Court President was Bold and Controversial' *Nation* (Bangkok, July 18, 2013) www.nationmultimedia.com/politics/Outgoing-court-president-was-bold-and-controversia-30210678.html accessed May 1, 2015; 'Updated: Court Battle Gains Some Heat' *Political Prisoners in Thailand* (27 April 2013) https://thaipoliticalprisoners.wordpress.com/2013/04/27/court-battle-gains-some-heat/ accessed July 15, 2015.

87 Decision 15–18/2556 [2013], Decision 1/2557 [2014], Decision 3–4/2557 [2014] Constitutional Court of Thailand.

References

Baker C. and Pongpaichit P., *A History of Thailand* (2nd edn, Cambridge University Press 2009).

Ginsburg T., 'Constitutional Afterlife: The Continuing Impact of Thailand's Postpolitical Constitution' (2008) 7 *International Journal of Constitutional Law* 83.

Harding A. and Leyland P., *The Constitutional System of Thailand* (Hart Publishing 2011).

Imaizumi S., 'The Political Reform and the Constitutional Court of Thailand' (Japanese External Trade Organization 2003).

Laothamatas A., 'A Tale of Two Democracies: Conflicting Perception of Elections and Democracy in Thailand' in R.H. Taylor (ed.), *The Politics of Elections in South East Asia* (Cambridge University Press 1996).

McCargo D., 'Network Monarchy and Legitimacy Crises in Thailand' (2005) 18 *Pacific Review* 499.

Nostitz N., 'The Red Shirts: From Anti-Coup Protesters to Social Mass Movement' in P. Chachavalpongpun (ed.), *Good Coup Gone Bad* (Institute of Southeast Asian Studies 2014).

Pongsudhirak T., 'Thailand since the Coup' (2008) 19 *Journal of Democracy* 140.

Saxer M., *Building the Good Society in Thailand: Resolving Transformation Conflict through Inclusive Compromise* (Friedrich-Ebert Stiftung 2014).

Supphasiri R., *Prawat Yǭ Kānmư̄ang Thai Nai Rǭp Thotsawat* [Brief Political Developments of Thailand in a Decade] (Post Book 2010).

Part III

Comparative perspectives

12 Courts, judicial review and the electoral process in Australia

An Antipodean perspective

Sarah Murray

Introduction

It is quite rare that electoral litigation is invoked in Australia. It is even rarer that an Australian election would be re-run due to concerns about a failure of process. The 2013 federal election was an exception to this trend. Following a federal election held on 7 September 2013, it transpired that the election result for the final two Senate positions (out of the six upper house seats) assigned to one of Australia's six States, Western Australia, was challenged. However, the discovery was made that the ability to undertake a recount of the State's votes was compromised by 1370 lost ballot papers, a number well in excess of the 14, or possibly 12, vote margin separating the contested seats. As a consequence of these extraordinary events, the 2013 half-Senate Western Australian election was declared void by the Court of Disputed Returns and Western Australian electors were sent back to polls in April 2014 to elect six Senators afresh.[1] A re-run such as this had only been ordered once before in Australia's electoral history (and then only for one Senate seat).[2]

Often, the involvement of the Court of Disputed Returns in Australian electoral cases is more dependent on the tightness of the contest between candidates than the gravity of the legal issues at stake.[3] This trend is exacerbated by the costs of funding challenges, the strictness of electoral litigious procedures and the political weight of the candidates involved. The limited nature of curial involvement in electoral disputes is also heightened by the fact that standard judicial review avenues are limited.[4] This chapter surveys the role of the courts and judicial review of the parliamentary electoral process in Australia at the federal level. I start with a brief description of the Australian constitutional structure and voting system. This is followed by an exploration of the function of the High Court as the federal Court of Disputed Returns in Australia, the place for the Commonwealth Parliament in electoral disputes and the recent case of *Australian Electoral Commission* v. *Johnston*.[5] The third section then traverses the degree to which the High Court defers to Parliament in matters of electoral legislative regulation.

Australian constitutional structure and voting system

Australia is a federation and constitutional monarchy, governed pursuant to the Commonwealth Constitution (Constitution), with the British monarch Australia's head of state and the Governor-General appointed as her representative. It draws on elements from the constitutional heritage of both the United States and the United Kingdom. Through federation, from 1 January 1901, Australia's six colonies united to form the Commonwealth of Australia, which saw governmental powers divided between the federal government and the Australian States, governed in turn by their own State constitutions. The federal government comprises a judicial, legislative and executive arm. The federal executive, including the Australian Prime Minister and members of cabinet, through principles of responsible and representative government, are drawn from the Commonwealth legislature, made up of the House of Representatives and the Senate.

Voting is compulsory in Australian federal elections and Section 245(1) of the Commonwealth Electoral Act 1918 (Cth) (CEA) provides that '[i]t shall be the duty of every elector to vote at each election'. Elections for the House of Representatives must be held at least every three years and, at these elections, half of the Senate (made up of Senators serving staggered six year terms) is also contemporaneously elected (subject to the possibility of a double dissolution election within the terms of Section 57 of the Constitution). A method of preferential voting is used to elect the 150 members of the House of Representatives. The 76 federal senators (12 for each State and two for the Australian Capital Territory and the Northern Territory, respectively) are chosen by proportional representation.

Function of the Australian High Court

The court of disputed returns

By the CEA, the Court of Disputed Returns' jurisdiction is the federal avenue for resolving disputes with respect to Commonwealth elections.[6] Sitting as the Court of Disputed Returns, the High Court can either hear an electoral petition or refer a matter to the Federal Court of Australia below it for resolution.[7] Decisions of the Court of Disputed Returns are final and not subject to appeal.[8] Electoral matters have been determined to be a part of the Court's jurisdiction and to constitute a judicial conferral (rather than an appointment upon a Judge in a personal capacity).[9] For constitutional reasons this latter distinction is significant because federal Judges can only be vested with federal judicial power,[10] subject to some limited and qualified exceptions.

Questions remain as to whether the right balance is struck between allowing sufficient access to the Court of Disputed Returns and preventing the floodgates to inane electoral petitions.[11] The ability to bring a petition to challenge an election is less a barrier than the procedural obstacles which apply to such a petition. These obstacles mean that the ability for a full judicial review of an election to be conducted is often quite limited.[12] The powers and procedures governing and limiting such review are provided for by the CEA. As an example, Section 355(e) of the CEA requires that every petition challenging an election[13] be filed within 40 days of the return of the writ to which it relates.[14] The Court has emphasised that such requirement is directed at 'certain[ty]' on the basis that the timely and 'fina[l]' resolution of a contested election is in 'the public interest'.[15] Further, general judicial review avenues are limited by express CEA provisions, such as Section 353 which precludes a challenge being brought by an elector to the validity of an election otherwise than in the Court of Disputed Returns.[16] The petition to the Court of Disputed Returns must not only set out the 'facts relied on to invalidate the election or return' (Section 355(a)) but it must 'be signed by a candidate at the election in dispute or by a person who was qualified to vote' (Section 355(c)) and 'be attested by 2 witnesses whose occupations and addresses are stated' (Section 355(d)). The Court has read these elements strictly so as to make it difficult for amendments to a petition to be made.[17]

Further, the powers of the Court are confined by the terms of the CEA. For instance, it cannot find a whole election entirely void[18] and a single petition, at least in the context of a challenge to the lower house of the Commonwealth Parliament, can only relate to a single electorate in which an elector voted or in which a candidate ran for election.[19]

Orr and Williams have espoused the need for some flexibility in the application of the CEA procedural provisions.[20] They have also reflected on the fact that curial intervention is also constrained by the need to show an impact on the choice of candidate[21] (see, for example, the recent case of *Johnston*)[22] and not just the size of their margin of victory.[23] As Isaacs J noted in *Kean* v. *Kerby*, in a case where there had been a one-vote margin in the contested seat, '[t]his Court of Disputed Returns is the only tribunal that can afford real and effective protection to electors maintaining their right of franchise'.[24]

The role of the Court of Disputed Returns also sits in the shadows of a remote constitutional possibility, cast by Section 47 of the Constitution. Section 47 provides:

> Until the Parliament otherwise provides, any question respecting the qualification of a senator or of a member of the House of Representatives, or respecting a vacancy in either House of the Parliament, and any question of a disputed election to either House, shall be determined by the House in which the question arises.

The Parliament did so 'otherwise provide' in 1902 with the enactment of Section 193(1) of the CEA, with its equivalent now being Section 354 of the 1918 CEA.[25] Section 354(1) provides: 'The High Court shall be the Court of Disputed Returns, and shall have jurisdiction either to try the petition or to refer it for trial to the Federal Court of Australia.'

The extent of this conferral of jurisdiction arose in *Sue* v. *Hill*, particularly in relation to whether Section 376 of the CEA affected the operation of Section 353(1) of the CEA such that questions of qualification or seat vacancies were outside the scope of Section 353(1) and were subject to a reference by the Commonwealth Parliament.[26] These provided:

> s 353(1): The validity of any election or return may be disputed by petition addressed to the Court of Disputed Returns and not otherwise.
>
> s 376: Any question respecting the qualifications of a Senator or of a Member of the House of Representatives or respecting a vacancy in either House of the Parliament may be referred by resolution to the Court of Disputed Returns by the House in which the question arises and the Court of Disputed Returns shall thereupon have jurisdiction to hear and determine the question.

Gleeson CJ, Gummow and Hayne JJ[27] and Gaudron J[28] found,[29] as in *Sykes* v. *Cleary*[30] and *In re Wood*,[31] that Section 47 was not referring to 'mutually exclusive' electoral questions. The majority therefore concluded that it was an error to assume that 'any question of a disputed election' was removed from a parliamentarian's qualifications to be a Senator or a Member of the House of Representatives.[32]

The question of a conflict of jurisdiction was also raised, but not resolved, by the Court.[33] Orr and Williams[34] discuss how this issue arose in parliamentary debates in the House of Representatives in relation to whether Mr Entsch, the member for Leichhardt, was disqualified from being a member of the House by Section 44(v) of the Constitution and whether, on a failed motion,[35] this should be referred to the Court of Disputed Returns, rather than dealt with by the Parliament.[36] Orr and Williams note that Section 368 of the CEA renders the Court of Disputed Returns' determination 'final and conclusive' and that a contemporaneous motion before Parliament 'might not defer the High Court from giving a different answer'.[37] Relatedly, Carney has noted that should a matter not be referred under Section 47, a conflict could arise between the chamber resolving a qualification issue contemporaneously brought before the High Court pursuant to the Common Informers (Parliamentary Disqualifications) Act 1975 (Cth).[38] Such a challenge could arise based on disqualification through constitutional requirements for sitting members set by Part IV of the Constitution. A judicial resolution in such a situation is arguably preferable but the current available forums mean that this is not inevitable.[39]

The Johnston *case*[40] *– the Western Australian Senate election debacle*

Section 7 of the Constitution provides that the 'Senate shall be composed of senators for each State, directly chosen by the people of the State'. Challenges to the validity of elections are not routinely brought.[41]

As noted above, the *Johnston* case is a recent exception to the trend and was the first time a half-Senate election for an entire State was re-run. This case followed an inquiry into the running of the WA election by Mick Keelty AO.[42]

While an initial request for a recount was refused, on appeal a recount of appropriately 96 per cent of WA Senate votes was ordered, at which point the number of missing ballot papers was discovered.[43]

Heard before Hayne J, his Honour found that the loss of the 1370 ballot papers from the Divisions of Pearce and Forrest meant that these voters were 'prevented from voting' within the terms of Section 365 of the CEA,[44] as their ballots were unable to be subject to the requisite scrutiny. Hayne J found that there were two prerequisites for determining the WA Senate election to be void on the basis of illegal practices: (1) 'that the result of the election was likely to be affected' and (2) 'that it is just that the candidate should be declared not to be duly elected or that the election should be declared void'.[45]

His Honour concluded that the election 'result declared was likely to be affected by illegal practices'[46] and, that as any records in relation to those missing papers were inadmissible, that the election on 7 September for six WA Senators was absolutely void and that a re-run of the election was essential, with the Commonwealth being required to pay all petitioners' costs, except for those of the Australian Electoral Commission.[47]

Conclusion

It remains to be seen whether the Court of Disputed Returns will begin to play a larger role in Australian elections. Federal elections are becoming increasingly complicated. This is not only as the country debates the merits of technological electoral changes,[48] but also through reform debates directed at the rise of minor and/or micro-parties[49] and the practical obstacles this has introduced (including some upper house Senate ballot papers of over one metre in length).[50] These debates have the potential to throw up new challenges, which land more parties on the steps of the Court of Disputed Returns.

The High Court and Parliament

Electoral legislative regulation – deference or interference by the High Court?

The Constitution is not particularly facilitative of constitutional rights challenges before the courts. It lacks a Bill of Rights and attempts to amend the Constitution to include voting rights in the 1970s and 1980s failed spectacularly.[51] Even Section 41, which could be read to confer a right to vote on 'adult person[s]', has been interpreted so as to be constitutionally obsolete.[52]

Constitutional attempts to challenge electoral legislation were traditionally confronted by a highly deferential High Court. While the Court accepted that the requirement in Sections 7 and 24 of the Constitution that the composition of the Senate and the House of Representatives be 'directly chosen by the people' did result in some constitutional limits, this often was not enough to result in constitutional success in challenges arguing for one-vote/one-value[53] or contesting the validity of electoral design or CEA provisions.[54] Instead, the High Court routinely found, by majority,[55] that such matters were to be determined by Parliament and not the Courts. This was in spite of the High Court using the 'directly chosen' constitutional requirement to find an 'implied freedom of political communication', which could invalidate federal or State legislation that burdened the communication of governmental or political matters without being 'reasonably appropriate or adapted to serve a legitimate end in a manner which is compatible with the maintenance of the constitutionally prescribed system of representative and responsible government'.[56]

However, in *Roach* v. *Electoral Commissioner*[57] and then *Rowe* v. *Electoral Commissioner*,[58] a majority of the High Court seemed to adopt a more interventionist approach which, in line with the proportionality implied freedom of political communication jurisprudence, resulted in electoral legislation being invalidated as unconstitutional.

In *Roach*,[59] by a split across the Court of four:two, the High Court held that it was unconstitutional by an application of the 'directly chosen by the people' requirement for legislation to preclude all prisoners, regardless of their term, from voting at federal elections. Universal suffrage, while potentially susceptible to permissible exceptions, did not justify such an exclusion from the franchise of the prison population.[60]

The majority in *Roach* found that any exclusion from the franchise needed to be justified by measures supported by a substantial reason, namely one that is reasonably appropriate and adapted to serve an end consistent and compatible with the maintenance of the constitutionally prescribed system of representative government.[61]

The failure to distinguish between serious and more trivial crimes and the length of a prisoner's imprisonment meant that this was not satisfied. Orr and Williams have commented that even the approach of the majority can be classed as conservative in that it represents less of a 'sword' than a 'partial shield' such that 'when the political process has granted the franchise to a group for a significant length of time, the right to vote of that group may become entrenched'.[62] They distinguish this from the High Court actively seeking to expand what suffrage means in Australia and point out that the Court needed to find more solid constitutional grounds for its electoral jurisprudence, rather than simply relying on what is effectively 'majoritarianism'.[63]

The minority were highly critical of the majority's reading of the 'directly chosen by the people' mandate. Hayne and Heydon JJ disputed that this phrase could inhibit the Parliament from determining the content of the franchise.[64] For Hayne J, it was a statement of 'generality' and not 'universality'.[65] Their Honours felt that the Parliament should not be limited by the 'common understanding of the time',[66] that the constitutional standard was a static one[67] and that something 'highly undesirable' in terms of the franchise did not equate to unconstitutionality.[68]

In *Rowe*,[69] again with a majority of four (this time composed of French CJ, Crennan, Gummow and Bell JJ), the Court found invalid provisions which closed the electoral roll shortly after electoral writs had been issued, affecting the eligibility of some 100,000 potential voters. Introduced on the premise of ensuring heightened electoral integrity, new voters only had until 8 p.m. on the day the writs were issued to enrol and only three days rather than seven days to transfer their enrolment.[70]

The majority determined that while not amounting to a direct disenfranchisement, the amendments practically disqualified voters who would otherwise have been eligible to vote at the 2010 election based on the 'directly chosen by the people' constitutional requirement.[71] French CJ sought to clarify that the 'common understanding' of the constitutional 'directly chosen by the people' phrase 'cannot now be diminished'[72] and that rather than being judicially determined arose out of 'a persistent view by the elected representatives of the people' of its meaning.[73]

For the majority, while accepting that these 100,000 eligible voters were strictly in contravention of the CEA, the Act operated so as to waive any penalty if enrolment did occur and hence put the 'civic right over the legal duty'.[74] The amending provisions in shortening the time period to enrol were found to lack a 'substantial reason',[75] to de-centre electoral 'participation' and to be 'disproportionate' in light of the impact on the franchise and the paucity of evidence of Australian electoral fraud.[76]

The minority judges from *Roach*, Hayne and Heydon JJ, were joined in *Rowe* by Kiefel J in finding that the otherwise eligible persons ('descamisados and other victims')[77] only had themselves to blame in failing to enrol in accordance with the CEA requirements and had infringed the Act by their tardiness.[78] Further, they did not agree that it was constitutionally possible for Australian democratic or electoral developments to alter somehow the import of the Constitution's 'directly chosen by the people' maxim,[79] or that it could require 'maximum participation'[80] or restrict the Commonwealth Parliament from regulating the enrolment periods. Furthermore, neither Hayne J nor Kiefel J was convinced by the proportionality arguments accepted by the majority in relation to the post-writ enrolment window.[81]

Interestingly, across both *Roach* and *Rowe*, the majority and minority accept that there must be judicial deference to political judgment. In *Rowe*, French CJ indicated 'that Parliament has a considerable discretion as to the means which it chooses to regulate elections and to ensure that persons claiming an entitlement to be enrolled are so entitled'.[82] Even in the recent decision of *Tajjour*, French CJ noted that 'Courts must not exceed their constitutional competence by substituting their own legislative judgments for those of parliament'.[83] For the minority, the 'spare' character of the Constitution's regulation of the franchise means that 'so much is left for the Parliament to provide'.[84]

However, a High Court bench split in relation to when the court should show deference to Parliament and when intervention is obligatory. For all of the judges, the 'directly chosen by the people' mandate becomes the crystallising factor. However, the majority's conception of this maxim is much richer than that of the minority.[85] For the majority, the 'directly chosen by the people' maxim is about maximising participation through a reading that is 'as expressive of the popular choice as practical considerations properly permit'[86] and which is chameleon-like in the way it responds to society's accepted mores and expectations.[87] Twomey contends that, worryingly, such an interpretation goes so far as to allow parliamentary amendment of the Constitution.[88] French CJ attempted to predict such a criticism by noting that he was not 'suggest[ing] that particular legislative procedures … can become constitutionally entrenched with the passage of time' but that instead parliaments are kerbed by the 'choice by the people' which can then make the 'alteration of a long-standing mechanism' unconstitutional.[89] Regardless, the majority's more luxuriant reading makes it harder for a law to withstand the High Court's gaze as there is a heightened potential for it to undermine the Court's conception of the constitutional mandate. This means a law, as analysed by the majority, is going to have a harder time being constitutionally valid,[90] and that following *Rowe*, even more prosaic electoral dimensions such as polling locations, ballot papers and enrolment procedures could be subject to greater scrutiny.[91] In contrast, a much more deferential outcome is inevitably bundled up in the methodological approach of the minority. The Court is, however, far from united and, with the bench's composition currently in a state of flux,[92] the continuance of the majority approach is not necessarily assured.

Conclusion

Uncertainty surrounds the Australian judicature's role in relation to the federal electoral process. In particular, it is uncertain whether electoral legislation adequately leaves the door open for electoral challenges to be brought and whether the courts are even the appropriate forum for such disputes to be ventilated. Similarly, divergent constitutional interpretations of the 'directly chosen by the people' mandate in Sections 7 and 24 of the Constitution mean that the jurisprudence of the High Court of Australia is far from unanimous as to when the Court should disturb federal electoral legislative regulation. The question of when judicial intervention is appropriate is not straightforward.[93] However, there clearly is a role for the courts to play, even if the precise boundaries surrounding this intervention are still the subject of debate.

Notes

1 *Australian Electoral Commission* v. *Johnston* (2014) 251 CLR 463 [106], [122] (Hayne J). The Joint Standing Committee on Electoral Matters described the ballot paper misadventure as the 'greatest failure in the history of the Australian Electoral Commission': Joint Standing Committee on Electoral Matters (2015) vii.
2 Australian Electoral Commission, *Annual Report 2013–2014* at 96.
3 Orr and Williams (2001) 73.
4 Australian Government (2009) [13.7]–[13.9]; Orr (2012). Note, however, availability of injunctive relief under s. 383 of the CEA.
5 *Johnston* (n. 1).

6 Australian States also have a similar jurisdiction conferred on Supreme Courts via State electoral legislation: e.g. Electoral Act 1992 (Qld), s. 137(1).
7 CEA, s. 354; for an excellent discussion of the history of the courts' involvement in electoral matters see Orr and Williams (2001) 55–61; Orr (2012).
8 CEA, s. 368. This was found to be constitutionally consistent with s. 73 of the Constitution: *Sue* v. *Hill* (1999) 199 CLR 462, 521 (Gaudron J). With a referral to the Federal Court, the constitutionalised prerogative writs may also be a potential avenue for judicial review in cases tainted by jurisdictional error: *Re Australian Electoral Commission; Ex parte Kelly* (2003) 77 ALJR 1307 [24] (Gummow J).
9 *Sue* v. *Hill* (n. 8) 480–486 (Gleeson CJ, Gummow and Hayne JJ), 514–523 (Gaudron J). As to the constitutionality of this conferral, see: *Re Brennan; Ex parte Muldowney* (1993) 116 ALR 619, 621–622 (Mason CJ); Walker (1997); Schoff (1997).
10 *R* v. *Kirby; Ex parte Boilermakers' Society of Australia* (1956) 94 CLR 254.
11 Australian Government (2009) [13.17].
12 Orr and Williams (2001) 93. See also Carney (2003) 183–184.
13 Section 353 of the CEA notes that a petition is the sole means of disputing the validity of an election or return.
14 *Rudolphy* v. *Lightfoot* (1999) 197 CLR 500.
15 Ibid. 508 (Gleeson CJ, Gaudron, McHugh, Gummow and Hayne JJ).
16 See further, Orr *et al.* (2003) 389.
17 Gageler (2003) 186, 192; Orr and Williams (2001) 76–77. See also *Re Berrill* (1978) 19 ALR 254, 255 (Gibbs ACJ, Stephen, Mason, Jacobs and Aickin JJ agreeing); *Sykes* v. *Australian Electoral Commission* (1993) 115 ALR 645, 648 (Dawson J); *McClure* v. *Australian Electoral Commission* (1999) 163 ALR 734, [9] (Hayne J); *Scott-Irving* v. *Oakeshott* [2009] FCA 487, [31]–[32]. Note s. 358(2) CEA: *Re Green* (2011) 85 ALJR 423.
18 *Muldowney* v. *Australian Electoral Commission* (1993) 178 CLR 34, 42 (Brennan ACJ); *Abbotto* v. *Commonwealth Electoral Commission* (1997) 144 CLR 352 (Dawson J).
19 See CEA, ss 221, 355(c); *Robertson* v. *Australian Electoral Commission* (1993) 116 ALR 407 (Toohey J); *Wheeley* v. *Australian Electoral Commissioner* [2005] FCA 473, [6] (Kiefel J). Cf. *Johnston* case where the WA Senate election was found to be void.
20 Orr and Williams (2001) 79 citing *Kean* v. *Kerby* (1920) 27 CLR 449, 458 (Isaacs J).
21 CEA, s. 362.
22 *Johnston* (n. 1) [2], [62], [102].
23 Ibid. [56] (Hayne J); Orr and Williams (2001) 71.
24 *Kean* (n. 20) 460.
25 *Sue* v. *Hill* (n. 8) 476–477 (Gleeson CJ, Gummow and Hayne JJ). For historical discussion see: *Schoff* (n. 9) 328–330.
26 *Sue* v. *Hill* (n. 8) 479 (Gleeson CJ, Gummow and Hayne JJ), 507 (Gaudron J).
27 Ibid. 479–480.
28 Ibid. 507–508.
29 Ibid. cf. 532, 538–539 (McHugh J), 562–565 (Kirby J), 571 (Callinan J).
30 (1992) 107 ALR 577, 579 (Dawson J).
31 (1988) 167 CLR 145, 160 (Mason CJ, Wilson, Brennan, Deane, Dawson, Toohey and Gaudron JJ).
32 *Sue* v. *Hill* (n. 8) 479 (Gleeson CJ, Gummow and Hayne JJ).
33 Ibid. 480.
34 Orr and Williams (2001) 64.
35 Commonwealth, *Parliamentary Debates*, House of Representatives, 10 June 1999, 6720, 6733.
36 Ibid. 6724 (Daryl Williams, Attorney-General). See also Orr *et al.* (2003) 386.

37 Orr and Williams (2001) 65.
38 Legislated pursuant to s. 46 of the Constitution. See Carney (2003) 184. See also *Sue* v. *Hill* (n. 8) 475 (Gleeson CJ, Gummow and Hayne JJ).
39 Ibid.
40 *Johnston* (n. 1).
41 Orr (2010) 211.
42 M. Keelty, 'Inquiry into the 2013 WA Senate Election' (December 2013) www.aec.gov.au/about_aec/Publications/Reports_On_Federal_Electoral_Events/2013/files/inquiry-into-the-2013-wa-senate-election.pdf accessed 1 September 2015.
43 Ibid. [43]–[48].
44 *Johnston* (n. 1) [95].
45 Ibid. [56].
46 Ibid. [105].
47 Transcript of Proceedings, *Australian Electoral Commission* v. *Johnston* [2014] HCATrans 32 (20 February 2014).
48 Joint Standing Committee on Electoral Matters (2014).
49 Hayden Cooper, 'The Rise of Micro Parties in the Senate' *ABC News* (9 September 2013) www.abc.net.au/news/2013-09-09/the-rise-of-the-micro-parties-in-the-senate/4946924 accessed 23 March 2015.
50 ABC News, 'Senate Ballot Paper Stretches Beyond a Metre in NSW' *ABC News online* (New South Wales, 14 August 2013) www.abc.net.au/news/2013-08-16/senate-ballot-paper-stretches-beyond-a-metre-in-nsw/4892934 accessed 23 March 2015.
51 See Twomey (2000) 151–153.
52 *R* v. *Pearson; Ex parte Sipka* (1983) 152 CLR 254. See also ibid. 126.
53 *Attorney-General (Cth); Ex rel McKinlay* v. *Commonwealth* (1975) 135 CLR 1; *McGinty* v. *Western Australia* (1996) 186 CLR 140.
54 *Judd* v. *McKeon* (1926) 38 CLR 380; *Langer* v. *Commonwealth* (1996) 186 CLR 302; *Mulholland* v. *Australian Electoral Commission* (2004) 220 CLR 181.
55 Cf. *McKinlay* (n. 53) 68–69 (Murphy J, dissenting).
56 *Lange* v. *Australian Broadcasting Corporation* (1997) 189 CLR 520, 567. For recent statements of the 'test' see: *Wotton* v. *Queensland* (2012) 246 CLR 1, [25] (French CJ, Gummow, Hayne, Crennan and Bell JJ); *Monis* v. *The Queen* (2013) 249 CLR 92, [61] (French CJ), [144]–[146] (Hayne J), [347] (Crennan, Kiefel and Bell JJ); *Unions NSW* v. *New South Wales* (2013) 88 ALJR 227, [35], [44] (French CJ, Hayne, Crennan, Kiefel and Bell JJ), [115] (Keane J).
57 (2007) 233 CLR 162.
58 (2010) 243 CLR 1.
59 *Roach* (n. 57).
60 Ibid. [7] (Gleeson CJ), [95] (Gummow, Kirby and Crennan JJ).
61 Ibid. [24] (Gleeson CJ), [85] (Gummow, Kirby and Crennan JJ).
62 Orr and Williams (2009) 124.
63 Ibid. and see 136.
64 Ibid. [145] (Hayne J), [179]–[180] (Heydon J).
65 Ibid. [112].
66 Ibid. [157]–[161] (Hayne J), [180] (Heydon J).
67 Ibid. [161] (Hayne J).
68 Ibid. [179] (Heydon J).
69 *Rowe* (n. 58).
70 Section 101 of the CEA required voters to enrol or change their enrolment details within 21 days of eligibility to do so; however, the amending provisions shortened the grace period that voters were given to attend to their electoral affairs after the calling of the election.
71 *Rowe* (n. 58) [24], [78] (French CJ), [154] (Gummow and Bell JJ), [381] (Crennan J).
72 For a critique of this argument see: Twomey (2012) 188–189.

73 *Rowe* (n. 58) [18]–[19]. See also [22].
74 Ibid. [370] (Crennnan J). See also [50], [78] (French CJ), [131], [161] (Gummow and Bell JJ).
75 Ibid. [25], [78] (French CJ), [157], [161] (Gummow and Bell JJ), [384] (Crennan J).
76 Ibid. [78] (French CJ), [167] (Gummow and Bell JJ), [384] (Crennan J).
77 Ibid. [271] (Heydon J).
78 Ibid. [216], [252] (Hayne J), [284], [288] (Heydon J), [402], [488] (Kiefel J).
79 Ibid. [202]–[203] (Hayne J), [292] (Heydon J), [415] (Kiefel J).
80 Ibid. [221]–[222] (Hayne J), [278], [279] (Heydon J), [412]–[413], [422] (Kiefel J).
81 Ibid. [249]–[263] (Hayne J), [479]–[489] (Kiefel J).
82 Ibid. [29]. See also [325] (Crennan J), [125]–[126] (Gummow and Bell JJ).
83 *Tajjour* v. *New South Wales* (2014) 88 ALJR 860, [36] (French CJ).
84 *Rowe* (n. 58) [200] (Hayne J).
85 Ibid. [132], [154].
86 Ibid. [154] (Gummow and Bell JJ).
87 Ibid. [18] (French CJ), [367] (Crennan J).
88 Twomey (2012) 189, 202.
89 *Rowe* (n. 58) [22].
90 For a detailed analysis of *Rowe* and comparative analysis see: Murray (2012).
91 Ibid. 329–330.
92 Since *Rowe* was decided, Gummow, Heydon, Crennan and Hayne JJ have stepped down. The new bench appointees of Gageler, Keane, Nettle and Gordon JJ present an opportunity to shake up the current majority position.
93 Orr *et al.* (2003) 386.

References

Australian Electoral Commission, *Annual Report 2013–2014* http://annualreport.aec.gov.au/annual-reports.html accessed 20 July 2015.

Australian Government, *Electoral Reform Green Paper: Strengthening Australia's Democracy* (Australian Government 2009).

Carney G., 'The High Court and the Constitutionalism of Electoral Law' in Graeme Orr, Bryan Mercurio and George Williams (eds), *Realising Democracy: Electoral Law in Australia* (Federation Press 2003).

Gageler S., 'Disputed Returns for Commonwealth Elections' in Graeme Orr, Bryan Mercurio and George Williams (eds), *Realising Democracy: Electoral Law in Australia* (Federation Press 2003).

Joint Standing Committee on Electoral Matters, *Second Interim Report on the Inquiry into the Conduct of the 2013 Federal Election: An Assessment of Electronic Voting Options* (Commonwealth of Australia 2014) www.aph.gov.au/~/media/02%20Parliamentary%20Business/24%20Committees/244%20Joint%20Committees/JSCEM/2013%20election%202nd%20interim/Full%20report.pdf accessed 23 March 2015.

Joint Standing Committee on Electoral Matters, *The 2013 Federal Election: Report on the Conduct of the 2013 Election and Matters Related Thereto* (Commonwealth of Australia 2015).

Murray S., 'Forcing Parliamentary Rollback: High Court Intervention in Australian Electoral Legislative Reform' (2012) 11(3) *Election Law Journal* 316.

Orr G., *The Law of Politics: Elections, Parties and Money in Australia* (Federation Press 2010).

Orr G., 'Judicial Review of the Administration of Parliamentary Elections' (2012) 23 *Public Law Review* 110.

Orr G. and Williams G., 'Electoral Challenges: Judicial Review of Parliamentary Elections in Australia' (2001) 23 *Sydney Law Review* 53.

Orr G. and Williams G., 'The People's Choice: The Prisoner Franchise and the Constitutional Protection of Voting Rights in Australia' (2009) 8(2) *Election Law Journal* 123.

Orr G., Mercurio B. and Williams G., 'Australian Electoral Law: A Stocktake' (2003) 2(3) *Election Law Journal* 383.

Schoff P., 'The Electoral Jurisdiction of the High Court as the Court of Disputed Returns: Non-Judicial and Incompatible Function' (1997) 25 *Federal Law Review* 318.

Twomey A., 'The Federal Constitutional Right to Vote in Australia' (2000) 28 *Federal Law Review* 125.

Twomey A., '*Rowe* v. *Electoral Commissioner: Evolution or Creationism*' (2012) 31(2) *University of Queensland Law Journal* 181.

Walker K., 'Disputed Returns and Parliamentary Qualifications: Is the High Court's Jurisdiction Constitutional' (1997) 20 *University of New South Wales Law Journal* 257.

13 Judicial review of the electoral process in Canada

Yasmin Dawood[1]

Introduction

The rules that govern the Canadian electoral process have two main sources. The first source of electoral rules is constitutional. The Charter of Rights and Freedoms explicitly protects the right to vote.[2] Section 3 of the Charter provides that every citizen has the right to vote for elections for the House of Commons or a provincial legislature and to be qualified for membership in those houses.[3] There are two additional Charter provisions that establish democratic rights. Section 4 sets a maximum duration of five years for the life of the House of Commons or a provincial legislature; this period can be extended in the event of a national crisis such as war, provided that two-thirds of the members vote for an extension.[4] Section 5 guarantees a sitting of Parliament and the legislatures at least once every year.[5] It is significant that the democratic rights protected under sections 3, 4, and 5 of the Charter cannot be overridden by the exercise of the notwithstanding clause in section 33. The second source of electoral rules is statutory. With respect to elections at the federal level, the Canada Elections Act provides a vast array of rules governing the eligibility of voters, the mechanics of voting on Election Day, the eligibility of candidates, the registration and conduct of political parties, campaign finance and electoral advertising, and the requirements for reporting and disclosure, among other topics. Provinces and municipalities in Canada have their own electoral statutes; however, the focus of this chapter will be on the rules that govern federal elections.

In Canada, the courts play an important role in adjudicating the disputes that arise over electoral rules. This chapter provides an overview of the role of the Supreme Court of Canada in regulating elections and certain aspects of the democratic process. The first section provides a general overview of the Court's approach to democracy and elections. The second section focuses on a few representative decisions in order to illustrate the function of the Court in overseeing the electoral process. The third section considers a few challenges facing the judicial supervision of elections and democracy.

The Supreme Court and electoral democracy

The Supreme Court has issued several decisions about the electoral process. These decisions have addressed a number of topics, including electoral redistricting, campaign finance, the rules regulating political parties, the disenfranchisement of prisoners, opinion polls, and the entitlement to vote.[6] Many of these cases have arisen under section 3 of the Charter, which provides that every citizen has the right to vote in federal and provincial elections.[7] Other cases have arisen under sections 2(b) and 2(d) of the Charter, which protect the freedoms of expression and association, respectively, and section 15, which guarantees equality.[8] This area of constitutional law is often referred to as 'the law of democracy.'

The Supreme Court has also played an important role in defining the meaning of democracy.[9] For example, the Court has described the principle of democracy as a 'fundamental value in our constitutional law and political culture.'[10] In its decisions, the Court has also emphasised the importance of section 3, declaring, for instance, that the 'right of every citizen to vote ... lies at the heart of Canadian democracy.'[11] In addition, the Court proclaimed that the 'right to vote is fundamental to our democracy and the rule of law.'[12]

In general, the Court has adopted what I call a 'bundle of rights' approach to its law of democracy cases. Under this bundle of rights approach, the Court has recognised multiple democratic rights, each of which is concerned with a particular facet of democratic governance and participation.[13] The Court has recognised the following four democratic rights in its election law jurisprudence: (1) the right to effective representation, (2) the right to meaningful participation, (3) the right to equal participation and (4) the right to a free and informed vote.[14]

The Court has described the first two rights – the right to effective representation and the right to meaningful participation – with specific reference to section 3's protection of the right to vote. The right to effective representation and the right to meaningful participation, respectively, are the purposes of section 3.[15] The Court has recognised two additional democratic rights – the right to equal participation and the right to a free and informed vote. The Court's recognition of these two rights is relevant for the Court's general understanding of the 'right to vote,' even though these rights do not attach specifically to section 3. Instead, these rights appear to be derived by the Court from an overarching constitutional commitment to the principle of democracy.[16]

The 'bundle of rights' approach has given the Court considerable flexibility in responding to a wide range of issues – such as electoral redistricting, campaign finance regulation, political equality, and the regulation of political parties. The Court's approach provides it not only with the ability to protect the activities of voting and standing for office as contemplated by the text of section 3, but also to regulate the structure of democratic institutions and the political system more broadly. By diversifying the concept of the 'right to vote' so that it includes a number of democratic rights, the Court has been able to intervene with respect to a wide array of political institutions and actors.

In addition, the Court's decisions are notable for paying attention both to the individual and to the institutional aspects of democratic rights. In my previous work, I have used the language of 'structural rights' to capture the particular nature of democratic rights.[17] Structural rights are individual rights that take into account the broader institutional framework within which these rights are defined, held, and exercised. Rights do not exist in a vacuum, but are instead exercised within an institutional framework that is constituted by relations of power. By recognising the dual individual–institutional nature of democratic rights, the Court has the ability to supervise various aspects of democratic governance.

The Supreme Court's election law cases

This section of the chapter provides a brief discussion of a representative sampling of the Supreme Court's decisions. It considers the Court's decisions on electoral redistricting, campaign finance, voting rights, and the entitlement to vote.

Electoral redistricting

In *Reference re Provincial Electoral Boundaries (Saskatchewan)*, the Court considered whether Saskatchewan's electoral boundaries violated the right to vote as protected by section 3 of the Charter.[18] The case arose because the governing Progressive Conservative party in Saskatchewan passed the Electoral Boundaries Commission Act (EBCA), which imposed various restrictions on the independent boundary commission that was charged with redrawing the provincial electoral map.[19] The EBCA required that the urban and rural ridings had to adhere to a strict quota, and that the urban ridings had to coincide with municipal boundaries. The legislation also allowed variances in the population sizes of the electoral districts that were within plus or minus 25 per cent of the provincial quotient.[20] As a result of these restrictions, urban voters were under-represented and rural voters were over-represented.[21] Not surprisingly, the EBCA enhanced the Progressive Conservatives' electoral support, which at the time was located primarily in the rural districts.

In a five-to-three decision, Justice McLachlin (as she then was) held on behalf of the majority that the electoral boundaries did not infringe the Charter.[22] The Court rejected the idea that electoral districts must adhere to the one-person, one-vote principle. In a key passage, Justice McLachlin stated that 'the purpose of the right to vote enshrined in s. 3 of the Charter is not equality of voting power per se, but the right to "effective representation." '[23] Justice McLachlin concluded that the disparity between the rural and urban areas did not violate the right to vote.[24] The involvement of the legislature did not 'render the process arbitrary or unfair' and the boundary commission was not 'unduly constrained' by EBCA.[25] This decision illustrates the Court's use of a bundle of rights approach to regulate an issue – electoral redistricting – that is not explicitly mentioned in the text of section 3.

In a dissenting opinion, Justice Cory concluded that there had been an infringement of section 3, and furthermore that the government had failed to justify the infringements under section 1. In particular, the government had provided no explanation as to why the legislature 'shackle[d] the Commission with the mandatory rural-urban allocation and the confinement of urban boundaries to municipal limits.'[26] He concluded that the 'fundamental right to vote should not be diminished without sound justification.'[27] The government, however, had failed to justify 'legislation which clearly has the effect of diminishing the rights of urban voters and reducing the representation of urban residents in the legislature.'[28] According to Justice Cory, legislative interference with the right to vote risked 'bringing the democratic process itself into disrepute.'[29]

Campaign finance

The Supreme Court has also considered whether the government is permitted to impose limits on third party spending. Third party spending refers to campaign spending that is conducted by individuals or groups that are neither candidates nor political parties. In *Libman* v. *Quebec (A.G.)*,[30] the Court considered the constitutionality of the third party spending limits set out in Quebec's Referendum Act. The Act laid forth the rules for the referendum on the Charlottetown Accord.[31] Robert Libman, who was president of the Equality Party, did not wish to join either the 'yes' or the 'no' position on the referendum question, and instead wished to advocate in favour of abstaining from the vote.[32] The referendum legislation, however, required that regulated expenses be incurred only through a national committee, which meant that individuals who supported neither option were limited to unregulated expenses.[33] Libman argued that these restrictions infringed the freedoms of expression and association and the right to equality.[34] He argued that any individual or group should have the right to receive public funding and to incur regulated expenses.[35]

The Court held that the restrictions infringed the freedom of political expression and could not be upheld under section 1 of the Charter.[36] It found that the provisions did not meet the minimal impairment test because the limits imposed on groups that do not affiliate themselves with the national committees are so restrictive that they amount to a total ban.[37] At the same time, the Court recognised that it was important to prevent 'the most affluent members of society from exerting a disproportionate influence by dominating the referendum debate through access to greater resources.'[38] As noted by Colin Feasby, the Court appeared to favour an 'egalitarian' approach to the rules governing spending during a referendum or an election.[39] The Court described the egalitarian aspect of spending limits as follows:

> [S]pending limits are essential to ensure the primacy of the principle of fairness in democratic elections. The principle of electoral fairness flows directly from a principle entrenched in the Constitution: that of the political

equality of citizens. If the principle of fairness in the political sphere is to be preserved, it cannot be presumed that all persons have the same financial resources to communicate with the electorate.[40]

The basic idea is that those with greater wealth should not be permitted to control the electoral process and thereby disadvantage those with less wealth; that is, disparities in private wealth should not be translated into disparities of political influence.[41]

The Court once again considered the constitutionality of third party spending limits in *Harper* v. *Canada*.[42] At issue in *Harper* was the constitutionality of third party spending limits as provided for in the Canada Elections Act.[43] Although the provisions of the Act had been struck down by the lower courts as violations of the Charter's guarantees of freedom of expression and association,[44] a six-to-three majority of the Supreme Court upheld the constitutionality of the third party spending limits. Writing for the majority, Justice Bastarache held that while the spending limits infringed the freedom of expression guarantee in section 2(b) of the Charter, the provisions were nonetheless justifiable under section 1.[45] The Court majority confirmed that Parliament had adopted an egalitarian model of elections, under which wealth is the main obstacle that prevents individuals from enjoying an equal opportunity to participate in the electoral process.[46] According to the Court, spending limits are required to prevent the most affluent citizens from 'monopolising election discourse' and thereby preventing other citizens from participating on an equal basis.[47] The Court held that although the spending limits infringed upon the freedoms of expression and association guaranteed by the Charter,[48] the provisions were nonetheless justifiable under section 1.[49]

In their dissenting opinion in *Harper*, Chief Justice McLachlin and Justice Major found that the spending limits failed the minimal impairment stage of the *Oakes* test because they imposed a 'virtual ban' on citizens who wished to participate in the political deliberation during the election period.[50] According to the dissent, the 'dangers posited are wholly hypothetical' because there is no evidence that wealthy citizens 'are poised to hijack this country's election process.'[51]

Voting rights

The Supreme Court has generally been very protective of the right to vote. For example, in *Sauvé* v. *Canada* (*Sauvé I*),[52] the Court struck down a blanket prohibition on inmate voting as provided for in section 51(e) of the Canada Elections Act on the ground that the limitation was not justifiable under section 1. The government subsequently amended the Act to prohibit voting by inmates who had been sentenced to a term of two years or more. In *Sauvé* v. *Canada* (*Sauvé II*),[53] however, a majority of the Court struck down this revised limitation on inmate voting.[54] Writing for a five-member majority, Chief Justice McLachlin struck the provision down as an unjustified violation of section 3.[55] The majority asserted that the 'right to vote is fundamental to our democracy and the rule of law and cannot be lightly set aside. Limits on it require not deference, but careful examination.'[56] In an important passage, Chief Justice McLachlin made a distinction between fundamental rights, on the one hand, and social and political policies, on the other:

> The core democratic rights of Canadians do not fall within a 'range of acceptable alternatives' among which Parliament may pick and choose at its discretion. Deference may be appropriate on a decision involving competing social and political policies. It is not appropriate, however, on a decision to limit fundamental rights.[57]

According to the majority, judicial deference was not appropriate when fundamental rights were at stake. By contrast, the dissenting justices described the issue as involving 'competing social or political philosophies relating to the right to vote.'[58] Writing for the dissenting justices, Justice Gonthier argued that the 'case rests on philosophical, political and social considerations which are not capable of "scientific proof." '[59] For this reason, the Court should defer to Parliament's judgment that temporary disenfranchisement enhances the rule of law and democracy.

The Court has also recognised the right of citizens to play a meaningful role in elections. In *Figueroa* v. *Canada*,[60] the head of the Communist Party of Canada challenged the constitutionality of a requirement that political parties must nominate candidates in at least fifty electoral districts in order to register as a political party.[61] Registered political parties are granted a number of benefits under the Canada Elections Act.[62] The Supreme Court held that the fifty-candidate rule violated section 3 and was not justifiable under section 1.[63] Writing for the six-member majority, Justice Iacobucci stated that section 3 includes 'the right of each citizen to play a meaningful role in the electoral process.'[64] The majority also found that political parties act 'as both a vehicle and outlet' for the participation of citizens in the electoral process.[65] The Court's decision added another right to the 'bundle of rights' that comprise the right to vote.

The Court has held that the section 3 right to vote does not apply to referenda. At issue in *Haig* v. *Canada*[66] was whether section 3 guaranteed the right to vote in the national referendum on the Charlottetown Accord.[67] In all provinces and territories except Quebec, the referendum took place under federal legislation.[68] In Quebec, the referendum took place under provincial legislation that imposed a six-month residency requirement on all voters.[69] Graham Haig, who had moved from Ontario to Quebec during the relevant period, was ineligible to vote in Quebec because he did not meet the six-month residency requirement and he was also ineligible to vote in Ontario because he no longer resided in an area covered by the federal legislation.[70]

Writing for the majority, Justice L'Heureux-Dubé stated that a 'referendum as a platform of expression is … a matter of legislative policy and not of constitutional law.'[71] As such, a referendum is not subject to section 2(b) of the

Charter in general because it is a 'creation of legislation.'[72] The majority also concluded that section 3 was clearly limited to the election of representatives to the provincial and federal legislatures, and hence did not guarantee the right to vote in a referendum.[73] In a dissenting opinion, Justice Iacobucci argued that Haig's section 2(b) rights were violated by the effect of the federal Referendum Act, and, moreover, that the violation could not be saved under section 1.[74] Justice Iacobucci argued that the two referenda, taken together, had a 'national character' that was intended to involve all Canadians.[75] Although Justice Iacobucci agreed with the view that the government is not obligated to hold referenda, or follow their results, he argued that if the government 'chooses to conduct a referendum, it must do so in compliance with the Charter.'[76]

More recently, there have been lower court cases involving voting rights. The British Columbia Court of Appeal recently upheld the constitutionality of voter identification requirements.[77] The Ontario Court of Appeal upheld the constitutionality of a rule that prevents non-residents from voting after spending five years abroad.[78] These cases raise questions about the scope and meaning of the constitutional right to vote. Both decisions have the effect of circumscribing the ability of citizens to cast a ballot. It is likely that these recent conflicts over the scope of the section 3 right to vote will one day be assessed by the Supreme Court.

Contested elections

In *Opitz* v. *Wrzesnewskyj*,[79] the Court considered how the entitlement to vote should be determined. The case arose out of a contested election result in the May 2011 federal election. In the Etobicoke Centre riding 52,794 votes were cast. Conservative MP Ted Opitz won the riding by a narrow twenty-six votes against Liberal incumbent Boris Wrzesnewskyj. The lower court set aside Opitz's win on the basis that seventy-nine ballots had procedural irregularities.[80] There was no evidence of fraud or corruption.

In a four-to-three decision, the Supreme Court overturned the lower court, thus averting a new election. In a majority decision by Justices Rothstein and Moldaver, the Court refused to 'disqualify the votes of several Canadian citizens based on administrative mistakes, notwithstanding evidence that those citizens were in fact entitled to vote.'[81] The majority stated that disenfranchising entitled voters would undermine public confidence in the electoral process.[82] The Court was also concerned that if annulments of elections were an easy process, the 'finality and legitimacy of election results will be eroded.'[83] For this reason, '[o] nly irregularities that affect the result of the election and thereby undermine the integrity of the electoral process are grounds for overturning an election.'[84]

Without delving into all the details of each contested ballot, it is worth noting that some of the mistakes made by election officials did not, according to the majority, arise to the level of an 'irregularity.'[85] The majority appeared to draw a distinction between 'irregularities,' which are 'serious administrative errors that are capable of undermining the electoral process' and mere mistakes.[86] After applying these standards to the contested ballots, the Court majority held that fifty-nine of the seventy-nine votes set aside by the lower court should be reinstated. As a result of the Court's re-assessment of the votes, Opitz won with a six vote margin.

The dissenting opinion was authored by Chief Justice McLachlin. According to the dissent, 'qualification' to vote is necessary but not sufficient for 'entitlement' to vote.[87] A voter must also satisfy the registration and identification requirements to be entitled to vote because these requirements are crucial for protecting the integrity of the electoral system.[88] The dissenting justices found that some of the mistakes made were sufficiently serious for those ballots to be set aside. The dissent argued that an annulment of the election would strengthen the public's confidence in the electoral process because it would signal that elections would not stand in the face of irregularities.[89]

Fairness, legitimacy, and the role of the court

The Supreme Court plays a vital role in protecting the fairness and legitimacy of the democratic process.[90] In this section, I briefly address two topics – partisan self-entrenchment and judicial deference – that raise particular challenges to the judicial review of the electoral process.

Partisan self-entrenchment

Partisan rule-making is a significant problem in the electoral arena. There are obvious incentives for the governing political party to craft election laws to provide it with an advantage at the next election. For example, many critics of the government's recent Fair Elections Act pointed out that the proposed changes benefitted the Conservative Party at the expense of the other political parties.[91] The Supreme Court of Canada, however, has yet to address the problem of the partisan manipulation of electoral laws.

In the United States, scholars have argued that courts should adopt the 'political markets' or 'structural' approach in their election law cases. According to the political markets theorists, dominant political parties have a propensity to 'lock up' political institutions in order to secure a partisan advantage.[92] For this reason, courts should intervene to prevent the political self-entrenchment of parties.[93]

Several scholars in the Canadian law of democracy literature have likewise argued for a political markets/structural approach to the Supreme Court of Canada's election law cases.[94] These scholars have applied the structural approach to a wide array of topics.[95] As described in the second section of this chapter, above, the electoral boundaries at issue in *Saskatchewan Reference* involved partisan rule-making, despite the existence of an independent boundary commission.[96] Another arena which raises the issue of partisan self-dealing is political finance, also known as campaign finance.[97] Given the incumbent-protecting effects of campaign finance regulations, commentators in the Canadian law of democracy field have raised structural concerns about the spending restrictions at issue in *Harper*[98] and the Accountability Act.[99] In general, courts should treat electoral laws with a certain amount of scepticism because elected officials have a propensity to enact laws that perpetuate their own power.

Judicial deference

In its law of democracy cases, the justices often have divergent approaches to the question of whether the Court should defer to Parliament with respect to electoral laws.[100] In *Harper*, for example, the Court majority was highly deferential to Parliament because it saw the electoral process as being presumptively 'political.' The majority stated that the workings of the electoral system are a 'political choice, the details of which are better left to Parliament.'[101] Since Parliament has the right to 'choose Canada's electoral model,' it is incumbent on the Court to defer to Parliament.[102] The Court was also very deferential to the government's social science evidence.[103]

A principal difficulty with judicial deference in the electoral realm, however, is the propensity of elected officials to engage in partisan rule-making. As Colin Feasby notes, the 'Court is uniquely suited, and Parliament is particularly ill-equipped, to police self-interested behaviour on the part of Parliament.'[104] Christopher Bredt and Markus Kremer argue that the Supreme Court should not defer to legislatures when they attempt to limit democratic rights.[105]

My own view is that the Court plays a vital role in protecting the fairness and legitimacy of the democratic process.[106] An overly deferential posture on the part of the Court, however, significantly diminishes the Court's ability to hold Parliament accountable for its regulation of the democratic process. As Chief Justice McLachlin observed in *Sauvé II*, 'it is precisely when legislative choices threaten to undermine the foundations of the participatory democracy guaranteed by the Charter that courts must be vigilant in fulfilling their constitutional duty to protect the integrity of this system.'[107] In particular, the risk posed by partisan self-dealing cannot be adequately addressed by a Court that is overly deferential to Parliament.[108]

I have argued for an alternative structural approach, one that is based on democratic rights, which could be used by the Court to address the problem of partisan rule-making.[109] The Court has already observed that section 3 'imposes on Parliament an obligation not to interfere with the *right of each citizen to participate in a fair election*.'[110] I suggest that this 'right to participate in a fair election' offers a promising way for the Court to ensure the fairness and legitimacy of the electoral process. By recognising a right to a fair and legitimate democratic process as a purpose of the right to vote, the Court would send a signal to Parliament that partisan rule-making is constitutionally impermissible. In this way, the Court could signal the broad standards of electoral integrity and fairness that would need to be met by Parliament.

Conclusion

The Supreme Court plays a vitally important role in the electoral process. In addition to defining the central democratic values that are at stake in elections, the Court has also issued decisions that have had a profound impact on the processes and institutions of democracy. The Court's decisions have affected diverse aspects of the electoral process, including electoral redistricting, campaign finance, voting rights, and contested elections. In general, the Court's role is to ensure the fairness and legitimacy of the democratic process. There are two challenges, however, to ensuring electoral fairness. The first challenge, partisan self-entrenchment, refers to the propensity of elected officials to engage in partisan rule-making. The second challenge is that the Court tends to adopt a deferential posture with respect to electoral laws. In general, this article has argued that judicial deference is misplaced with respect to electoral laws. Instead of deferring, the Court could use a rights-based approach to ensure the fairness and integrity of the electoral process.

Notes

1 This chapter is adapted from Yasmin Dawood, 'The Role of Courts and Judgments in Elections' in *The Informed Citizens' Guide to Elections: Electioneering Based on the Rule of Law*, special edition of the *Journal of Parliamentary and Political Law* (Carswell 2015).

2 Canadian Charter of Rights and Freedoms, Part I of the Constitution Act, 1982, being Schedule B to the Canada Act 1982 (UK), 1982, c. 11 [Charter].

3 Charter, s. 3.

4 Charter, s. 4.

5 Charter, s. 5.

6 *Reference re Provincial Electoral Boundaries (Saskatchewan)*, [1991] 2 SCR 158, 81 DLR (4th) 16 [*Saskatchewan Reference*] (electoral boundary drawing); *Sauvé* v. *Canada (Attorney General)*, [1993] 2 SCR 438, 64 CRR (2d) 1 [*Sauvé I*] (inmate voting rights); *Haig* v. *Canada (Chief Electoral Officer)*, [1993] 2 SCR 995, 105 DLR (4th) 577 [*Haig*] (residency requirements during referenda); *Harvey* v. *New Brunswick (Attorney General)*, [1996] 2 SCR 876, 137 DLR (4th) 142 [*Harvey*] (membership in provincial legislatures); *Libman* v. *Quebec (Attorney General)*, [1997] 3 SCR 569, 151 DLR (4th) 385 [*Libman*] (referendum spending limits); *Thomson Newspapers Co.* v. *Canada (Attorney General)*, [1998] 1 SCR 877, 159 DLR (4th) 385 [*Thomson Newspapers*] (public opinion polls); *Sauvé* v. *Canada (Attorney General)*, 2002 SCC 68, [2002] 3 SCR 519 [*Sauvé II*] (inmate voting rights); *Figueroa* v. *Canada (Attorney General)*, 2003 SCC 37, [2003] 1 SCR 912 [*Figueroa*] (benefits for political parties); *Harper* v. *Canada (Attorney General)*, 2004 SCC 33, [2004] 1 SCR 827 [*Harper*] (third party election spending); *R* v. *Bryan*, 2007 SCC 12, [2007] 1 SCR 527 [*Bryan*] (distribution of election results); *Opitz* v. *Wrzesnewskyj*, 2012 SCC 55, [2012] 3 SCR 76 [*Opitz*] (contested elections and the entitlement to vote).

7 Charter, s. 3.

8 Feasby (2007) 539 (defining the law of the political process as encompassing decisions that fall under ss 3, 2, and 15).

9 Dawood (2013b) 258.

10 *Reference re Secession of Quebec*, [1998] 2 SCR 217 at para. 61, 161 DLR (4th) 385.

11 *Sauvé II* (n. 6) at [1].

12 Ibid. at [9].
13 Dawood (2013b) 254–255.
14 Ibid. at 255.
15 *Saskatchewan Reference* (n. 6) 183; *Figueroa* (n. 6). When determining the scope and meaning of a Charter right, the Court employs a 'purposive approach,' which focuses on the purpose underlying the right or the interests that the right was meant to protect. *R* v. *Big M Drug Mart*, [1985] 1 SCR 295 at [116].
16 Dawood (2013b) 255.
17 Dawood (2012) 503–504.
18 *Saskatchewan Reference* (n. 6).
19 Electoral Boundaries Commission Act, ss 1986–87–88, c. E-6.1.
20 *Saskatchewan Reference* (n. 6) at [190].
21 Ibid. at [169].
22 Ibid. at [197].
23 Ibid. at [183].
24 Ibid. at [197].
25 Ibid. at [194].
26 Ibid. at [173], Cory J, dissenting.
27 Ibid. at [174], Cory J, dissenting.
28 Ibid.
29 Ibid. at [172], Cory J, dissenting.
30 *Libman* (n. 6).
31 Ibid. at [1].
32 *Harper* (n. 6) at [60].
33 *Libman* (n. 6) at [14].
34 Ibid. at [2], [27].
35 Ibid. at [18].
36 Ibid. at [35], [85].
37 Ibid. at [82].
38 Ibid. at [41].
39 Feasby (1999) 31–32.
40 *Libman* (n. 6) at [47].
41 Sunstein (1995); Fiss (1996).
42 *Harper* (n. 6).
43 See Canada Elections Act, SC 2000, c. 9. For a discussion of the *Harper* decision, see Geddis (2004) paras 18–25; Dawood (2013c) 307–309.
44 [2001] 93 Alta LR (3d) 281; [2002] 14 Alta LR (4th) 4.
45 *Harper* (n. 6) at [66], [121].
46 Ibid. at [62], citing Feasby (1999).
47 Ibid. at [61].
48 Ibid. at [66].
49 Ibid. at [121].
50 Ibid. at [35], McLachlin CJ and Major J dissenting.
51 Ibid. McLachlin CJ and Major J dissenting.
52 *Sauvé I* (n. 6).
53 *Sauvé II* (n. 6). For an analysis of the case, see Brown (2003).
54 Canada Elections Act, RSC 1985, c. E-2, s. 51(e).
55 *Sauvé II* (n. 6) at [62].
56 Ibid. at [9].
57 Ibid. at [13].
58 Ibid. at [67], Gonthier J dissenting.
59 Ibid.
60 *Figueroa* (n. 6).
61 Ibid. at [3].

62 Ibid. at [4].
63 Ibid. at [90].
64 Ibid. at [25].
65 Ibid. at [39].
66 *Haig* (n. 6).
67 Ibid. at [1019].
68 See Referendum Act, SC 1992, c. 30.
69 See Referendum Act, RSQ c. C-64.1.
70 *Haig* (n. 6) 1009.
71 Ibid. at [1041].
72 Ibid. at [1040].
73 Ibid. at [1033].
74 Ibid. at [1062], Iacobucci J dissenting.
75 Ibid, Iacobucci J dissenting.
76 Ibid. at [1065].
77 *Henry* v. *Canada (Attorney General)*, 2014 BCCA 30, 301 CRR (2d) 216 Ryan JA.
78 *Frank* v. *Canada (Attorney General)*, 2015 ONCA 536 (CanLII).
79 *Opitz* (n. 6).
80 2012 ONSC 2873, 110 OR (3d) 350.
81 *Opitz* (n. 6) at [1].
82 Ibid.
83 Ibid. at [2].
84 Ibid.
85 Ibid. at [90], [93], [100], [107].
86 Ibid. at [24].
87 Ibid. at [140].
88 Ibid.
89 Ibid. at [140], [147], McLachlin CJ dissenting.
90 Dawood (2012) 504.
91 Remarks of Professor Yasmin Dawood on Bill C-23, An Act to Amend the Canada Elections Act, before the Standing Committee on Procedure and House Affairs, Parliament of Canada (March 31, 2014).
92 Issacharoff and Pildes (1998) 644–646.
93 Pildes (2004) 41.
94 For an extended discussion of the structural approach in Canada, see Dawood (2012) 503–504, 511–518.
95 Feasby (2007); Feasby (2006) 243; MacIvor (1996); Manfredi and Rush (2008); Pal (2011); Dawood (2006); Dawood (2012).
96 Fritz (1999–2000) 4; Carter (2011) 320–321.
97 Feasby (2006); Dawood (2012).
98 Manfredi and Rush (2008) 108.
99 Federal Accountability Act, SC 2006, c. 9. For discussions of the Accountability Act, see Feasby (2007) 517, 528–529; MacIvor (2008) 105–107.
100 Dawood (2013a) 84–87.
101 *Harper* (n. 6) at [87].
102 Ibid.
103 Dawood (2014) 188–191.
104 Feasby (2005) 288.
105 Bredt and Kremer (2005) 21–27.
106 Dawood (2012) 504.
107 *Sauvé II* (n. 6) at [15].
108 Dawood (2012) 556–561.
109 Ibid. 503–508.
110 *Figueroa* (n. 6) at [51].

References

Bredt C. and Kremer M., 'Section 3 of the *Charter*: Democratic Rights at the Supreme Court of Canada' (2005) 17 *National Journal of Constitutional Law* 19.

Brown D., '*Sauvé* and Prisoners' Voting Rights: The Death of the Good Citizen?' (2003) 20 *Supreme Court Law Review* (2d) 297.

Carter M., 'Ambiguous Constitutional Standards and the Right to Vote' (2011) 5 *Journal of Parliamentary and Political Law* 309.

Dawood Y., 'Democracy, Power, and the Supreme Court: Campaign Finance Reform in Comparative Perspective' (2006) 4 *International Journal of Constitutional Law* 269.

Dawood Y., 'Electoral Fairness and the Law of Democracy: A Structural Rights Approach to Judicial Review' (2012) 62 *University of Toronto Law Journal* 499.

Dawood Y., 'Democracy and Dissent: Reconsidering the Judicial Review of the Political Sphere' (2013a) 63 *Supreme Court Law Review* (2d) 59.

Dawood Y., 'Democracy and the Right to Vote: Rethinking Democratic Rights Under the Charter' (2013b) 51 *Osgoode Hall Law Journal* 251.

Dawood Y., 'Freedom of Speech and Democracy: Rethinking the Conflict Between Liberty and Equality' (2013c) 26 *Canadian Journal of Law and Jurisprudence* 293.

Dawood Y., 'Democracy and Deference: The Role of Social Science Evidence in Election Law Cases' (2014) 32 *National Journal of Constitutional Law* 173.

Feasby C., '*Libman* v. *Quebec (A.G.)* and the Administration of the Process of Democracy under the *Charter*: The Emerging Egalitarian Model' (1999) 44 *McGill Law Journal* 5.

Feasby C., 'Freedom of Expression and the Law of the Democratic Process' (2005) 29 *Supreme Court Law Review* (2d) 237.

Feasby C., 'The Supreme Court of Canada's Political Theory and the Constitutionality of the Political Finance Regime' in Keith Ewing and Samuel Issacharoff, eds, *Party Funding and Campaign Financing in International Perspective* (Hart Publishing 2006) 243.

Feasby C., 'Constitutional Questions about Canada's New Political Finance Regime' (2007) 45 *Osgoode Hall Law Journal* 514.

Fiss O., *The Irony of Free Speech* (Harvard University Press 1996).

Fritz R., 'Challenging Electoral Boundaries Under the *Charter*' (1999–2000) 5 *Review of Constitutional Studies* 1.

Geddis A., 'Liberté, Egalité, Argent: Third Party Election Spending and the *Charter*' (2004) 42 *Alberta Law Review* 429.

Issacharoff S. and Pildes R., 'Politics as Markets: Partisan Lockups of the Democratic Process' (1998) 50 *Stanford Law Review* 643.

MacIvor H., 'A Missed Opportunity: Political Finance and the Federal Accountability Act' (2008) 1 *Journal of Parliamentary and Political Law* 105.

MacIvor H., 'Do Canadian Political Parties form a Cartel?' (1996) 29 *Canadian Journal of Political Science* 317.

Manfredi C. and Rush M., *Judging Democracy* (Broadview Press 2008).

Pal M., 'Breakdowns in the Democratic Process and the Law of Canadian Democracy' (2011) 57:2 *McGill Law Journal* 299.

Pildes R., 'Foreword: The Constitutionalization of Democratic Politics' (2004) 118 *Harvard Law Review* 29.

Sunstein C., *Democracy and the Problem of Free Speech* (2nd edn, Free Press 1995).

14 Regulation by charter

Judicial review of elections in South Africa

Kareem Crayton

In modern democracies, courts play a crucial role in balancing two distinct yet significant ideals in governance: one-person–one-vote and the rule of law. Each of these concepts is traceable to a theory of civic equality. The basic feature of every free and fair democratic election is that the persons who are to be governed enjoy an equal opportunity to select those who will be responsible for the governing. In the United States, for instance, the concept is bound up in the now universal concept of 'one person one vote,' which remains a crucial (if also theoretically complex) foundational principle in modern democracies.[1] Winning the endorsement of a majority of those persons who are qualified electors is the most common threshold used to determine what the public's will is.

Similarly, the precept that the rule of law is sovereign in democracies draws on the notion of civil equality as well. Just as every citizen living in a democracy is expected to enjoy equal standing with respect to voicing preferences at the polls, so too does each person have the fundamental right to seek formal redress for legal injury. Generally, this expectation of fair and equal access to justice calls for some kind of adjudicatory process conducted by a neutral arbiter and decided according to established law.[2] Often, these ideas are housed within the legal concept of due process, which includes a basic dignitary component.[3] While nations may differ in the manner that they determine how much judicial process is due under certain circumstances, the general expectation is that rulings are consistent and irrespective of wealth or privilege. This concept is equally relevant to the fairness principle as it is to the institutional independence of the judiciary.[4]

In both contexts, then, the democratic system proceeds on the view that certain basic rights and obligations must be available to citizens regardless of their level of power, influence, or standing. Yet, the business of the court, the forum where the rule of law is most typically invoked and vindicated, operates in a manner that is not easily suited to address the conflicts that arise during an election. Judges are expected to minimise or avoid altogether any explicit political motivations in their handling of legal conflicts.[5] Their work depends upon the neutral, consistent application of law to facts. Political alliances and loyalties, which are common (and encouraged) in the electoral sphere, have no legitimate place in the courtroom. In fact, the exercise of legal rights as enforced by the judicial power is usually the refuge of minority groups as a structural shield against the unbridled imposition of the majority's will – even the kind of legislative policies that might prevail in the voting booth.[6]

The principle of voter equality, by contrast, proceeds in a largely different context. Unlike a case involving minority rights, a majority (where legitimately expressed) typically is entitled to the benefits and power associated with governing authority. And unlike the aspirations towards neutrality in adjudication, locating the majority's viewpoint in an election most fundamentally depends upon aggregating the expression of voter preferences in the electoral process. One major aim of democracy is to establish public mandates that are well-supported by links of accountability between the voters and their elected representatives.[7] Candidates and parties therefore are encouraged to compete for votes in the political marketplace during campaigns and, after elections, to perform in office according to the majority's will.[8] Accordingly, the expression of equally valued preferences is central to the enterprise of electioneering and campaigns.

The question arises, then, how the judiciary can or should function in the set of cases on its docket where these two related yet distinct tenets of democratic life intersect. When the courts are called to rule on the regulation of the political process, what role should they play? Can they maintain the neutral position of arbiter of rights where the stakes of the political process can be quite obvious and where its decisions inevitably will have political ramifications? If this judicial puzzle is solvable, then how might courts try to address the inherent conflicts between the two spheres of public life?

Three possible approaches to judicial management of election cases

A three-part typology illustrates the different ways that courts can address the challenge of fashioning and interpreting rules to manage the electoral process. Courts, for example, may utilise their power to create rules and standards to resolve challenges in election cases. This first approach generally has great purchase in states where the governing legal structure provides little direction (if any) for how legal problems of this type should be resolved. This approach is well illustrated, for example, in the manner that the United States Supreme Court developed the one-person–one-vote doctrine.[9] Today, this rule enjoys a respected place in constitutional law (indeed, international law), but its origin story involves a healthy dose of judicially driven theorising and rule-making.[10] For all of its merits, the approach remains open to critique as new issues emerge that test the bounds of the rules once established and ideological shifts within the institution itself raise doubts about the continued respect for the earlier rule.[11]

At the other end of the spectrum, a court may opt to abdicate any serious role in resolving these conflicts. Where an external entity is responsible for handling election conflicts, the court may defer more heavily to that entity's choices in deciding how to run the political process. Only in limited instances will the courts intervene to upend the policy decisions taken by non-judicial actors in respect for their expertise and discretion. Some courts in the European Union direct non-political or independent entities to manage elections; however, even these actors can find themselves subject to litigation challenges. Under these conditions, the judiciary may avoid risks to its own institutional credibility in resolving the clashes between the two equality principles by limiting its attention to a straightforward review of the choices of the external actor in question. Particularly where the institutional position of the judiciary is unstable, the expertise of external agencies can serve as an important buffer to the vitriol that can often follow from the most heated and controversial election challenges.

Lying between these two types of judicial regulation, the courts may appeal to a constitutional framework directly in answer to an election challenge. Where the applicable governing charter (usually a modern one) provides express direction that points more explicitly towards a solution in a case, the Court can turn its attention squarely on applying traditional tools of legal interpretation to support its rulings. Absent from this second option is a strong institutional effort to craft a new regime from whole cloth; rather, the effort purports only to clarify existing language. Ironically, the state where this type of adjudication has often occurred for election cases is South Africa, a country that features an otherwise powerful Constitutional Court. This Court has developed a record of turning to constitutional provisions in election cases rather than its available authority to fashion decidedly new rules on an as-needed basis.

Taken together, these case types represent the spectrum of options that are available for courts in most democratic systems. Of course, there rarely is an 'ideal' method for handling these cases; there are both challenges and advantages associated with each approach. However, this analysis does indicate that some approaches may well be better suited than others as a means of election regulation under distinct conditions.

Illustrations of the South African approach

One of the more modern modes of regulating elections can be found in the South African Constitutional Court, which reflects the third approach to managing election cases. This court possesses an extraordinarily large well of authority to regulate in this area. Unlike courts in the United States, where the source of most regulatory action emanates primarily from judicial theorising, South Africa's judiciary regulates through enforcement of terms that are more clearly enumerated in the nation's Constitution.[12] Among the modern national governing charters in the world, South Africa's Constitution has been hailed as an exemplar for establishing a sophisticated and largely effective electoral framework for industrialised democracies.[13]

The judiciary's place in the maintenance of this constitutional system is quite central. Partly resulting from the apartheid era in which the rule of law was largely subject to legislative will (and the legislature was itself anti-democratic), the new republic's regime emphasises that the Constitution serves as the sovereign authority for the nation and the Constitutional Court as its ultimate vindicator.[14] Accordingly, the judicial power stands as the final guarantor of all of the rights and structures that establish the democratic system. This special position is reflected in several of the Court's internal practices, including the creation of 'direct access,' allowing individual litigants in extraordinary circumstances to bypass the normal appellate process and immediate hearing in the Court.[15]

The Court has, as a result, approached its role of adjudication quite seriously in a variety of cases. Beyond the formal rules of the Court, the members' informal handling of their caseload reflects a careful management of their power. In internal practices, for example, the members of the Court rely on consensus based decision-making to avoid sharp divisions of ideology or ethnic identity in opinions.[16] The eleven justices also work to ensure that their pronouncement of judgment in cases appeals to the principles in the Constitution. This interest in grounding decisions in the provisions of the Constitution is at once a means of building public confidence and reliance on the charter and also a means of protecting the judiciary's own institutional capital – i.e. the authority and credibility to render decisions in especially difficult cases.

In practice, the South African approach to decision-making in election cases (where political concerns are likely highest) reflects its interest in relying explicitly on constitutional commitments. A brief comparison helps to illustrate specific ways that South Africa's system has parted ways with its American counterpart. Unlike the American system, where rights have been developed through judicial theorising in a line of cases, the right to vote is enumerated in South Africa's Constitution as an affirmative guarantee.[17] Every citizen enjoys a series of political rights that are enumerated in Chapter 2, Section 19 of the Constitution. The provision also recognises the citizen's rights associated with the broad freedoms to 'make political choices' ranging from the formation of parties to campaigning.[18] At the same time, the South African Constitution establishes rights that are more systemic than individual (the preferred approach for assigning rights in the American system) – including an entitlement of all citizens to maintain 'free, fair, and regular elections.'[19] Interestingly, this provision would seem to impose an obligation on the government to ensure a process that complies; the closest that the American Constitution comes to this idea can be found in the so-called Guarantee Clause, which the US Supreme Court has long ruled a dead letter (and non-justiciable).[20] And with respect to the scope of the definition of voting, the South African Constitution makes clear that protections not only relate to balloting itself (which must remain secret) but also extend to more peripheral matters like campaigning and holding an elective office with few restrictions.[21]

To be sure, the notable advantage of the South African constitutional system is its establishment during the modern era, which left great latitude to the system's designers. These benefits include the ability to frame these provisions with a keen awareness of the likely political actors that would emerge and also the lessons from the policy experiences in other democracies – including the United States. Perhaps the most important factor that explains why this nation has succeeded is that these provisions were crafted with full view of its own political history under apartheid – including many of the frustrations and anxieties of the previous regimes.[22] Insofar as this new charter proceeds after an extended and infamous period of state-enforced racial inequality in the political sphere, there remains an awareness of the need to correct the past state wrongs against a majority of its people.

What also distinguishes this constitutional system from the US model is its full embrace of the pre-eminent role for the rule of law principle. The Constitution is recognised as the sovereign power in the country, and the nation's Constitutional Court is the entity that is vested with the authority to interpret and vindicate the rights and principles contained therein.[23] Thus, because the terms of this Constitution are far-reaching, the scope of the Court's authority also has the potential to enact quite massive effects in the state and society. Accordingly, the problems of regulating politics and elections are rather naturally expected to find their way into the Constitutional Court, at least when they raise recognisable constitutional problems.

The cases described below have placed South Africa's judiciary quite squarely in the position of addressing a novel question of law that carried broad implications on the nature of the election system. In an effort to respond to the legal challenge, the Court turned not to its own inherent authority but instead to the provisions of the Constitution itself as the means to reach an answer that would address the conflict.

The first illustration of the Court's action is a constitutional challenge to several legislative reforms meant to enable national and local legislators to switch parties subsequent to their election to Parliament. Opponents of the policy filed a suit alleging that the proposed rule changes would violate the Constitution, since there were no provisions in the charter that permitted 'floor crossing.'[24] The possible consequences of the reform were quite dire for the smaller political parties of the nation, since their sustained growth would be at risk if members could switch their allegiances to other parties after they won elected office. The claimants also pressed concerns about more systemic harms that could follow if the Court did not rule in their favour. If upheld, the challenged policy would violate the core values of governance contained in the Constitution. If the floor crossing practice were permitted, they asserted, the foundational guarantees that South Africa would maintain a multi-party election system based on proportional representation would be eroded.[25]

Rather than enact its own articulation of a rule or standard with an appeal to political theory, the Constitutional Court dealt with this case by sticking rather closely to the terms laid out in the Constitution. The justices unanimously found that none of the highlighted constitutional provisions specifically prohibited the practice of floor crossing. Both pluralism and proportionality were acknowledged as bedrock constitutional principles, but the Court declined to hold that either was inherently inconsistent with permitting members to switch parties. And since the litigants could not point to any other constitutional provision or theory to support their objections, the Court concluded that the reform posed no problems. For the justices, the constitutional provisions were less specific directives than concepts that left room for policy-making. Proportionality, for example, was a concept entrenched in multiple ways in other nation's systems – all of which (to varying degrees) might be said to satisfy the basic mandate. The Court pointed out that it had agreed to fast-track its consideration of this case (acknowledging its special role in providing access in order to police constitutional norms), but it also found that there was simply no sound basis for striking down or further regulating the changes to the manner of party alignment in Parliament.

A second election case where the justices even more explicitly appealed to the very structure of the Constitution to resolve an election dispute involved the allocation of governmental power. In *Electoral Commission* v. *Langenberg Municipality*, the Court issued a preliminary statement about jurisdiction that relied on the Constitution to establish that states have an obligation to comply with the constitutional order.[26] In this case, the challenged policy was developed by an independent agency whose main purpose was allocating the resources and machinery needed to run elections in South Africa. The specific policy involved the provision of mobile voting stations that helped provide ballot access to persons living in very remote areas of the country; the relevant statute directed that the Commission consider providing these stations for any given area by taking into account factors including population density and distance to access other voting facilities.

In its substance, this case was about the scope of the government's obligation to make voting accessible to citizens. The claimants in the case, residents in a remote community, sought judicial intervention to force the governing agency to offer additional voting equipment to accommodate voters living in a far removed town. Without access to the machinery, residents would need to walk dozens of miles to find the nearest polling station, which claimants viewed as a practical limit on their right to vote. According to the agency, though, removing this equipment from the affected community was simply unavoidable; it was the result of difficult resource limitations that were of primary importance in the decision.

The major constitutional question that the Court described as a matter of 'future importance' related to the ability of the plaintiffs to establish legal standing. A special provision of the Constitution sets out a special set of non-litigative procedures for the resolution of conflicts deemed 'intergovernmental disputes.'[27] To the extent that the Independent Election Commission (IEC) of South Africa (an entity that certainly performed public functions) was deemed an arm of government, the lawsuit with a municipality could not proceed. Thus, the primary question was whether the decision taken by the IEC was subject to a challenge in the courts.

On this question, the Court concluded that the agency was not an arm of government and was therefore subject to answer the lawsuit at issue. Just as fascinating as the answer to this question was the Court's analysis in justifying this conclusion. The opinion acknowledged the public aspects of the policy work done by the IEC, which included the maintenance of free and fair elections as described in the Constitution. Yet the legal status of these independent agencies was not identical to other more typical governmental bodies that are described in the other parts of the Constitution as organs of the state. The President and Parliament have a duty to coordinate their policy views and understanding of constitutional law to avoid courtroom battles, for example, they are each mentioned in the provision setting out the duty for cooperation.

By contrast, the Court reasoned, the IEC's special function places it in a distinct category from these other entities. It is properly characterised as part of a broader category of agencies – a state institution which serves the democratic system outside the governmental sphere. This view of the nation's governing structure acknowledges the connectedness of the different entities responsible for the management of election policy, but it also emphasises the necessity of locating independent agencies as subject to the Constitution and the law. The structure of the Constitution makes this distinction in order to support the maintenance of the independence of the agency. Otherwise, the Commission would be more likely sensitive to the policy preferences of political actors like Parliament or the President. In recognition that the independence of the agency 'does not exist in the air,' the Court maintains a distinctive place for the Commission within the political system.

While this reasoning might appear in a consideration of function, the Court's analysis largely starts and ends with an assessment of the language and structure of the Constitution. While not a strict construction of the document, the ruling does impose a loyalty to the clear principles of independence established in the constitutional structure.

A third case that presents a straightforward application of Constitutional principles to overturn the application of national policy comes in *Minister of Home Affairs* v. *National Institute for Crime Prevention* (*NICRO*).[28] Unlike the two previous cases, this challenge appeared to rely most directly on a commitment in the Constitution guaranteeing the right to vote for every citizen. The claimants argued that parliamentary amendments to the Electoral Act wrongfully denied the franchise to certain classes of convicted persons while they were completing their terms in prison custody. The policy enjoyed widespread popular support, as evidenced by its relatively swift approval within Parliament. As in many countries, curtailing the freedoms of the imprisoned population in South Africa (one with very few defenders in public life) carries very little resistance from identifiable constituencies in majoritarian politics.

Although the justices did not all agree about the final outcome of this case, they did speak with unity and clarity about the terms under which the claim ought to be analysed. The language of the Constitution left little question that the right to vote was an important one and that the presumption of the relevant language was to provide the franchise to all citizens equally. Indeed, this starting point was obvious not only from the text of the language describing this right but also from the nation's political experience with the apartheid system, in which political rights were severely limited for the majority of the population. The point of the new democratic regime was to eliminate the racial classifications evident in the allocation and enjoyment of the franchise. For both textual and historical reasons, the Court noted that the national government held a special duty to ensure that its resulting policies to regulate voting meet the sacred obligation to secure this right for all persons.

Importantly, recognising the infringement of a constitutional right posed major implications for the Court's review of record evidence. The Constitution directs that, to be upheld, any policy purporting to curtail a clearly established right must meet demanding standards of review outlined in the limitations clause.[29] In practical consequence, the recognition shifted the burdens of production and of proof from the claimants to the state. In practice, the provision requires judges to make an assessment of the array of factors that the state considered in adopting the infringing policy. The court's overall goal in this process is to assess the competing factors associated with pursuing the qualification. Where the court finds that the various concerns justify the policy, the state will be upheld as a permissible or justifiable limit on rights.

As mentioned above, the unremarkable part of the *NICRO* decision is its recognition that the right to vote is a core value in the Constitution. The provision's language could hardly be more specific on the point. Aside from the formulations of the relevant interests in the case, the two wings of the Court parted ways with the correct application of the limitations clause. In the majority's view (led by the Chief Justice), the lost benefit of access to the election system was significant enough to demand that the state articulate quite compelling reasons for its policy. And following from the observation that this analysis required more subjective reasoning, the majority also took account of the country's rather pernicious history of denying the franchise. That analysis effectively heaped additional burdens on to the state to demonstrate something more than a legitimate exercise rationale for enacting this kind of restrictive legislation.

The dissenting justices, by comparison, afforded greater weight in their limitations analysis to the evidence that would frame the denial of the franchise as conditionally justifiable. According to these members, the analysis had to consider more carefully the prevalence of crime. This reality posed a need to find ways that the state could signal distaste for unlawful behaviour and also the unavailability of less restrictive forms of punishment. Under these conditions, said the dissenters, disqualifying this class of citizens was amply warranted due to wrongdoing by those convicted along with the rationale of deterrence and punishment in the law. State officials had represented to the court that the ongoing surge in violence could be curtailed by the enforcement of the law. So while they acknowledged that the limitations clause was the correct locus of inquiry, the dissenters followed a very different (and ultimately more forgiving) analytical path than did the majority.

Taken together, these election cases engaged by the Constitutional Court in South Africa, are illustrations of how judicial authority may be evoked to manage electoral problems. The distinctive approach in this nation's courts is that instead of drawing on its own authority to create doctrine, the Constitutional Court resolves questions of voter access and governing procedure with direct reference to the provisions in the Constitution for guidance. Whereas the US system is quite sparing – so much so that its sparse and sometimes opaque terms sustain live, modern conflicts, the South African approach directs great energy to leveraging the Constitution's structure and process to direct outcomes.

To be clear, this Court certainly developed a sense of how the actors in the electoral system ought to operate while also taking full account of the implications of its decisions. Yet part of the justification for the focus on the terms of the Constitution is the fact that the statements are not especially far ideologically from the established text. The Court has been able to articulate a vision for the political system with very few logical steps from the relevant text for support. Accordingly, the solutions to conflicts over politics remain closely linked to the apparent structure set forth in the Constitution. Indeed, the cases mentioned above address a simple foundational question that is quite germane to the work that judicial actors do – determining whether the matter at hand properly interprets a provision or deciding whether an agency falls within the ambit for judicial review.

Conclusions

The above cases illustrate how the Court can play a key role in the democratisation process and management of the election system. At least three points can be made in light of the manner in which South Africa's Constitutional Court has addressed these problems. First, these cases highlight how central constitutional courts can be in mediating the political process, sometimes in the primary, high-profile context of reviewing legislation and actions for their constitutionality. Second, the courts tend to demand in these cases a shared sense of purpose within the membership. The challenges to courts when regulating the political process come where its members appear sharply divided, especially in ways that reflect societal divisions in normal politics. And, third, the message that seems apparent for most courts is that power need not always be exercised to its fullest extent. Even where a court is authorised to take action, leaving other actors in the political system to mediate a conflict, can sometimes be an ideal strategy. This does not necessarily mean abdicating any role in the process, but it may mean limiting one's attention in a manner that relies more on other actors involved in the process rather than a strict adherence to administer adjudicatory powers in traditional fashion.

Taken together, each of these cases provides some insight about the challenges for courts as they regulate the political process. While appeals to structure and history certainly matter, the situations show that individual choices by the courts in articulating constitutional principles can be used to respond to the political problems, especially during a crisis. In pursuing answers, courts continually grapple with the balance between these equality principles using the best tools available. Ultimately, their decisions, while not always based on consensus, help to develop understandings within the country about their electoral process and, more generally, the democratic project.

Notes

1 See *Reynolds* v. *Sims*, 377 US 533 (1964).
2 See UN General Assembly (1966) 171, 'All persons shall be equal before the courts and tribunals.'
3 See Ackerman (2012).
4 See, e.g. Kaufman (1979); Ferejohn (1998).
5 Hellman (2007).
6 Henrard (2002) 147–148.
7 Ferejohn (1999).
8 Ibid.
9 See *Baker* v. *Carr*, 369 US 186 (1962); *Reynolds* v. *Sims*, 377 US 533 (1964).
10 See Gerken (2002).
11 See *Evenwel* v. *Abbott*, 1:14-cv-335 (Western District of Texas, 2015); Garrett Epps, 'One Person One Vote?' *Atlantic* (31 May 2015). The most salient question before the US Supreme Court in its 2015–16 term will be whether the equal population standard allows states like Texas to exclude undocumented persons (i.e. non-citizen residents) from its tally for each district population.
12 Sachs (1997).
13 Ibid.
14 Dickson (1997).
15 Sachs (1997).
16 Ibid.
17 See Constitution of South Africa, Ch. 2, Sec. 19.
18 Ibid.
19 Ibid. Ch. 2, Sec. 19(2).
20 See *Luther* v. *Borden*, 48 US 1 (1849); US Constitution Art. IV, Sec. 4; Weinberg (1994).
21 See Constitution of South Africa, Ch. 2, Sec. 19(3)(a)–(b).
22 See Webb (1998).
23 Ibid.
24 See *United Democratic Movement* v. *President of the Republic of South Africa and Others*, 2003 (1) SA 495; 2002 (11) BCLR 1179 (4 October 2002).
25 See Constitution of South Africa, Ch. 1, Sec. 1(d).
26 2001 (9) BCLR 883 (CC) (7 June 2001).
27 See Constitution of South Africa, Sec. 41(2)(b).
28 2004 (5) BCLR 445 (CC) (3 March 2004).
29 See Constitution of South Africa, Ch. 2, Sec. 7(3), Sec. 36(1). The relevant language of the Limitation Clause reads:

> The rights in the Bill of Rights may be limited only in terms of law of general application to the extent that the limitation is reasonable and justifiable in an open and democratic society based on human dignity, equality and freedom, taking into account all relevant factors, including –
>
> (a) the nature of the right;
> (b) the importance of the purpose of the limitation;
> (c) the nature and extent of the limitation;
> (d) the relation between the limitation and its purpose; and
> (e) less restrictive means to achieve the purpose.
>
> (2) Except as provided in subsection (1) or in any other provision of the Constitution, no law may limit any right entrenched in the Bill of Rights.

References

Ackerman L., *Human Dignity: Lodestar of Equality in South Africa* (Juta and Co. 2012).

Dickson B., 'Protecting Human Rights through a Constitutional Court: The Case of South Africa' (1997) *Fordham Law Review* 531.

Epps G., 'One Person One Vote?' *Atlantic* (31 May 2015).

Ferejohn J., 'Independent Judges, Dependent Judiciary: Explaining Judicial Independence' (1998) 72 *Southern California Law Review* 353.

Ferejohn J., 'Accountability and Authority: Toward a Theory of Political Accountability' in Adam Przeworski and Susan C. Stokes (eds), *Democracy, Accountability, and Representation* (Cambridge University Press 1999).

Gerken H., 'The Costs and Causes of Minimalism in Voting Cases: Baker v. Carr and Its Progeny' (2002) 80 *North Carolina Law Review* 1411.

Hellman A.D., 'Justice O'Connor and "The Threat to Judicial Independence": The Cowgirl Who Cried Wolf?' (2007) 39 *Arizona Law Review* 845.

Henrard K., *Minority Protection in Post-Apartheid South Africa: Human Rights, Minority Rights, and Self-Determination* (Praeger 2002).

Kaufman I.R., 'Chilling Judicial Independence' (1979) 88 *Yale Law Journal* 684.

Sachs A., 'South Africa's Unconstitutional Constitution: The Transition from Power to Lawful Power' (1997) 41 *St. Louis University Law Journal* 1249.

UN General Assembly, International Covenant on Civil and Political Rights, Art. XIV 16 December 1966, United Nations, Treaty Series, vol. 999, available at: www.refworld.org/docid/3ae6b3aa0.html (accessed 31 August 2015).

Webb H., 'The Constitutional Court of South Africa: Rights Interpretation and Comparative Constitutional Law' (1998) 1 *University of Pennsylvania Journal of Constitutional Law* 205.

Weinberg L., 'Political Questions and the Guarantee Clause' (1994) 65 *University of Colorado Law Review* 887.

Index

Page numbers in *italics* denote tables.